Amazon Web Services Bootcamp

Develop a scalable, reliable, and highly available cloud
environment with AWS

Sunil Gulabani

BIRMINGHAM - MUMBAI

Amazon Web Services Bootcamp

Commissioning Editor: Vijin Boricha
Acquisition Editor: Namrata Patil
Content Development Editor: Deepti Thore
Technical Editor: Nirbhaya Shaji
Copy Editor: Safis Editing
Project Coordinator: Shweta H Birwatkar
Proofreader: Safis Editing
Indexer: Priyanka Dhadke
Graphics: Jisha Chirayil
Production Coordinator: Shraddha Falebhai

First published: March 2018

Production reference: 1290318

Published by Packt Publishing Ltd.
Livery Place
35 Livery Street
Birmingham
B3 2PB, UK.

ISBN 978-1-78829-445-4

www.packtpub.com

`mapt.io`

Mapt is an online digital library that gives you full access to over 5,000 books and videos, as well as industry leading tools to help you plan your personal development and advance your career. For more information, please visit our website.

Why subscribe?

- Spend less time learning and more time coding with practical eBooks and Videos from over 4,000 industry professionals

- Improve your learning with Skill Plans built especially for you

- Get a free eBook or video every month

- Mapt is fully searchable

- Copy and paste, print, and bookmark content

PacktPub.com

Did you know that Packt offers eBook versions of every book published, with PDF and ePub files available? You can upgrade to the eBook version at `www.PacktPub.com` and as a print book customer, you are entitled to a discount on the eBook copy. Get in touch with us at `service@packtpub.com` for more details.

At `www.PacktPub.com`, you can also read a collection of free technical articles, sign up for a range of free newsletters, and receive exclusive discounts and offers on Packt books and eBooks.

Contributors

About the author

Sunil Gulabani is a software engineer based in India. He is currently working on Java EE and the AWS Cloud platform. He is also a cloud evangelist who helps IT folks to leverage the AWS cloud platform for their business needs. He has insightful knowledge on designing microservices, system architecture and integration, data modeling, relational databases, and NoSQL in order for an application to achieve high throughput.
He has authored the following books:

- Developing RESTFul Web Services with Jersey 2.0
- Amazon S3 Essentials
- Practical Amazon EC2, SQS, Kinesis, and S3

In loving memory of my elder brother, Kailash Gulabani, who inspired everyone around him to face the challenges in life with grace. I am grateful to the Almighty God for giving me all the strength to chase my dreams. To my parents for their endless love and blessings. My wife, Priya, whose love, affection, encouragement, and prayers make me able to get such success and honor. Thank you for understanding and inspiring me always.

About the reviewers

GogulaRaja S. R. is a DevOps engineer at Cloudenablers Inc, a product-based company in Chennai, India. He takes care of analyzing and setting up the environments in the public cloud for the customers. He has also worked extensively with automation technologies (Chef and Ansible). He possesses the ability to deep dive into a specific area whenever the need arises and make sense of it quickly.

I would like to thank my parents, friends, and my company for providing their love and support.

Dhwani Dyer is a software engineer from India. She's done her bachelor's from Gujarat University and master's from Gujarat Technological University and is currently working at Infostretch as an implementation analyst on Java-based applications. She's interested in freelancing for development, AWS, Jenkins, and Relational Database. She's keen interest in writing tech blogs, book reviews, and is actively involved in knowledge sharing communities with knowledge of Java, HTML, CSS, AWS, Linux basic, data modeling, relational database, and has experience on the client side too.

First and foremost, I would like to thank my parents and sisters for standing beside me throughout my career. They are my inspiration and motivation for continuing to improve my knowledge and move my career forward. I also wish to thank all my friends, colleagues, and project coordinator, Shweta Birwatkar. Thanks for everything.

Packt is searching for authors like you

If you're interested in becoming an author for Packt, please visit authors.packtpub.com and apply today. We have worked with thousands of developers and tech professionals, just like you, to help them share their insight with the global tech community. You can make a general application, apply for a specific hot topic that we are recruiting an author for, or submit your own idea.

Table of Contents

Preface

AWS is at the forefront of cloud computing today. Businesses are adopting AWS Cloud because of its reliability, versatility, and flexible design.

The book will guide you to build and manage highly reliable and scalable applications and services on AWS. Also, you will be learning all the necessary skills to design, deploy, and manage your applications and services on the AWS cloud platform. Initially, we will walk you through various web services offered by Amazon. This will help you to get a high-level of understanding of different services.

Moving forward, we will be exploring Amazon IAM, EC2, S3, RDS, and more, to get you well-versed with core Amazon services. Each chapter will contain different ways to access AWS resources such as AWS Management Console, AWS CLI, AWS SDK (Java), and Cloud Formation. Later, you may choose any of the ways to create your cloud infrastructure. The book also contains easy-to-follow hands-on steps, tips, and recommendations, along with security and troubleshooting concepts.

By the end of the book, you will be able to create a highly secure, fault-tolerant, and scalable environment for your applications to run on.

Let's play with Amazon Web Services!

Who this book is for

This book targets IT professionals and system administrators looking at designing, deploying, and managing your applications and services on the AWS cloud platform. Developers looking at building highly scalable cloud-based services will also find this book useful. A basic understanding of AWS would be beneficial.

What this book covers

Chapter 1, *Getting Started with AWS*, briefs you about the basics of cloud computing and what Amazon Web Services (AWS) offers in cloud computing ecosystem. We will have walkthrough on different services offered by Amazon and sign-up processes.

Chapter 2, *Configuring IAM*, explains how to manage the access to AWS resources. This is a central security service around which all different AWS resources are surrounded for access management.

Chapter 3, *Building Server Using EC2*, helps you to build highly available and scalable applications using EC2 instances. We will learn how to configure the load balancer and auto-scaling feature, which helps to scale our application dynamically.

Chapter 4, *Storing Files on S3*, demonstrates how to utilize the cloud storage for more than one. We will learn about how to store data to and retrieve data from S3 and host a static HTML website.

Chapter 5, *Managing RDS*, lets you set up and operate database over the cloud. We will learn about different database engines supported by Amazon RDS and how to set up the MySQL database instance.

Chapter 6, *Implementing DynamoDB – NoSQL Database*, lets you create and operate a DynamoDB table. We will talk about auto-scaling the provisioned throughput on the DynamoDB table and secondary indexes, and then we have an example that will demonstrate CRUD operations.

Chapter 7, *Implementing Caching Using ElastiCache*, guides you through creating a caching server on the AWS cloud. We will learn about caching servers supported by the Amazon ElastiCache service and how to set up the infrastructure.

Chapter 8, *Triggering Notifications*, lets you create an SNS topic and send notifications to subscribers. We will also talk about push notifications on mobile devices and desktops.

Chapter 9, *All about CloudWatch*, explains how to monitor the AWS resources and applications to make sure they are up and running. You will learn about different features of CloudWatch, such as Alarm, Metrics, Logs, and Events.

To get the most out of this book

There are a few considerations to follow the examples in this book: a text editor or IDE (I use IntelliJ IDEA), internet access, and admin rights to your machine to install software.

Download the example code files

You can download the example code files for this book from your account at www.packtpub.com. If you purchased this book elsewhere, you can visit www.packtpub.com/support and register to have the files emailed directly to you.

You can download the code files by following these steps:

1. Log in or register at www.packtpub.com.
2. Select the **SUPPORT** tab.
3. Click on **Code Downloads & Errata**.
4. Enter the name of the book in the **Search** box and follow the onscreen instructions.

Once the file is downloaded, please make sure that you unzip or extract the folder using the latest version of:

- WinRAR/7-Zip for Windows
- Zipeg/iZip/UnRarX for Mac
- 7-Zip/PeaZip for Linux

The code bundle for the book is also hosted on GitHub at https://github.com/PacktPublishing/Amazon-Web-Services-Bootcamp. In case there's an update to the code, it will be updated on the existing GitHub repository.

We also have other code bundles from our rich catalog of books and videos available at https://github.com/PacktPublishing/. Check them out!

Download the color images

We also provide a PDF file that has color images of the screenshots/diagrams used in this book. You can download it here: http://www.packtpub.com/sites/default/files/downloads/AmazonWebServicesBootcamp_ColorImages.pdf.

Conventions used

There are a number of text conventions used throughout this book.

`CodeInText`: Indicates code words in text, database table names, folder names, filenames, file extensions, pathnames, dummy URLs, user input, and Twitter handles. Here is an example: "To create the Redis ElastiCache cluster, first we need to create the security group using the `AWS::EC2::SecurityGroup` type".

A block of code is set as follows:

```
AmazonElastiCache amazonElastiCache = AmazonElastiCacheClientBuilder
        .standard()
        .withClientConfiguration(getClientConfiguration())
        .withCredentials(getCredentials())
        .withRegion(getRegions())
        .build();
```

When we wish to draw your attention to a particular part of a code block, the relevant lines or items are set in bold:

```
AmazonElastiCache amazonElastiCache = AmazonElastiCacheClientBuilder
        .standard()
        .withClientConfiguration(getClientConfiguration())
        .withCredentials(getCredentials())
        .withRegion(getRegions())
        .build();
```

Any command-line input or output is written as follows:

```
export PATH=~/.local/bin:$PATH
```

Bold: Indicates a new term, an important word, or words that you see onscreen. For example, words in menus or dialog boxes appear in the text like this. Here is an example: "Choose the **Account type** of your choice, and provide the required details, and click **Create Account and Continue**."

Warnings or important notes appear like this.

Tips and tricks appear like this.

Get in touch

Feedback from our readers is always welcome.

General feedback: Email `feedback@packtpub.com` and mention the book title in the subject of your message. If you have questions about any aspect of this book, please email us at `questions@packtpub.com`.

Errata: Although we have taken every care to ensure the accuracy of our content, mistakes do happen. If you have found a mistake in this book, we would be grateful if you would report this to us. Please visit `www.packtpub.com/submit-errata`, selecting your book, clicking on the Errata Submission Form link, and entering the details.

Piracy: If you come across any illegal copies of our works in any form on the Internet, we would be grateful if you would provide us with the location address or website name. Please contact us at `copyright@packtpub.com` with a link to the material.

If you are interested in becoming an author: If there is a topic that you have expertise in and you are interested in either writing or contributing to a book, please visit `authors.packtpub.com`.

Reviews

Please leave a review. Once you have read and used this book, why not leave a review on the site that you purchased it from? Potential readers can then see and use your unbiased opinion to make purchase decisions, we at Packt can understand what you think about our products, and our authors can see your feedback on their book. Thank you!

For more information about Packt, please visit `packtpub.com`.

Getting Started with AWS 1

Cloud computing is driving the IT industry to restructure the application workflow. It offers low-cost services for IT resources over the internet and a pay-as-you-go pricing model. Under cloud computing, IT resources can be utilized on demand. So, you don't need to pay for unused resources or any upfront fees to provision any hardware in advance.

Amazon Web Services (AWS) is a leading cloud services provider. AWS offers different services in various graphical regions, which can be chosen by customers based on their requirements. With AWS, we can create high availability and fault tolerant applications with minimal configurations. AWS reduces the stress of managing on-premises physical servers and allows us to focus on application layers.

The following topics will be covered in this chapter:

- Introduction to AWS
- Sign-up process
- Regions
- Installation of the AWS CLI

Introduction to AWS

AWS is a cloud computing platform offered by Amazon. It offers a large set of services that can be utilized in various forms. AWS caters for different services, including infrastructure, networking, storage, databases, security, and many more. These different services can be used in the application life cycle. Also, AWS offers a **pay-as-you-go** pricing model, which means that the user will only pay for services being used, so the user doesn't have to pay any upfront fees to acquire hardware resources.

AWS offers a web service interface for all services. We can also integrate AWS services via web services with various software to make our application management easier. AWS offers multiple regions to create AWS services.

The user has the choice to select the regions based on the application usage so that latency is low. Each region has multiple **Availability Zones** (**AZ**), which means you have an option to select Availability Zones where the application will reside, to avoid failure when one availability zone is down but another may be up.

Services offered by AWS

AWS offers a wide range of services under different categories. The following are some of the services that are offered by AWS.

Compute

Compute offers a computing platform where we can create virtual servers, and deploy and run our applications:

- **Elastic Compute Cloud** (**EC2**): AWS EC2 is a web service interface that allows users to create and configure *compute machines* in the cloud. It offers scalable compute machines with minimal configuration and reduces overall time to boot new servers.
- **EC2 Container Service** (**ECS**): AWS ECS allows you to work with Docker-enabled applications. We don't need to deal with the installation or configuration of prerequisite software to run on the cluster. ECS runs on Amazon EC2 clusters, so it can scale seamlessly.
- **Lightsail**: AWS Lightsail is used to launch virtual private servers. Lightsail offers low-cost computing servers that can be utilized by small and medium-sized businesses (SMBs).
- **Elastic Beanstalk**: AWS Elastic Beanstalk is used for deploying and handling applications without worrying about the infrastructure it is going to run. We simply upload the application's deployable file and Elastic Beanstalk automatically handles capacity provisioning, load balancing, auto scaling, and application health monitoring.
- **Lambda**: AWS Lambda is a serverless computing service where we don't need to manage servers and can focus on the business logic. AWS Lambda code will be executed based on requests and it can scale automatically.
- **Batch**: AWS Batch allows us to execute multiple jobs automatically. It can execute applications and container images on EC2 instances to accomplish certain tasks.

Storage

AWS offers a wide range of cloud storage services used by applications and for archival purposes:

- **Simple Storage Service (S3)**: AWS S3 is an object-based storage service over the web. We can store any amount of data and it can be retrieved from anywhere over HTTP. We can also host a static HTML website on S3.
- **Elastic File System (EFS)**: AWS EFS is a scalable file storage system that can be used with EC2 instances. EFS can be automatically scaled up and down based on files being added or removed. EFS can also be mounted on an external server residing outside the Amazon ecosystem.
- **Glacier**: AWS Glacier is a low-cost storage service that can be used for data archiving and infrequently used data. Glacier offers a reliable, secure, and cost-effective storage service.
- **Storage Gateway**: AWS Storage Gateway is an interface that helps to connect an on-premise storage infrastructure with an AWS storage infrastructure. Storage Gateway offers multiple storage solution types, including file gateway, volume-based, and tape-based types.

Database

AWS offers a variety of database services that can be used for storing application data in RDMSes, NoSQL databases, and caching servers:

- **Relational Database Service (RDS)**: AWS RDS is a cloud relational database offered by Amazon that makes it easy to configure and provide scalability. AWS RDS offers a wide range of databases to choose from, including Amazon Aurora, MySQL, PostgreSQL, MariaDB, Microsoft SQL Server, and Oracle. Amazon also provides a database migration service that can be used by consumers to migrate on-premise or external databases to the Amazon Cloud.
- **DynamoDB**: AWS DynamoDB is a fully managed NoSQL service that provides high performance and scalability. It handles databases in a distributed manner so that consumers do not have to deal with the administration of the database. Consumers will be directly dealing with tables with unlimited storage and they can store and retrieve data.

- **ElastiCache**: AWS ElastiCache provides a data caching service that can be an in-memory data store that improves application performance. ElastiCache offers two open source in-memory data stores, Redis and Memcached. The user can configure clusters of caching servers that can automatically handle failover.
- **Redshift**: AWS Redshift is a fully managed data warehouse service provided by Amazon. Redshift allow us to connect via SQL-based clients and business intelligence tools and is focused on analytics. It also offers fast query execution over a large set of datasets.

Networking and content delivery

AWS offers solutions for running companies' infrastructures under a secured cloud. It can deliver content using the **Content Delivery Network (CDN)** for low latency, and can expose DNS and REST APIs for applications running on the cloud:

- **Virtual Private Cloud (VPC)**: AWS VPC allows us to create private and public networks where we can create different Amazon services. Those services will run under our virtual network in the same way as those running on on-premise data centers. We have authority to configure the IP address range, subnets, network gateways, and security layers.
- **CloudFront**: AWS CloudFront is a global CDN that helps to cache data over edge locations and provide data to the requester faster. The CDN helps to minimize cost and deliver content with low latency.
- **Direct Connect**: AWS Direct Connect is a dedicated network service where a consumer can connect an on-premise data center directly to the Amazon network. This helps to reduce the time lag for data transmission and we can configure the connections to increase capacity.
- **Route 53**: AWS Route 53 is a **Domain Name System (DNS)** where we can route our request to AWS infrastructures, such as EC2, RDS, or other services. It also has the capability to route to non-AWS infrastructures. It provides scalability and high availability for the Domain Name System service, so users can rely on it. Route 53 is IPv6 compliant.
- **API Gateway**: AWS API Gateway is a service that exposes the front entry point (URL) for an application. API Gateway helps to build, monitor, and secure APIs, and can scale at any level. We can redirect the API calls to either AWS Lambda, web applications running on EC2, or any other servers.

Migration

AWS offers migration services that reduce the complexity and time for companies to migrate to the cloud:

- **AWS Migration Hub**: AWS Migration Hub allows us to monitor the progress of an application's migration within AWS resources and other partnering software tools. This makes it easier for us to get a high level of understanding about the migration's progress.
- **Application Discovery Service**: AWS Application Discovery Service is an intelligent service that collects and summarizes the usage of applications and their dependent services running on on-premise servers. This service can be where a user wants to migrate a system and wants to collect information about the on-premise server and find out about the dependent applications. It stores the collected data in the Application Discovery Service database, which will be in an encrypted format. Users can then export the data in CSV or XML format.
- **Database Migration Service (DMS)**: AWS DMS is a service that helps to migrate databases from an on-premise server to the Amazon Web Services cloud. It provides support for same-origin vendor database migration, such as Oracle to Oracle, and cross-origin vendor database migration, such as Oracle to MySQL.
- **Server Migration Service (SMS)**: AWS SMS is an automated service that migrates your on-premise server workload to AWS. This service can be scheduled and can take incremental migration as well.
- **Snowball**: Snowball is a petabyte-scale data transfer service whereby a user can migrate a large number of datasets from one system to AWS or vice versa. Transferring large amounts of data will incur a heavy cost for data transition over the network and may cause security concerns. So to overcome this, Snowball provides an appliance where we can attach an appliance to our local network and transfer the data.

Development tools

AWS offers development tools, such as code storage repositories and building tools for managing deployment strategies:

- **CodeStar**: AWS CodeStar is a tool where we can create, manage, and work on software projects. It comes with easy integration with other AWS services, such as CodeCommit, CodePipeline, CodeBuild, CodeDeploy, and others. It also supports various programming languages, such as C#, HTML5, Java, Node.js, Ruby, PHP, and Python.

- **CodeCommit**: AWS CodeCommit is a code repository service fully managed by AWS. It provides private Git repositories for enterprises to use as source control. CodeCommit is also compatible with Git tools.
- **CodeBuild**: AWS CodeBuild is a build service that compiles source code, executes tests, and creates deployable or consumable files. CodeBuild is a fully managed service provided by AWS. It scales as per user requirements and is charged based on minutes used to build the code.
- **CodeDeploy**: AWS CodeDeploy is an automated application deployment service. CodeDeploy supports deployment to EC2 instances and on-premise servers, and can take deployable files from various locations, such as GitHub, AWS S3 Bucket, and Bitbucket.
- **CodePipeline**: AWS CodePipeline is an automated service to release an application. CodePipeline allows us to visualize the build and deploy process. We can create multiple stages where CodePipeline first builds your application, executes tests, deploys to the pre-production environment via CodeDeploy or any other deployment process, and then moves to the production environment.
- **Cloud9**: AWS Cloud9 provides an **Integrated Development Environment (IDE)** that resides on the cloud and can be accessed from the browser. Cloud9 allows us to write, run, and debug applications in many languages, such as JavaScript, PHP, Python, Java, and many more.
- **X-Ray**: AWS X-Ray provides analysis of the application, which is useful for developers, architects, or product leads. It provides performance analysis of the application and its connected services. This analysis can later be used to identify any performance issues or errors in the system.

Management tools

AWS offers management tools to monitor applications, create an entire application stack in one shot, and support services:

- **CloudWatch**: AWS CloudWatch is a monitoring service that can give you overall system health analysis, metrics collected from AWS services, log viewing, and alarms configured on metrics, which take certain actions based on the alarm triggered. We can also have custom application metrics stored on CloudWatch Metrics, which can also be used for alarm configuration or dashboard views.
- **AWS Auto Scaling**: The AWS Auto Scaling service monitors our application and can auto scale based on the configuration. We can configure Auto Scaling for various AWS resources to manage high load and build performance-optimized and cost-effective applications.

- **CloudFormation**: AWS CloudFormation is a service that creates the entire infrastructure of an application. This helps users to create entire infrastructures in one go, instead of creating each AWS resource individually.
- **CloudTrail**: AWS CloudTrail audits the API calls made to your AWS account. It tracks the API calls made from the AWS Management Console, AWS SDKs, the AWS CLI, and from different AWS services. This helps to monitor the AWS resources being utilized and make them more secure.
- **Config**: The AWS Config service tracks the configuration changes of AWS resources. We can easily see whether any changes occurred in the configuration of AWS resources and can take action accordingly.
- **OpsWorks**: AWS OpsWorks is a Chef and Puppet based configuration management service. Chef and Puppet are automated configuration management tools that help to manage your server configuration using their templates.
- **Service Catalog**: AWS Service Catalog is a service that maintains a list of services that can be used on the AWS account. This helps companies to track and maintain governance of AWS resources being utilized as per their policies.
- **Systems Manager**: AWS Systems Manager provides an interface to manage operational data from multiple AWS resources. We can group multiple AWS resources as groups for an application and can view operational data or detect any issues going on within these groups of resources.
- **Trusted Advisor**: AWS Trusted Advisor helps to guide you in implementing AWS best practices. It observes the AWS service and provides recommendations on how to reduce cost, achieve performance, secure resources, and implement fault tolerance.
- **Managed Services**: AWS Managed Services is a support service that provides AWS infrastructure management and lets you focus on application management. Managed Services frees you from infrastructure operations such as monitoring. It applies patches on AWS resources, security, regular backups, and more.

Media services

AWS offers media services such as video conversion, real-time video streaming for analytics and machine learning, broadcasting videos, and more:

- **Elastic Transcoder**: AWS Elastic Transcoder is a service to transcode the media file which can be executed on various devices, such as mobile phones, tablets, and PCs. Elastic Transcoder frees developers from worrying about supporting the media files on various devices. Elastic Transcoder creates the different versions for us to support various devices.

- **Kinesis Video Streams**: AWS Kinesis Video Streams is a service to ingest videos over the Kinesis stream. Using Kinesis Video Streams, we can run analytics, apply machine learning, and process video data.
- **MediaConvert**: AWS MediaConvert allows us to convert video files into the multiple formats that are used from various devices.
- **MediaLive**: AWS MediaLive allows us to stream videos live over multiple devices, such as televisions, smartphones, tablets, and so on. We don't need to worry about the infrastructure for broadcasting the videos, as Amazon takes care of it.
- **MediaPackage**: AWS MediaPackage provides a secure way to deliver videos over the internet. Based on the load for a specific video stream, AWS MediaPackage scales automatically so that the user doesn't experience any difficulties.
- **MediaStore**: AWS MediaStore is a storage service for media. It provides live video streaming for videos that are stored in MediaStore.
- **MediaTailor**: AWS MediaTailor allows us to add advertisements to individual video streams based on the user's choice. It can also measure the metrics for ads, and reports can be formed accordingly.

Machine learning

AWS offers artificial intelligence services that use machine learning capabilities:

- **Amazon SageMaker:** Amazon SageMaker allows us to build, run, train, and deploy machine learning models. It simplifies the process of building and training the models, which are generally complex, in real time.
- **Amazon Comprehend:** Amazon Comprehend is based on **natural language processing (NLP)**. It has the ability to analyze text data and apply machine learning to identify various results.
- **AWS DeepLens:** AWS DeepLens provides an AI-enabled video camera where developers can make use of machine learning models. AWS DeepLens can be integrated with Kinesis Video Stream, AWS IoT devices, SQS, SNS, S3, and more.
- **Amazon Lex:** AWS Lex is used to build conversational applications. Lex uses **natural language understanding (NLU)** and **automatic speech recognition (ASR)**, which can be used to build conversational applications.

- **Machine Learning:** AWS **Machine Learning (ML)** is a service to create machine learning models from data. Users don't need to know about complex machine learning algorithms; AWS ML does this for you. ML also provides APIs to extract predictions based on the data you provided.
- **Amazon Polly:** AWS Polly is a text-to-life speech conversion service. Polly supports multiple languages and voices, which can be used in speech-based applications.
- **Rekognition:** AWS Rekognition is an image recognition service that can extract text, objects, scenes, and faces from images. It also provides search capabilities for faces in images.
- **Amazon Transcribe:** Amazon Transcribe allows us to create text files out of audio files stored on S3. It becomes easy for developers to use the service directly, without having knowledge about how the speech needs to be converted to text.
- **Amazon Translate:** Amazon Translate is a service that has the ability to translate one language to another language by applying complex neural machine learning and deep learning models.

Security, identity, and compliance

AWS offers security to access its cloud services. This helps administrators or companies to manage access to entire AWS services and secure applications using SSL certificates:

- **Identity and Access Management (IAM)**: AWS Identity and Access Management is a service that provides secured access to AWS resources. Using IAM, we can verify authentication and authorization to use AWS services.
- **AWS Cognito**: This allows us to create and log in users for authentication and authorization to applications. The administrator can manage the permissions to be provided to certain users. Cognito also integrates with social identities, such as Facebook, Twitter, Amazon, and so on. Cognito also syncs data across the user's devices, which benefits the user experience, making it possible to have all data across all devices.
- **GuardDuty**: AWS GuardDuty is a threat detection service that monitors AWS resources. It can detect any unauthorized access or unusual API calls, so that we can take precautions to protect our AWS resources.

- **Inspector**: AWS Inspector is an automated tool that finds security and compliance vulnerabilities on AWS services. This tool creates detailed reports based on the severity of the vulnerability.

- **Certificate Manager**: AWS Certificate Manager allows you to create and manage the Secure Sockets Layer/Transport Layer Security for use with different AWS services that are exposed over the internet. Using Certificate Manager, you can deal with the renewal of certificates without impacting your applications over AWS.

- **Directory Service**: AWS Directory Service allows us to use Microsoft **Active Directory** (**AD**) on AWS. Using this service, IT administrators can set up access to AWS services for users and groups, and enable single sign-on applications.

- **WAF and Shield**: The AWS **Web Application Firewall** (**WAF**) helps us to monitor HTTP/HTTPS requests for AWS CloudFront or AWS Application Load Balancer. Using AWS WAF, we can apply rules to control access to CloudFront or Application Load Balancer. AWS Shield helps us to protect from **distributed denial of service** (**DDoS**) attacks.

- **Artifact**: AWS Artifact provides AWS security and compliance reports and agreements. This service is available at no additional cost. AWS Artifact provides reports with various accreditation bodies. AWS Artifact also covers agreements for a **Non-Disclosure Agreement** (**NDA**) and **Business Associate Addendum** (**BAA**).

- **Amazon Macie**: Amazon Macie is a security service that uses machine learning for discovering, classifying, and protecting your data stored on AWS. It identifies sensitive data and monitors for security breaches. Reports are displayed on the dashboard and alerts are generated for any security concerns.

- **AWS Single Sign-On**: AWS **Single Sign-On** (**SSO**) allows us to have centrally managed SSO for our AWS account and applications. This helps to centrally manage the user access and sign-on process at the organization level.

- **CloudHSM**: AWS CloudHSM (**Hardware Security Module**) allows you to create and use your encryption keys on AWS. These encryption keys can easily be integrated with applications using APIs, such as the **PKCS #11, Java Cryptography Extensions** (**JCE**), and **Microsoft CryptoNG** (**CNG**) libraries.

Analytics

AWS offers an analytics compute engine that performs complex algorithms on data on demand:

- **Athena:** AWS Athena is a query service that analyzes data on AWS S3. Athena supports standard queries over S3 data. It doesn't have any infrastructure to be managed, and we just need to pay for the queries being executed.
- **Elastic MapReduce (EMR):** AWS Elastic MapReduce is based on the Hadoop framework, which provides fast processing of a large set of data stores using EC2 instances. AWS EMR supports a wide range of frameworks, such as HBase, Apache Spark, Presto, and Flink. AWS EMR can be integrated with various AWS services, such as S3 and DynamoDB.
- **CloudSearch:** AWS CloudSearch is a search service that can be integrated with applications. CloudSearch can search a large set of data from various sources. AWS CloudSearch also scales as per the load, so users don't need to do any manual actions in order to achieve scalability.
- **ElasticSearch Service:** AWS ElasticSearch Service is a managed service that allows users to create an ElasticSearch cluster in AWS. ElasticSearch is an open source search engine used for searching and analytics.
- **Kinesis:** AWS Kinesis provides streams that can be used for processing real-time data streaming. It also provides Firehose, which is responsible for delivering data records received on streams to respective AWS services. It also provides Kinesis Analytics, which can be used via standard SQL.
- **Data Pipeline:** AWS Data Pipeline is an automated service that processes data from one source and moves it to destinations on AWS. It has the ability to perform complex processing, it can handle workloads, it has highly availability of resources, and more.
- **Quicksight:** AWS Quicksight is a business analytics tool that generates visual reports based on data. It automatically generates several visual graphs and analysis reports from static and dynamic data sources.
- **AWS Glue:** AWS Glue is an **extract, transform, and load (ETL)** service that is used for analytics purposes. AWS Glue takes a data source as input and creates the table definition automatically in the AWS Glue Data Catalog. Then, the user can query the data over AWS Glue.

Internet of Things

AWS offers **Internet of Things (IoT)** solutions that can be connected to embedded devices:

- **AWS IoT:** AWS IoT is a service that allows you to connect devices with AWS services. It has the ability to make devices interact with applications and send data to and from then. AWS IoT provides an SDK that helps you to connect to devices.
- **IoT Analytics:** AWS IoT Analytics allows us to apply analytics on IoT data which is unstructured in nature. It allows us to filter, transform, and enhance the data based on the type of data.
- **IoT Device Management:** AWS IoT Device Management allows us to manage IoT devices at a central location. Using this, we can manage a device's inventory and configurations, and provide **over-the-air (OTA)** updates easily.
- **Amazon FreeRTOS**: Amazon FreeRTOS is an operation system for microcontrollers that securely connects to AWS services, such as AWS Greengrass and AWS IoT Core.
- **AWS Greengrass**: AWS Greengrass is local software that performs computation, messaging, caching, and data syncing with connected devices. It can also act based on local events generated by devices. AWS Greengrass-supported devices can also transmit data to other devices with the AWS IoT SDK.

Contact center

AWS offers customer service on demand, which makes it easier for companies to manage it:

- **Amazon Connect**: Amazon Connect is a customer contact center service. Using Amazon Connect, we can quickly set up a customer contact center and scale as per our needs. It also provides metrics and reporting that help to manage customer queries by contacting the right customer care agents.
- **Pinpoint**: AWS Pinpoint helps to analyze app usage and campaign based on the statistics. It monitors app usage behavior, which users to target and send notifications to, at what time, and so on. It also supports multiple messaging channels, such as push notifications, text messages, or email.
- **Simple Email Service (SES)**: AWS Simple Email Service provides an effective email platform that can be used for sending and receiving emails. We can configure our own domain for email addresses. The infrastructure and maintenance requirements of email servers are costly and complex, so by using SES, we can get rid of infrastructure and maintenance activities.

2. Provide **Contact Information**: Here, we need to provide the contact information of the AWS account holder:

Figure 1.1: Contact Information

Choose the **Account type** as per your choice, provide the required details, and click **Create Account and Continue**.

3. Provide **Payment Information**: Here we will provide the payment information. AWS will charge us based on our AWS account billing:

Figure 1.3: Payment Information

4. **Phone Verification**: Here we need to verify our phone number:

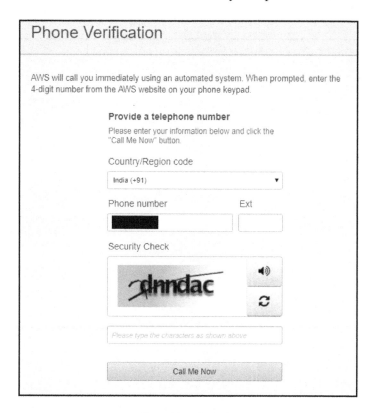

Figure 1.4: Phone Verification

Update your details if there are any changes and click **Call Me Now**. A code will be displayed on the screen and simultaneously you will get a call from Amazon to verify your phone number. Please verify it by providing the displayed code when called, and once verified, you can see on the window that your phone is verified and you will be redirected to the next screen.

5. Select a **Support Plan**: Here, we need to choose a support plan that we need for our AWS account:

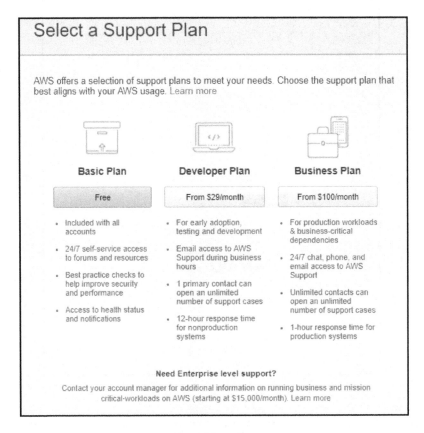

Figure 1.5: Support Plan

For our example, we are good with the **Basic** support plan, which is **Free**. Click **Free** and you will be redirected to the AWS Registration Confirmation Page.

Sign-in process

You have an AWS Account created and now we can sign in to the AWS Management Console to start using the services. Go to `https://console.aws.amazon.com`:

Figure 1.6: Sign-in page

Provide the AWS account **Email** address and click **Next**:

Figure 1.7: Sign in - Password

Provide the **Password** of your AWS account and click **Sign in** to log in to the AWS
Management Console:

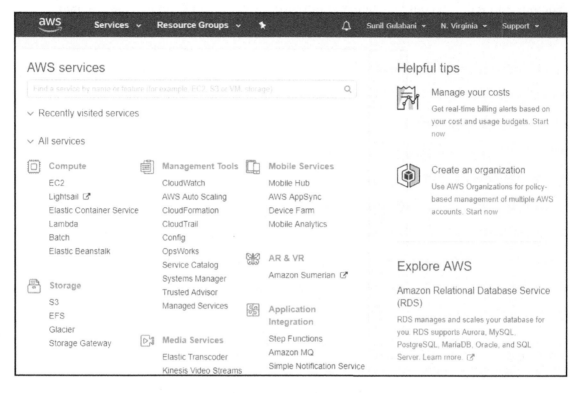

Figure 1.8: AWS Management Console

Regions

AWS offers services in multiple regions. This helps to reduce latency for an application. It is
important to choose a specific region where customers are going to use your application.
The following are the regions available for users:

- US East (Northern Virginia)
- US East (Ohio)
- US West (Northern California)
- US West (Oregon)
- Canada (Central)
- EU (Ireland)

- EU (Frankfurt)
- EU (London)
- EU (Paris)
- Asia Pacific (Singapore)
- Asia Pacific (Sydney)
- Asia Pacific (Seoul)
- Asia Pacific (Tokyo)
- Asia Pacific (Mumbai)
- South America

To know which services are supported in each region, please visit `https://aws.amazon.com/about-aws/global-infrastructure/regional-product-services/`.

Installing the AWS CLI

The AWS **Command Line Interface (CLI)** is one of the ways to interact with AWS services. We will be showcasing CLI commands to use certain services in forthcoming chapters. So, as a prerequisite, we will install the AWS CLI on our machine.

Windows

To install the AWS CLI on Windows, we can install it directly by using MSI Installer or by using `pip` (package manager for Python). We will demonstrate the installation using MSI Installer:

1. Download the installer from the following link, as per your machine's compatibility:

   - **64-bit:** `https://s3.amazonaws.com/aws-cli/AWSCLI64.msi`
   - **32-bit:** `https://s3.amazonaws.com/aws-cli/AWSCLI32.msi`

2. Execute MSI Installer and follow the instructions.
3. Once installed, you can check the installation by using the following command:

   ```
   aws --version
   ```

The following output should be visible on the command line. The version may vary if you are installing older or later versions:

```
C:\WINDOWS\System32>aws --version
aws-cli/1.11.133 Python/2.7.9 Windows/8 botocore/1.6.0
```

Figure 1.9: AWS CLI version

Linux

To install the AWS CLI on a Linux machine, we need to install `pip` (a package manager for Python):

1. Download the script for installing `pip`:

   ```
   curl -O https://bootstrap.pypa.io/get-pip.py
   ```

2. Install `pip`:

   ```
   python get-pip.py --user
   ```

3. Add the `pip` installation path in the environment variables:

   ```
   export PATH=~/.local/bin:$PATH
   ```

4. Verify the `pip` installation:

   ```
   pip --version
   ```

5. Install the AWS CLI:

   ```
   pip install awscli --upgrade --user
   ```

6. Once installed, you can check the installation using the following command:

   ```
   aws --version
   ```

The following output should be visible on the command line. The version may vary if you are installing older or later versions:

```
[root@ip-172-31-18-198 ec2-user]# aws --version
aws-cli/1.11.133 Python/2.7.5 Linux/3.10.0-693.el7.x86_64 botocore/1.6.0
[root@ip-172-31-18-198 ec2-user]#
```

Figure 1.10: AWS CLI version - Linux

Summary

In this chapter, we covered an overview of AWS and the various services offered by AWS. It is very important to choose the appropriate service, which can be efficient, reliable and cost effective. We also covered steps for creating an AWS account, the regions offered by AWS, and the installation of the AWS CLI, which will be used in the future chapters.

In the next chapter, we will be learning about the **Identity and Access Management (IAM)** service, which is a core part of AWS.

Configuring IAM
2

In this chapter, we will be covering the core security service of AWS—AWS IAM. Identity and Access Management, referred to as IAM, is a central part, which surrounds all AWS services. For an enterprise, big or small, data security is the most important aspect that needs to be tightened. In this chapter, we will demonstrate how we can create and administer IAM users, groups, roles, and policies using AWS Management Console, AWS CLI, AWS SDK – Java, and CloudFormation.

In this chapter, we will cover the following topics:

- Policies
- Roles
- Groups
- Users

Identity and Access Management (IAM) is the most important service of the AWS cloud. It is used to provide access to other AWS resources. Each AWS resource has access restrictions and permissions that are being governed by IAM. It allows us to provide granular-level permissions to users or AWS resources to access other AWS resources. At base, we have Policies, which allow and deny actions on the AWS resources. Next is Roles, which can have multiple policies attached, and this can be associated with AWS resources so that they can assume a role and get access to the AWS resources. IAM also allows us to create groups, which is a logical entity to club multiple policies and this can be associated with IAM users. So, when we create an IAM user, and associate it with a group, it means the user can get access to all the AWS resources mentioned in the group's policies. It becomes easier to provide and manage access based on groups. If a user moves from one business group to another in the same organization, the administrator will only change the group assignment for a particular user.

AWS IAM also provides access to the federated users, which reside outside IAM. Federated users can assume roles and get access to the AWS resources. Federated users are given short-lived access rights to AWS resources and are more secure in nature.

Policies

A Policy is a JSON document that contains a list of permissions to allow or deny access to AWS resources. A single policy can be attached to one or more IAM user, group, and role. AWS IAM Policies provides the following two types of policies:

- **AWS Managed Policies**: These policies are governed by AWS. These policies are created for common use cases so that IT administrators can directly use these policies instead of creating new ones.
- **Customer Managed Policies**: These policies are custom made under your AWS account. The customer can define specific resource-based permissions and can modify them as and when needed.

The following is the sample customer-managed policy document:

```
{
    "Version": "2012-10-17",
    "Statement": [
        {
            "Effect": "Allow",
            "Action": [
                "s3:*"
            ],
            "Resource": "arn:aws:s3:::awsbootcamp-bucket"
        }
    ]
}
```

The preceding policy allows all (s3:*) actions on s3 bucket (awsbootcamp-bucket). Effect can take either an Allow or Deny value. Action may contain multiple AWS resource actions and resource can also take multiple **Amazon Resource Name (ARN)** values as an array.

ARN allows us to uniquely identify the AWS resources. For more information on ARN, visit https://docs.aws.amazon.com/general/latest/gr/aws-arns-and-namespaces.html.

We can also provide resource-based permissions to some of the AWS resources such as AWS S3 Bucket, AWS SQS, AWS SNS, and AWS Glacier vault. The following is a sample of the resource-based policy:

```
{
    "Version": "2012-10-17",
    "Statement": [{
        "Principal": {
```

```
            "AWS": [
                "arn:aws:iam::AWS-ACCOUNT-ID:root"
            ]
        },
        "Effect": "Allow",
        "Action": [
            "s3:*"
        ],
        "Resource":  "arn:aws:s3:::awsbootcamp-bucket"
    }]
}
```

The preceding policy contains an additional field, `Principal`, which might contain the AWS User Account ID, AWS User, or AWS Service for which permissions will be granted.

We can also have multiple policy statements defined in a single policy document. Let's see how to add multiple policy statements:

```
{
  "Version": "2012-10-17",
    "Statement": [{
        "Effect": "Allow",
        "Action": [
            "s3:*"
        ],
        "Resource":  "arn:aws:s3:::awsbootcamp-bucket"
    }, {
        "Effect": "Allow",
        "Action": [
            "s3:*"
        ],
        "Resource":  "arn:aws:s3:::awsbootcamp-bucket-2"
    }]
}
```

Let's look at different ways to create AWS IAM Policies.

AWS Management Console

AWS Management Console allows us to create and manage the Policies using the user interface, which provides easier navigation for users to understand things better.

Creating a policy

The following steps will guide you to create a policy:

1. Go to AWS IAM Management Console at `https://console.aws.amazon.com/iam/home` and click on Policies from the left navigation, or you can directly go to `https://console.aws.amazon.com/iam/home#/policies`. Under Policies, you can see AWS Managed Policies and Customer Managed Policies.

2. Click on the **Create Policy** button:

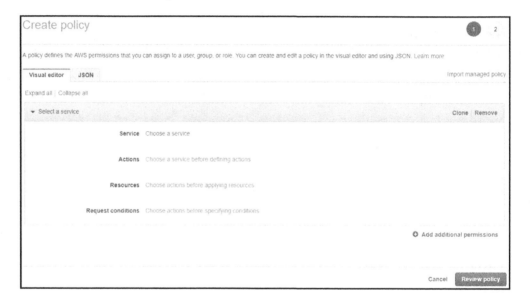

Figure 2.1: Create policy

Here, we can either create our own custom policy or import a managed policy. Importing a managed policy will require us to import and attach the policy document to our new policy that needs to be created. To create a policy from scratch, we can use VisualEditor or JSON Editor. VisualEditor helps us avoid making mistakes while providing actions and resources. We will go with VisualEditor and do the following:

- **Choose a service**: Choose a service for which you want to provide permissions. We will choose the S3 service.
- **Select actions**: Select actions based on what permissions you want to provide. We will select All S3 actions (`s3:*`).

- **Resources**: We can either select all resources (*) access or provide specific resource ARNs to which we need to provide access.
- **Request conditions**: We can provide additional restrictions such as what can be the Source IP, Source ARN, UserAgent, Referer, and SourceVpc. In our case, we will not add any request conditions.

3. By clicking on **Add Additional Permissions**, you can add a new policy document. Once you are done with selection policies and permissions, click on **Review Policy**:

Figure 2.2: Review policy

- We will need to provide the following details:
    - **Name**: Type in AmazonS3FullAccess. You can provide a friendly name which depicts your policy.
    - **Description**: Type in AmazonS3FullAccess. You can provide any description of your choice.
    - **Summary**: Review the policies that were selected in the previous step.

Once you are done, click on **Create Policy**:

Figure 2.3: Policy Created

AWS CLI

AWS CLI allows us to use the IAM service via the scripts. Scripts can be automated to execute IAM CLI commands, which can create and manage policies, groups, roles, and users. For accessing via the CLI, you need to configure the access key ID, the secret key, and grant IAM service access accordingly.

 If you are accessing AWS CLI for the first time, you need to create a user having access for IAM services.

To execute the CLI script, open Command Prompt.

Creating a policy

The following command creates customer-managed policies under your AWS account:

```
aws iam create-policy ^
--policy-name "AmazonS3FullAccess" ^
--policy-document file://PolicyDocument.json ^
--path "/" ^
--description "Amazon S3 Full Access Policy"
```

The following is the policy document used to create a policy
named `PolicyDocument.json`:

```
{
  "Version": "2012-10-17",
  "Statement": [{
    "Effect": "Allow",
    "Action": [
      "s3:*"
    ],
    "Resource": "arn:aws:s3:::my-bucket"
  }]
}
```

The following are the options, which can be used with create-policy:

Parameters	Optional	Description
`--policy-name`	False	This is a friendly name, which describes your policy.
`--policy-document`	False	This is the policy JSON document, which contains AWS resources and actions allowed or denied on them.
`--path`	True	This is the path of the policy. If the path is not provided, the default / (slash) is considered.
`--description`	True	This is a friendly description, which describes your policy.

Creating a policy version

The following command creates a new policy version for a specific customer-managed
policy:

```
aws iam create-policy-version ^
--policy-arn "arn:aws:iam::123456789012:policy/AmazonS3FullAccess" ^
--policy-document file://NewPolicyDocument.json ^
--set-as-default
```

The following is the policy document used to create a policy version
named `NewPolicyDocument.json`:

```
{
  "Version": "2012-10-17",
  "Statement": [{
    "Effect": "Allow",
```

```
      "Action": [
        "s3:*"
      ],
      "Resource": "arn:aws:s3:::my-bucket-2"
  }]
}
```

The following are the options, which can be used with create-policy-version:

Parameters	Optional	Description
--policy-arn	False	This is the customer-managed policy ARN to which a new version needs to be created
--policy-document	False	This is the policy JSON document, which contains AWS services and actions allowed on it
--set-as-default or --no-set-as-default	True	This specifies whether a new policy version is set as default

AWS SDK – Java

AWS SDK allows us to use the IAM service via the SDK in multiple languages so that we can customize it as per our choices. To access the IAM service, we need to create the AmazonIdentityManagement object as follows:

```
AmazonIdentityManagement amazonIdentityManagement =
AmazonIdentityManagementClientBuilder
        .standard()
//.withClientConfiguration(getClientConfiguration())
        .withCredentials(getCredentials())
        .withRegion(Regions.US_EAST_1)
        .build();

public ClientConfiguration getClientConfiguration() {
  return new ClientConfiguration()
          .withProxyUsername("PROXY_USERNAME")
          .withProxyPassword("PROXY_PASSWORD")
          .withProtocol(Protocol.HTTPS)
          .withProxyHost("PROXY_HOSTNAME")
          .withProxyPort(80);
  }

public AWSCredentialsProvider getCredentials() {
  //  return new AWSStaticCredentialsProvider(new
```

```
BasicAWSCredentials("ACCESS_KEY", "SECRET_KEY"));
    return new ProfileCredentialsProvider("aws-bootcamp");
}
```

When your code is executed behind the proxy server, you need to set the client configuration properties. We can use any of the Credentials Provider techniques to create the `AWSCredentialsProvider` object. Here, we have added access key ID and secret key in the `C://Users/{USER}/.aws/credentials` file with the profile name `aws-bootcamp`.

Creating a policy

The following code creates a customer-managed policy under your AWS account:

```
String policyName = "AmazonS3FullAccess";
String description = "S3 Full Access On my-bucket";
String policyDocument = readFromFile("PolicyDocument.json");
String policyARN =
    createPolicy(policyName, description, policyDocument);

........

public String createPolicy(
    String policyName,
    String description,
    String policyDocument) {

    CreatePolicyRequest createPolicyRequest =
        new CreatePolicyRequest()
        .withPolicyName(policyName)
        .withDescription(description)
        .withPolicyDocument(policyDocument);

    CreatePolicyResult createPolicyResult =
        amazonIdentityManagement
        .createPolicy(createPolicyRequest);

    return createPolicyResult.getPolicy().getArn();
}
```

The following is the policy document used to create the policy `PolicyDocument.json`:

```
{
    "Version": "2012-10-17",
    "Statement": [{
        "Effect": "Allow",
        "Action": [
```

```
            "s3:*"
        ],
        "Resource":  "arn:aws:s3:::my-bucket"
    }]
}
```

Creating a policy version

The following code creates a new policy version for a specific customer-managed policy:

```
String newPolicyDocument = readFromFile("NewPolicyDocument.json");

updatePolicy(policyARN, newPolicyDocument);

. . . . . . . .

public String updatePolicy(
        String policyARN,
        String policyDocument) {

    CreatePolicyVersionRequest createPolicyVersionRequest =
            new CreatePolicyVersionRequest()
                    .withPolicyArn(policyARN)
                    .withPolicyDocument(policyDocument)
                    .withSetAsDefault(true);

    CreatePolicyVersionResult createPolicyVersionResult =
            amazonIdentityManagement.
                    createPolicyVersion(
                        createPolicyVersionRequest);

    return createPolicyVersionResult
            .getPolicyVersion()
            .getVersionId();
}
```

The following is the policy document used to create a policy version NewPolicyDocument.json:

```
{
    "Version": "2012-10-17",
    "Statement": [{
      "Effect": "Allow",
      "Action": [
        "s3:*"
      ],
```

```
    "Resource": "arn:aws:s3:::my-bucket-2"
  }]
}
```

AWS CloudFormation

AWS CloudFormation provides an efficient way to create and manage AWS resources. We define the AWS resources in the template file, which can be either in JSON or YAML format. We will be covering CloudFormation examples in JSON format. We can add multiple AWS resources in a single template and refer to it as stack. We can create CloudFormation stack using the AWS Management Console, CLI, or SDK.

To create a customer-managed policy, we need to use the AWS::IAM::ManagedPolicy type as follows:

```
"AmazonS3FullAccess": {
    "Type": "AWS::IAM::ManagedPolicy",
    "Properties": {
      "ManagedPolicyName": "AmazonS3FullAccess",
      "Description": "S3 Full Access On my-bucket",
      "Path": "/",
      "PolicyDocument": {
        "Version": "2012-10-17",
        "Statement": [{
          "Effect": "Allow",
          "Action": [
            "s3:*"
          ],
          "Resource": "arn:aws:s3:::my-bucket"
        }]
      }
    }
  }
```

This will create a managed policy.

Role

AWS IAM Role allows an entity to assume a role and get the permissions to access the AWS resources. The entity can be a federated user, a cross-account user, or an AWS resource. Consider we have an Amazon EC2 instance as an Entity and want to access Amazon S3. So to get access, we need to attach the IAM Role (having permissions to access S3) to our EC2 instance. So now, the EC2 instance can assume the role and get the permissions to access S3.

Let's look at different ways to create the AWS IAM Role.

AWS Management Console

The AWS Management Console allows us to create and manage the Role.

Creating a role

The following steps will guide you to create a role:

1. Go to AWS IAM Management Console at `https://console.aws.amazon.com/iam/home` and click on Roles from the left navigation or directly go to `https://console.aws.amazon.com/iam/home#/roles`
2. Under Roles, you can see a list of AWS IAM Roles created under your account (if any)
3. Click on the **Create role** button:

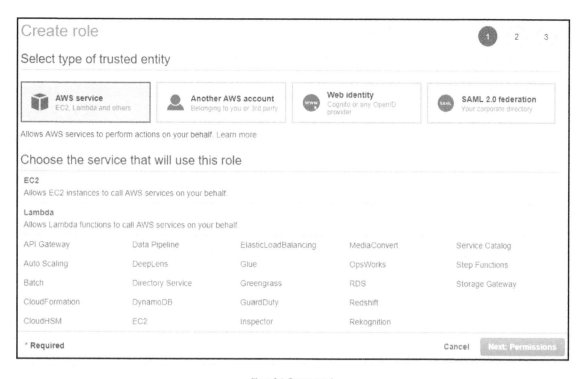

Figure 2.4: Create new role

Here, we need to select the type of trusted entity for our role:

- **AWS service**: This is used when a role needs to perform specific actions from a specific AWS service
- **Another AWS account**: This is used when you want a different AWS account of your own or a third-party AWS account needs access
- **Web Identity**: This is used when you want to allow access to federated users using some external web identity or **OpenID Connect (OIDC)**
- **SAML 2.0 federation**: This is used when you want to allow access to federated users using SAML 2.0

For our example, we will use **AWS service**. Under **Choose the service that will use this role**, select **EC2** and click on **Next: Permissions**.

4. The next step is to **Attach permissions policies**:

Figure 2.5: Attach Policy to Role

Here, we can filter the policy to ease the selection process. We will select the **AmazonS3FullAccess** checkbox and click on **Next: Review**.

5. The next step is to provide the role name, description, and review the trusted entities and policies that were attached in the previous step:

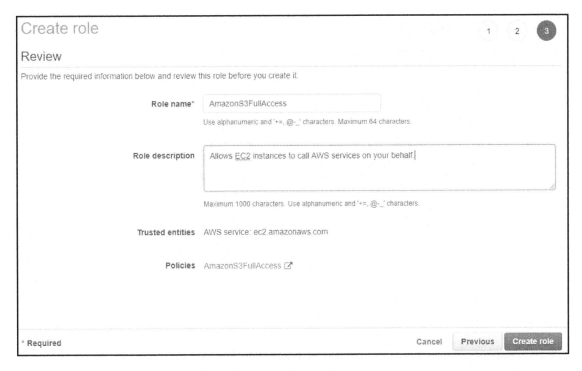

Figure 2.6: Set role name and review

Once verified, click on **Create role**:

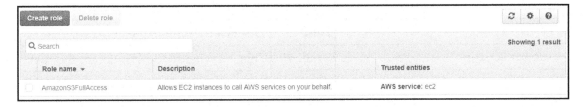

Figure 2.7: Role created

Once a role is created, we can add or remove managed policies and inline policies under a newly created role as per our requirements.

AWS CLI

To execute the CLI script, open Command Prompt.

Creating a role

The following command creates the IAM role under your AWS account:

```
aws iam create-role ^
--role-name "AmazonS3FullAccessRole" ^
--description "Amazon S3 Full Access Role" ^
--path "/" ^
--assume-role-policy-document file://Trust-Relationships.json
```

The following is the trust relationship policy document used to create a role named `Trust-Relationships.json`:

```
{
  "Version": "2012-10-17",
  "Statement": [
    {
      "Effect": "Allow",
      "Principal": {
        "Service": "ec2.amazonaws.com"
      },
      "Action": "sts:AssumeRole"
    }
  ]
}
```

The following are the options which can be used with create-role:

Parameters	Optional	Description
--role-name	False	This is a friendly name of the role.
--description	True	This is a friendly description of the role.
--path	True	This is the path of the role. If the path is not provided, the default / (slash) is considered.
--assume-role-policy-document	False	This is the trust relationship policy document that defines permissions to the service to assume the role.

Attaching managed policies

The following command attaches the managed policies to the role. By attaching the policies, all permissions defined in the policies are applicable while assuming the role:

```
aws iam attach-role-policy ^
--role-name "AmazonS3FullAccessRole" ^
--policy-arn "arn:aws:iam::123456789012:policy/AmazonS3FullAccess"
```

The following are the options, which can be used with `attach-role-policy`:

Parameters	Optional	Description
--role-name	False	This is the role name to which the policy needs to be attached
--policy-arn	False	This is the policy ARN, which needs to be attached

Creating an inline role policy

The following command creates an inline role policy. Inline role policies will be specific to this role only; we cannot reuse this policy:

```
aws iam put-role-policy ^
--role-name "AmazonS3FullAccessRole" ^
--policy-name "S3FullAccessOnMyBucket2" ^
--policy-document file://NewPolicyDocument.json
```

The following is the policy document used to create the inline role policy named NewPolicyDocument.json:

```
{
  "Version": "2012-10-17",
  "Statement": [{
    "Effect": "Allow",
    "Action": [
      "s3:*"
    ],
    "Resource": "arn:aws:s3:::my-bucket-2"
  }]
}
```

The following are the options, which can be used with put-role-policy:

Parameters	Optional	Description
--role-name	False	This is the role name to which the inline policy will be created
--policy-name	False	This is a friendly name for the policy
--policy-document	False	This is the policy JSON document that defines permissions to AWS services

AWS SDK – Java

AWS SDK allows us to create and manage AWS IAM Roles. To access the IAM service, we need to create the AmazonIdentityManagement object as described in the policy's AWS SDK - Java section.

Creating a role

The following code creates the IAM role under your AWS account:

```
String roleName = "AmazonS3FullAccess";

 String roleDescription = "S3 Full Access";

String assumeRolePolicyDocument =
readFromFile("assumeRolePolicyDocument.json");

String roleARN = createRole(roleName, roleDescription,
assumeRolePolicyDocument);
. . . . . . . .

public String createRole(
        String roleName,
        String description,
        String assumeRolePolicyDocument) {
    CreateRoleRequest createRoleRequest =
            new CreateRoleRequest()
                    .withRoleName(roleName)
                    .withDescription(description)
                    .withAssumeRolePolicyDocument(
                            assumeRolePolicyDocument);
```

```
CreateRoleResult createRoleResult =
        amazonIdentityManagement.
                createRole(createRoleRequest);

    return createRoleResult
            .getRole()
            .getArn();
}
```

Attaching managed Policies

The following code will attach managed Policies to our role:

```
attachRolePolicy(roleName, policyARN);
........
public void attachRolePolicy(
        String roleName,
        String policyARN) {

    AttachRolePolicyRequest attachRolePolicyRequest =
            new AttachRolePolicyRequest()
                    .withRoleName(roleName)
                    .withPolicyArn(policyARN);

    AttachRolePolicyResult attachRolePolicyResult =
            amazonIdentityManagement.
                    attachRolePolicy(attachRolePolicyRequest);
}
```

Creating an inline role policy

The following code will create a new inline role policy, which cannot be reused to attach to any other role as it is specific to this role only:

```
String inlineRolePolicyName = "S3FullAccessOnMyBucket2";

String inlineRolePolicyDocument =
readFromFile("newPolicyDocument.json");

putRolePolicy(roleName, inlineRolePolicyName,
inlineRolePolicyDocument);
........

public void putRolePolicy(
        String roleName,
```

```
            String policyName,
            String policyDocument) {
    PutRolePolicyRequest putRolePolicyRequest =
            new PutRolePolicyRequest()
                    .withRoleName(roleName)
                    .withPolicyName(policyName)
                    .withPolicyDocument(policyDocument);

    PutRolePolicyResult putRolePolicyResult =
            amazonIdentityManagement.
                    putRolePolicy(putRolePolicyRequest);
}
```

AWS CloudFormation

To create a role, we need to use the AWS::IAM::Role type as we've done in the following code:

```
"AmazonS3FullAccessRole": {
   "Type": "AWS::IAM::Role",
   "Properties": {
     "AssumeRolePolicyDocument": {
       "Version": "2012-10-17",
       "Statement": [{
         "Effect": "Allow",
         "Principal": {
           "Service": ["ec2.amazonaws.com"]
         },
         "Action": ["sts:AssumeRole"]
       }]
     },
     "Path": "/",
     "Policies": [{
       "PolicyName": "S3FullAccessOnMyBucket2",
       "PolicyDocument": {
         "Version": "2012-10-17",
         "Statement": [{
           "Effect": "Allow",
           "Action": [
             "s3:*"
           ],
           "Resource": "arn:aws:s3:::my-bucket-2"
         }]
       }
     }],
     "ManagedPolicyArns": [{
```

```
      "Ref": "AmazonS3FullAccess"
    }],
    "RoleName": "AmazonS3FullAccessRole"
  }
}
```

The preceding CloudFormation script will create a role, which has access to the S3 bucket `my-bucket-2`, and this role can only be assumed from EC2 instances.

Group

AWS IAM Group allows us to group multiple policies together, which can then be attached to IAM Users. This group provides the flexibility to IT administrators to manage groups based on admins, developers, teams, departments, or organizations. The group contains a list of policies, which contain permissions to access AWS resources.

Let's look at different ways to create the AWS IAM Group.

AWS Management Console

The AWS Management Console allows us to create and manage the groups.

Creating a group

Create a new group under your AWS account using the following steps:

1. Go to AWS IAM Management Console at `https://console.aws.amazon.com/iam/home` and click on Groups from the left navigation or you can directly go to `https://console.aws.amazon.com/iam/home#/groups`
2. Under Groups, you can see a list of the groups you created

3. Click on the **Create New Group** button:

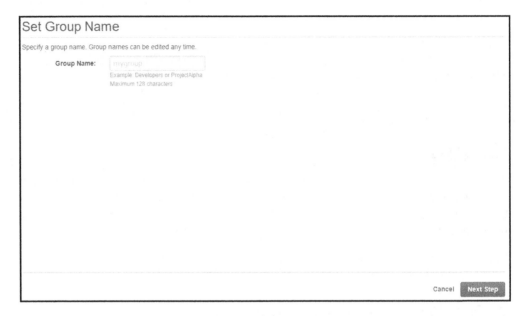

Figure 2.8: Set Group Name

Provide a friendly name for the group to be created and click on **Next Step**

4. The next step is to click on **Attach Policy** under group:

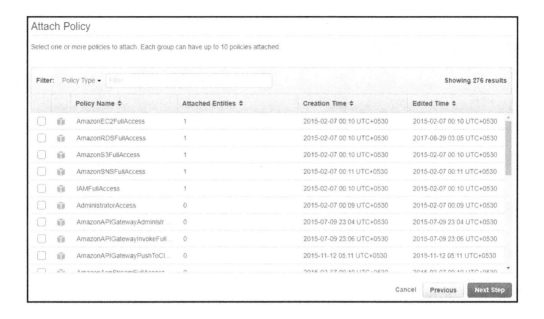

Figure 2.9: Attach Policy

Select the managed policies you want to attach to group and click on **Next Step**.

5. The next step is to **Review** the group and attach the policy:

Figure 2.10: Review Group

Click on **Create Group**:

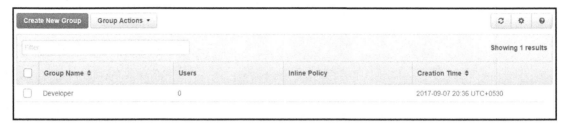

Figure 2.11: Group Listing

Once Group is created, it is ready to get associated with IAM User. Later in this chapter, we will attach this Group to User. We can also modify the group's managed policies and inline policies.

AWS CLI

To execute the CLI script, open Command Prompt.

Creating a group

The following command creates a new group under your AWS account:

```
aws iam create-group ^
--group-name "Developer" ^
--path "/"
```

The following are the options, which can be used with create-group:

Parameters	Optional	Description
--group-name	False	This is a friendly name for the group.
--path	True	This is the path of the group. If the path is not provided, the default / (slash) is considered.

Attaching a group policy

To attach the managed policy under the group, use the following code:

```
aws iam attach-group-policy ^
--group-name "Developer" ^
--policy-arn "arn:aws:iam::123456789012:policy/AmazonS3FullAccess"
```

The following are the options, which can be used with attach-group-policy:

Parameters	Optional	Description
--group-name	False	This is the name of the group under which the policy will be attached
--policy-arn	False	This is the policy ARN that needs to be attached

Adding a group policy – Inline

Add an inline policy under the group. If the same policy name is available under the group, it will update it:

```
aws iam put-group-policy ^
--group-name "Developer" ^
--policy-name "S3FullAccessOnMyBucket2" ^
--policy-document file://NewPolicyDocument.json
```

The following is the policy document used to create the inline group policy **NewPolicyDocument.json**:

```
{
  "Version": "2012-10-17",
  "Statement": [{
    "Effect": "Allow",
    "Action": [
      "s3:*"
    ],
    "Resource": "arn:aws:s3:::my-bucket-2"
  }]
}
```

The following are the options, which can be used with put-group-policy:

Parameters	Optional	Descriptions
--group-name	False	This is the name of the group
--policy-name	False	This is the name of the policy that needs to be created
--policy-document	False	This is the policy JSON document that defines permissions to AWS services

AWS SDK – Java

AWS SDK allows us to use the IAM service via the SDK. To access the IAM service, we need to create the `AmazonIdentityManagement` object as described in Policy's AWS SDK - Java section.

Create Group

Create a new group under your AWS account using the following code:

```
String groupName = "Developer";

 createGroup(groupName);
........
public void createGroup(
        String groupName) {
    CreateGroupRequest createGroupRequest =
            new CreateGroupRequest()
                    .withGroupName(groupName);

    CreateGroupResult createGroupResult =
            amazonIdentityManagement.
                    createGroup(createGroupRequest);
}
```

Attaching a group policy

The following code attaches the managed policy under the group:

```
attachGroupPolicy(groupName, policyARN);
........
public void attachGroupPolicy(
        String groupName,
        String policyARN) {
    AttachGroupPolicyRequest attachGroupPolicyRequest =
            new AttachGroupPolicyRequest()
                    .withGroupName(groupName)
                    .withPolicyArn(policyARN);

    AttachGroupPolicyResult attachGroupPolicyResult =
            amazonIdentityManagement.
                    attachGroupPolicy(attachGroupPolicyRequest);
  }
```

Adding a group policy – Inline

Add inline policy under the group. If the same policy name is available under the group, it will update it:

```
String inlineGroupPolicyName = "S3FullAccessOnMyBucket2";

String inlineGroupPolicyDocument =
    readFromFile("NewPolicyDocument.json");

putGroupPolicy(groupName, inlineGroupPolicyName,
      inlineGroupPolicyDocument);
........

public void putGroupPolicy(
        String groupName,
        String policyName,
        String policyDocument) {
    PutGroupPolicyRequest putGroupPolicyRequest =
            new PutGroupPolicyRequest()
                    .withGroupName(groupName)
                    .withPolicyName(policyName)
                    .withPolicyDocument(policyDocument);
```

```
        PutGroupPolicyResult putGroupPolicyResult =
              amazonIdentityManagement.
                    putGroupPolicy(putGroupPolicyRequest);
    }
```

NewPolicyDocument.json

```
    {
        "Version": "2012-10-17",
        "Statement": [{
          "Effect": "Allow",
          "Action": [
            "s3:*"
          ],
          "Resource": "arn:aws:s3:::my-bucket-2"
        }]
    }
```

AWS CloudFormation

To create a role, we need to use the AWS::IAM::Group type as shown here:

```
    "Developer": {
        "Type": "AWS::IAM::Group",
        "Properties": {
          "GroupName": "Developer",
          "ManagedPolicyArns": [{
            "Ref": "AmazonS3FullAccess"
          }],
          "Path": "/",
          "Policies": [{
            "PolicyName": "S3FullAccessOnMyBucket2",
            "PolicyDocument": {
              "Version": "2012-10-17",
              "Statement": [{
                "Effect": "Allow",
                "Action": [
                  "s3:*"
                ],
                "Resource": "arn:aws:s3:::my-bucket-2"
              }]
            }
          }]
        }
    }
```

The preceding CloudFormation script will create a group with customer-managed policy `AmazonS3FullAccess` attached and an inline policy on S3 bucket `my-bucket-2`.

Users

IAM User is an entity, which will be accessing AWS resources. The entity can be a person or an application that needs fixed credentials to access AWS resources. The IAM user allows us to generate credentials to access the AWS Management Console or generate programmatic access credentials to access from AWS CLI or AWS SDK. The IAM User can have Groups or Policies attached to get the required AWS resource permissions.

Let's look at different ways to create AWS IAM Users.

AWS Management Console

The AWS Management Console allows us to create and manage the Users.

Create an user

Create a new user under your AWS account using the following steps:

1. Go to the AWS IAM Management Console and click on **Users** from the left navigation pane or you can directly go to `https://console.aws.amazon.com/iam/home#/users`. Under **Users**, you can see a list of users created under your AWS account.

2. Click on the **Add user** button:

Figure 2.12: Add User

We will need to provide the following details:

- **Username**: Type in aws-bootcamp or your choice of username.
- **Access type**: Here, we need to select the type of access we want to give to the user. We will select both the access types.

On enabling **AWS Management Console access**, you will be prompted to provide a password, which can be **Autogenerated password** or **Custom password**. Also, you can define whether the user needs to reset the password on first login:

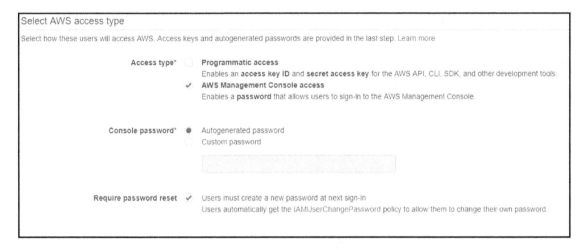

Figure 2.13: Select Access Type

Once the details are provided, click on **Next: Permissions.**

3. The next step is to set permissions for the **user**:

Figure 2.14: Set Permissions for user

It provides options to provide permissions to the user as follows:

- **Add a user to the group**: You can add this new user to the existing group, which has defined a set of permissions. This step is optional; you can add a user to **Group**(s) at a later stage, even after creating the user.

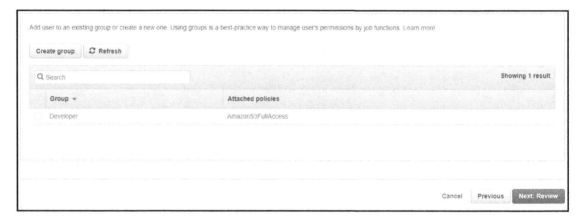

Figure 2.15: Add user to group

Select the group(s) and click on **Next: Review**.

- **Copy permissions from the existing user**: This will copy all the permissions from an existing user so that you don't need to attach group(s) or policies explicitly. It will have the same group(s) and inline policies the existing user has. This option is useful when a new user joins an organization and you need to provide the same access as that of the existing user:

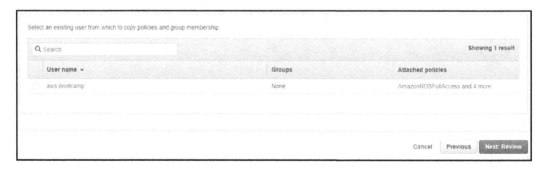

Figure 2.16: Copy permissions from existing user

Select the user and click on **Next: Review**.

- **Attach existing policies directly**: Here you can attach the managed policies directly. This step is optional; you can attach the policies at a later stage, even after creating the user:

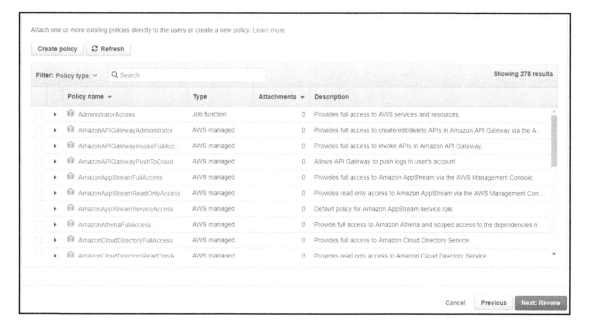

Figure 2.17: Attach existing policies directly

 Attaching policies directly is not a good practice. Instead, you should provide permissions using group(s).

Select the policies and click on **Next: Review**.

4. For our example, we will add a user to the group. The next step is to review and click on **Create user**:

Figure 2.18: Review User

5. The user will be created and you can download the **Access key ID** and **Secret access key** from this screen:

Figure 2.19: User Created

You should download the .csv file or save credentials at a secure location as this contains credentials to access AWS services.

The secret access key is only available on this screen. If you failed to save or misplaced the secret key, it won't be recoverable. In that case, you need to generate another access key ID and secret access key.

Once you have saved the credentials, click on **Close**:

Figure 2.20: User Listing

AWS CLI

AWS CLI allows us to use the IAM service via the scripts. For accessing via the CLI, you need to configure the access key ID and secret key and grant access to the IAM service accordingly.

 If you are accessing AWS CLI for the first time, you need to create a user having access to IAM services.

To execute the CLI script, open Command Prompt.

Create an user

The following command creates a new user under your AWS account:

```
aws iam create-user ^
--user-name "Sunil" ^
--path "/"
```

The following are the options, which can be used with create-user:

Parameters	Optional	Description
--user-name	False	This is a friendly name that identifies the entity or application.
--path	True	This is the path of the user. If the path is not provided, the default / (slash) is considered.

Creating an access key

The following command creates the access key ID and secret access key for the user:

```
aws iam create-access-key ^
--user-name "Sunil"
```

The following are the options, which can be used with create-access-key:

Parameters	Optional	Description
--user-name	True	This is the username for which the access key needs to be created. If the username is not provided, the access key is created for the user who is signing the request.

This command returns the access key ID and secret access key, which need to be stored at a secure location. Using this access key ID and secret access key, you will be able to access AWS services.

Creating a login profile

Let's create a login profile for the user specified, so that the user is able to access it via the AWS Management Console with the help of the following command:

```
aws iam create-login-profile ^
--user-name "Sunil" ^
--password "abcd1234" ^
--password-reset-required
```

The following are the options, which can be used with create-login-profile:

Parameters	Optional	Description
--user-name	False	This is the username for which the login profile needs to be created
--password	False	This is the password for the login profile
--password-reset-required or --no-password-reset-required	True	This specifies whether the user needs to reset the password on first sign in or not

Adding a user to the group

Add a user to the specified group so that the user has permissions to AWS services described under group:

```
aws iam add-user-to-group ^
--user-name "Sunil" ^
--group-name "Developer"
```

The following are the options, which can be used with add-user-to-group:

Parameters	Optional	Description
--user-name	False	This is the username, which will be added under group
--group-name	False	This is the group name to which the user will be added

Attaching a user policy

Attach the specified managed policy to the user:

```
aws iam attach-user-policy ^
--user-name "Sunil" ^
--policy-arn "arn:aws:iam::123456789012:policy/AmazonS3FullAccess"
```

The following are the options, which can be used with attach-user-policy:

Parameters	Optional	Description
--user-name	False	This is the username to which the policy needs to be attached
--policy-arn	False	This is the policy ARN that needs to be attached

AWS SDK – Java

AWS SDK allows us to use the IAM service via the SDK. To access the IAM service, we need to create the `AmazonIdentityManagement` object as described in the Policy's AWS SDK - Java section.

Creating a user

Create a new user under your AWS account:

```
String userName = "Sunil";

createUser(userName);
........

public void createUser(
        String userName) {
    CreateUserRequest createUserRequest =
            new CreateUserRequest()
                    .withUserName(userName);

    CreateUserResult createUserResult =
            amazonIdentityManagement.
                    createUser(createUserRequest);
}
```

Create an access key

Create an access key ID and secret access key for the user:

```
String accessKeyId = createAccessKey(userName);
........

public String createAccessKey(
        String userName) {
```

```
CreateAccessKeyRequest createAccessKeyRequest =
        new CreateAccessKeyRequest()
                .withUserName(userName);

CreateAccessKeyResult createAccessKeyResult =
        amazonIdentityManagement.
                createAccessKey(createAccessKeyRequest);

return createAccessKeyResult
        .getAccessKey()
        .getAccessKeyId();
}
```

This service returns the access key ID and secret access key, which need to be stored at a secure location. Using this access key ID and secret access key, you will be able to access AWS services.

Creating a login profile

Create a login profile for the user specified so that the user is able to access via the AWS Management Console:

```
createLoginProfile(userName, "abcd1234");

. . . . . . . .

public void createLoginProfile(
        String userName,
        String password) {
    CreateLoginProfileRequest createLoginProfileRequest =
            new CreateLoginProfileRequest()
                    .withUserName(userName)
                    .withPassword(password)
                    .withPasswordResetRequired(true);

    CreateLoginProfileResult createLoginProfileResult =
            amazonIdentityManagement.
                    createLoginProfile(createLoginProfileRequest);
}
```

Adding a user to a group

Add a user to a specified group so that the user has permissions to AWS services described under the group:

```
addUserToGroup(userName, groupName);

........

public void addUserToGroup(
        String userName,
        String groupName) {
    AddUserToGroupRequest addUserToGroupRequest =
            new AddUserToGroupRequest()
                    .withUserName(userName)
                    .withGroupName(groupName);

    AddUserToGroupResult addUserToGroupResult =
            amazonIdentityManagement.
                    addUserToGroup(addUserToGroupRequest);
}
```

Attaching a user policy

Attach the specified managed policy to the user:

```
attachUserPolicy(userName, policyARN);

........

public void attachUserPolicy(
        String userName,
        String policyARN) {
    AttachUserPolicyRequest attachUserPolicyRequest =
            new AttachUserPolicyRequest()
                    .withUserName(userName)
                    .withPolicyArn(policyARN);

    AttachUserPolicyResult attachUserPolicyResult =
            amazonIdentityManagement.
                    attachUserPolicy(attachUserPolicyRequest);
}
```

AWS CloudFormation

To create a user, we need to use the `AWS::IAM::User` type:

```
"IAMUser": {
    "Type": "AWS::IAM::User",
    "Properties": {
      "Groups": [{
        "Ref": "Developer"
      }],
      "LoginProfile": {
        "Password": "abcd1234",
        "PasswordResetRequired": true
      },
      "ManagedPolicyArns": [{
        "Ref": "AmazonS3FullAccess"
      }],
      "Path": "/",
      "Policies": [{
        "PolicyName": "S3FullAccessOnMyBucket2",
        "PolicyDocument": {
          "Version": "2012-10-17",
          "Statement": [{
            "Effect": "Allow",
            "Action": [
              "s3:*"
            ],
            "Resource": "arn:aws:s3:::my-bucket-2"
          }]
        }
      }],
      "UserName": "Sunil"
    }
  }
```

The preceding template snippet will create a user along with a login profile, managed inline policy attached, and the group to which the user will be added.

To create an access key ID and secret access key for a specific user, we need to use the `AWS::IAM::AccessKey` type:

```
"UserCredentials" : {
    "Type" : "AWS::IAM::AccessKey",
    "Properties" : {
      "UserName" : { "Ref" : "IAMUser" }
    }
  }
```

This creates the access key ID and secret access key. So, to get the values, we need to add in the output as follows:

```
"Outputs": {
    "AccessKey" : {
      "Value" : { "Ref" : "UserCredentials" }
    },
    "SecretKey" : {
      "Value" : {
        "Fn::GetAtt" : [ "UserCredentials", "SecretAccessKey" ]
      }
    }
  }
```

In the output tab of CloudFormation Stack, we can see the values of **Access Key ID** and **Secret Access Key**.

Summary

In this chapter, we have covered how to create and manage AWS Identity and Access Management. We learned about IAM policy, role, group, and user using AWS Management Console, CLI, and SDK Java. IAM is a core part of AWS services, which provides security and permissions to access AWS services.

In the next chapter, we will be learning about EC2 and how we can build scalable applications on EC2.

Building Servers Using EC2

3

Cloud servers are a new infrastructure (rather than on-premises servers) for running applications. Cloud servers are virtual remote machines that can be accessed via the internet. Software can be configured on cloud severs as per our needs. It becomes easy for IT or system administrators to manage cloud servers with minimal configuration, rather than handling traditional on-premise servers. Cloud servers are cheap and offer pay-as-you-go pricing models. So, it becomes inexpensive for small as well as large companies. It also offers a variety of operating system flavors to use. So, we can choose whichever operating system is best suited to our requirements or applications.

In this chapter, we will cover the following topics:

- EC2 instance types
- **Amazon Machine Images (AMI)**
- Key pairs
- Security groups
- EC2 instances
- Elastic Load Balancer
- Auto Scaling groups
- Elastic Block Storage

Elastic Compute Cloud (EC2) allows us to create virtual machines on the Amazon cloud. EC2 offers a wide range of computing machines with different hardware and operating systems. EC2 provides advanced security and elasticity, which allows us to create and deploy highly scalable and fault-tolerant applications. Using EC2, we can reduce the time taken to procure the computing machine, as creating a server and deploying our applications can be done in fewer steps. Also, we don't need to pay any upfront fees for the procurement of machines. They are charged on a pay-as-you-go basis. We can deploy and run any application on EC2, as it offers a virtual machine. You can create any number of EC2 instances under your account.

There are some limits to the number of high-capacity servers that can be created, but these limits can be increased by sending a request to Amazon.

EC2 also allows us to attach storage volumes, which can be used by applications. Storage volumes can be temporary or persistent. This also allows us to manage server access by defining the IP addresses, protocols, and ports.

Amazon EC2 has different pricing models:

- **On-demand**: On-demand instances are useful where we need short-term instances. When you don't know whether you need an instance for a longer time, then you may go with on-demand instances. Amazon charges you based on hours for on-demand instances.
- **Reserved instances**: Reserved instances are used when we know we want our servers to be up and running for a longer period of time, say, more than 1 year. This helps us to reduce the cost by 75% when compared to on-demand instances. We need to purchase reserved instances based on instance types and pay the upfront fees.
- **Spot instances**: Spot instances help us to reduce the cost, as we need to bid for the instances. If Amazon has spare instances in its fleet, you may get them. These instances can be terminated within 2 minutes by Amazon by giving notification. These types of instances are useful when we want to perform small activities and we are not hampered if the instances are terminated in between activities.
- **Dedicated hosts**: Dedicated hosts are often used by AWS customers who want their EC2 instances to run on isolated physical hardware. Other AWS customer instances are not running on this dedicated host hardware.

EC2 instance types

Amazon offers a wide range of computing instance types. They differ in CPUs, storage, memory, and networking performance capability. These instance types are split into five categories:

- General purpose
- Compute optimized
- Memory optimized
- Accelerated computing
- Storage optimized

For more information on instance types, please visit
https://aws.amazon.com/ec2/instance-types.

Amazon Machine Images

An **Amazon Machine Image** (**AMI**) contains a configuration for creating EC2 instances. With a single AMI, we can create multiple EC2 instances. An AMI may contain the configuration of the virtual server, pre-installed software packages, root devices, and much more. It helps users to reuse the AMI for different EC2 instances. Amazon also provides an option for users to create a custom AMI that will include their custom configurations. Amazon also allows us to share the AMI with other AWS accounts and AWS Marketplace.

Key pairs

Key pairs are used to log in to the EC2 instances. They act like access credentials to EC2 instances. They use public-private keys to encrypt and decrypt the login credentials. While creating EC2 instances, we need to associate key pairs so that the user can use them to log in using SSH.

Store key pairs at a secure location because they act as a password for users to connect to your EC2 instance. If the key pair is lost, we cannot recover it. So, we need to generate another key pair and relaunch the EC2 instance with the new key pair.

AWS Management Console

Go to the AWS EC2 Management Console at https://console.aws.amazon.com/ec2/home.

Creating key pairs

Create a new key pair under your AWS account:

1. Click **Key pairs** under **NETWORK and SECURITY** in the left menu.

2. Click **Create Key Pair.** Provide a friendly name in the **Key pair name** input field:

Figure 3.1: Creating a key pair

Usually, a key pair name should be able to identify the entity as an application or user, or department/group name. Click **Create**:

Figure 3.2: Listing key pairs

The key pairs file, `aws-bootcamp.pem`, will be downloaded on your machine. Store this key pair file in a secure location.

AWS CLI

To execute the CLI script, open Command Prompt.

Creating key pairs

Create a new key pair under your AWS account:

```
aws ec2 create-key-pair ^
--key-name "aws-bootcamp"
```

The following are the options that can be used with `create-key-pair`:

Parameters	Optional	Descriptions
`--key-name`	False	Friendly key name which identifies the entity as an application or user or department/group name

This command returns the private key and key fingerprint, which needs to be saved to a file at a secure location.

AWS SDK - Java

To access EC2 services, we need to create the `AmazonEC2` object as:

```
AmazonEC2 amazonEC2 = AmazonEC2ClientBuilder
                    .standard()
//                  .withClientConfiguration(getClientConfiguration())
                    .withCredentials(getCredentials())
                    .withRegion(Regions.US_EAST_1)
                    .build();
```

The `ClientConfiguration` and `AWSCredentialsProvider` objects are created in the same way as we did in `Chapter 2`, *Configuring IAM*.

Creating key pairs

Create a new key pair under your AWS account:

```
String keyPairName = "aws-bootcamp";
 String keyPairPrivateMaterial = createKeyPair(keyPairName);
 ........
public String createKeyPair(
String keyName) {
CreateKeyPairRequest createKeyPairRequest =
 new CreateKeyPairRequest()
.withKeyName(keyName);
CreateKeyPairResult createKeyPairResult =
 amazonEC2.createKeyPair(
createKeyPairRequest);
KeyPair keyPair = createKeyPairResult.getKeyPair();
String privateKey = keyPair.getKeyMaterial();
return privateKey;
}
```

Save `keyPairPrivateMaterial` to a file, as this contains the private key which we will be able to use to log in to an EC2 instance.

Security groups

A security group acts as a firewall for our EC2 instance. We can restrict access to our EC2 by defining on which protocol, port, and IP address EC2 is accessible. We can also define a CIDR block so that a group of IP addresses are able to access EC2 instances.

AWS Management Console

Go to AWS EC2 Management Console at `https://console.aws.amazon.com/ec2/home`.

Creating a security group

Create a new security group under your AWS account:

Click **Security Groups** under **NETWORK & SECURITY** in the left menu. Click **Create Security Group**:

Figure 3.3: Creating a security group

Provide a friendly security group name, description, and the VPC you want to create this security group. Also, we need to add a rule for inbound access. In our case, we will add a rule for SSH (port 22), which will allow us to access an EC2 instance from any source (IP address). We can also provide an outbound rule, which will allow us to access specific destinations only. By default, the outbound rule is configured to access port 0-65535 and to all destinations:

Figure 3.4: Outbound security group rule

Once the rules are added, click **Create**:

Figure 3.5: Security group listing

AWS CLI

To execute the CLI script, open Command Prompt.

Creating a security group

Create a new security group under your AWS account:

```
aws ec2 create-security-group ^
--group-name "aws-bootcamp" ^
--description "Security Group for AWS Bootcamp" ^
--vpc-id "vpc-a1cbefd8"
```

The following are the options that can be used with `create-security-group`:

Parameters	Optional	Descriptions
`--group-name`	False	Friendly name.
`--description`	False	Friendly description.
`--vpc-id`	True	VPC ID under which the security group will be created. If we don't provide a VPC ID, the default VPC ID will be created.

Adding an inbound rule

Add an inbound rule under the specified security group:

```
aws ec2 authorize-security-group-ingress ^
--group-id "sg-f529f186" ^
--protocol "tcp" ^
--port 22 ^
--cidr "0.0.0.0/0"
```

or

```
aws ec2 authorize-security-group-ingress ^
--group-name "aws-bootcamp" ^
--protocol "tcp" ^
--port 22 ^
--cidr "0.0.0.0/0"
```

The following snippet will add multiple permissions:

```
aws ec2 authorize-security-group-ingress ^
--group-name "aws-bootcamp" ^
--ip-permissions
"IpProtocol=tcp,FromPort=22,ToPort=22,IpRanges=[{CidrIp=0.0.0.0/0},{CidrIp=
10.0.0.0/24}]"
```

The following snippet will allow access from the source security group of the same AWS Account ID or another one:

```
aws ec2 authorize-security-group-ingress ^
--group-name "aws-bootcamp" ^
--protocol "tcp" --port 22 ^
--source-group "default" ^
--group-owner "123456789012"
```

The following are the options that can be used with `authorize-security-group-ingress`:

Parameters	Optional	Descriptions
`--group-id`	True	Group ID, under which the inbound rule will be added. This can be used instead of `--group-name`.
`--group-name`	True	Group name under which the inbound rule will be added. This can be used instead of `--group-id`.
`--protocol`	True	The IP protocol. Valid values can be TCP, UDP, ICMP, all.
`--port`	True	Single integer port or range (min-max) that will be opened to access from sources.
`--cidr`	True	The CIDR IP range, which allows access to a defined port.
`--ip-permissions`	True	Single or multiple IP permissions.
`--source-group`	True	Name or ID of the source security group. Either the source group or CIDR can be given.
`--group-owner`	True	AWS Account ID in which the source security group is created.

AWS SDK – Java

To access EC2 services, we need to create the `AmazonEC2` object, as described in the key pair's AWS SDK - Java section.

Creating a security group

Create a new security group under your AWS account:

```
String groupName = "aws-bootcamp";
 String groupDescription = "Security Group for AWS Bootcamp";
 String groupId = createSecurityGroup(groupName, groupDescription);
........
public String createSecurityGroup(
String groupName,
String groupDescription) {
CreateSecurityGroupRequest createSecurityGroupRequest =
 new CreateSecurityGroupRequest()
```

```
.withGroupName(groupName)
.withDescription(groupDescription);
CreateSecurityGroupResult createSecurityGroupResult =
 amazonEC2.createSecurityGroup(
createSecurityGroupRequest);
return createSecurityGroupResult.getGroupId();
}
```

Adding an inbound rule

Add an inbound rule under the specified security group:

```
int sshPort = 22;
 String cidr = "0.0.0.0/0";
 authorizeSecurityGroupIngress(groupName, sshPort, cidr);
........
public void authorizeSecurityGroupIngress(
String groupName,
 int port,
String cidr) {
AuthorizeSecurityGroupIngressRequest request =
 new AuthorizeSecurityGroupIngressRequest()
.withGroupName(groupName)
.withIpProtocol("tcp")
.withCidrIp(cidr)
.withToPort(port)
.withFromPort(port);
 /*IpPermission ipPermission =
createIpPermission(port, cidr);
request.withIpPermissions(ipPermission);*/
AuthorizeSecurityGroupIngressResult result =
 amazonEC2.
authorizeSecurityGroupIngress(request);
}
private IpPermission createIpPermission(
 int port,
String cidr) {
IpRange ipRange = new IpRange()
.withCidrIp(cidr);
IpPermission ipPermission =
 new IpPermission()
.withIpProtocol("tcp")
```

```
.withFromPort(port)
.withToPort(port)
.withIpv4Ranges(ipRange);
return ipPermission;
}
```

We can either use the IP permission to set multiple permissions in a single request, or add multiple requests using individual calls.

AWS CloudFormation

To create a security group, we need to use the AWS::EC2::SecurityGroup type:

```
"AWSBootcampSecurityGroup": {
    "Type": "AWS::EC2::SecurityGroup",
    "Properties": {
        "GroupName" : "aws-bootcamp",
        "GroupDescription": "Enable access via port 22 and 80",
        "SecurityGroupIngress": [{
            "IpProtocol": "tcp",
            "FromPort": "22",
            "ToPort": "22",
            "CidrIp": "0.0.0.0/0"
        },{
            "IpProtocol": "tcp",
            "FromPort": "80",
            "ToPort": "80",
            "CidrIp": "0.0.0.0/0"
}]
    }
  }
```

EC2 instance

An EC2 instance is a virtual server running on Amazon. An EC2 instance service is exposed as a web service, whereby a user can provision a computing platform to run their application.

AWS Management Console

Go to AWS EC2 Management Console at https://console.aws.amazon.com/ec2/home.

Launching an instance

Create a new EC2 instance:

1. Click **Instances** under **INSTANCE** on the left menu.
2. Click **Launch Instance**.
3. **Choose an Amazon Machine Image (AMI).** As discussed in the AMI section, we need to choose an AMI that has the required pre-installed software package:

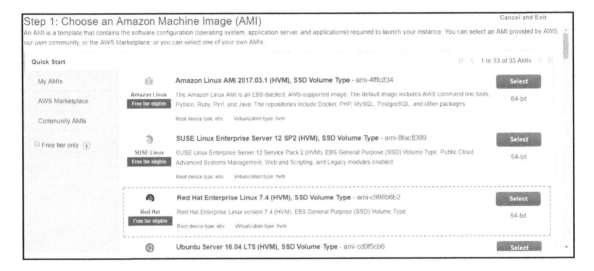

Figure 3.6: Choosing an AMI

Here, we can see that we have the option to select the AMI from different sources:

- **My AMIs**: Choose from your own custom created AMI.
- **AWS Marketplace**: You can choose from AWS Marketplace where third parties have created AMIs for public use. These AMIs may be freely available or you may be charged.
- **Community AMIs**: You can choose from Community AMIs, which are listed by third parties who have made their AMI public.

If you are a new user on the AWS account, you are eligible to use different AWS services under the free tier for a certain period of time.

 Go to `https://aws.amazon.com/free/` to find more about the AWS free tier

In our case, we will select **Red Hat Enterprise Linux 7.4 (HVM), SSD Volume Type**. Click **Select**.

4. Choose an instance type: In this step, we need to choose the instance type we want to create. This defines the computing capacity we need our EC2 instance to have:

Figure 3.7: Choosing an instance type

We will select **t2.micro**, which comes under the **Free Tier**. Click **Next: Configure Instance Details**.

5. Configure the instance: Provide the details as per your requirements:

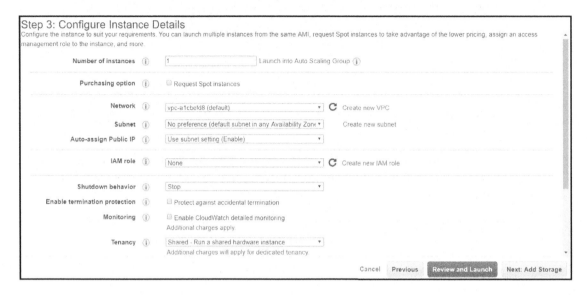

Figure 3.8: Configuring instance details

We can also provide a shell script that will be executed when the instance is created. This shell script can contain some software packages or applications to install on the instance:

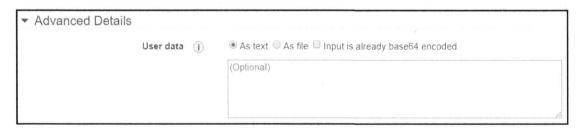

Figure 3.9: Configuring instance advanced details

Click **Next: Add Storage**.

6. Add the storage: We can add additional volume in this step. You can increase the size of the volume as per your requirements:

Figure 3.10: Adding storage

Here, the **Delete on Termination** checkbox is selected, which means the volume will be deleted when the instance is terminated. If you want to keep the volume even after the instance is terminated, deselect this checkbox. Click **Next: Add Tags**.

7. Add the tags: In this step, we can add tags to the EC2 instance and volume. Tags are used to easily manage AWS resources by providing similar tags. As we did in our book example, we will add tags with **key** as **Name** and **value** as **AWS Bootcamp**, so in future, if we want to know which EC2 instance belongs to which category, we can identify it using tags:

Figure 3.11: Adding tags

Click **Next: Configure Security Group**.

8. Configure the security group: In this step, we will create a new security group or select an existing security group:

Figure 3.12: Configuring a security group

To select an existing security group, click on the **Select an existing security group** radio button. This will list the security groups created under your account:

Figure 3.13: Selecting an existing security group

Select the appropriate security group and click **Review and Launch**.

9. Review and launch: Review the configuration and click **Launch**:

Figure 3.14: Review and launch

10. Create a new key pair or select an existing key pair: In this step, choose an existing key pair or create a new key pair:

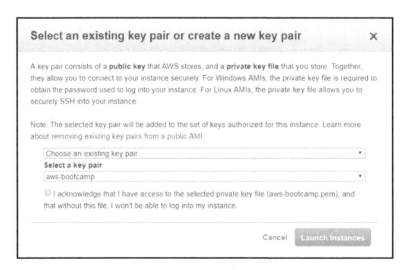

Figure 3.15: Selecting a key pair

Click on the checkbox for acknowledging that you have the pem file of the selected key pair so that you can access the EC2 instance and then click **Launch Instances**.

11. The instance is launched: We have now finished launching a new EC2 instance:

Figure 3.16: Launch status

To view the launch logs, click on the **View launch log** link and if you want to view the list of instances, click **View Instances**.

12. View the instances: Here you can view the instances that have been created under your AWS account:

Figure 3.17: Viewing instances

We can see the instance state is **running**, which means the instance has been created and is running. We can verify the instance by connecting to it using the SSH client.

Connecting to the EC2 instance

In the previous section, we created an EC2 instance using AWS Management Console. In this section, we will connect to an EC2 instance using an SSH client, PuTTY:

1. Open `PuttyGen.exe`: PuTTYgen is the key generator tool for generating keys:

Figure 3.18: Opening PuTTYgen

Click **Load**, which will load an existing private key, `aws-bootcamp.pem`:

Figure 3.19: Loading the pem file

Click **OK**.

2. (Optional) Provide the **Key Passphrase** for securing your private key usage.

3. Click **Save private key** as `aws-bootcamp.ppk`. Open `Putty.exe`: Putty is an SSH and telnet client that allows us to connect to remote machines:

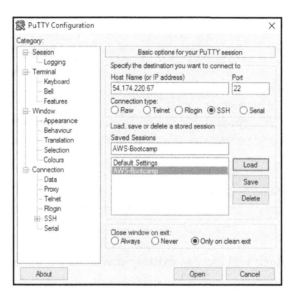

Figure 3.20: Putty

Provide the following details:

- **Host Name (or IP address)**: Provide the public IP address of the EC2 instance, `54.174.220.67`, which can be obtained from the View Instances page
- **Private key file for authentication**: Expand **SSH** on the left menu, click **Auth**, and click **Browse** to select the `aws-bootcamp.ppk` file
- After providing the details, click **Open**

4. **Putty Security Alert**: You will be asked to add the server's host key to the cache in the registry. This will be requested when you connect to the remote machine for first time from your local machine:

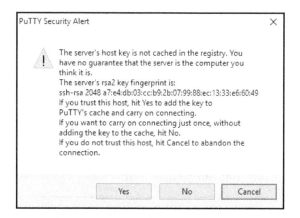

Figure 3.21: Adding the server host key in the registry

5. You will be asked for the login user: Provide `ec2-user` as the username. This username varies as per operating system:

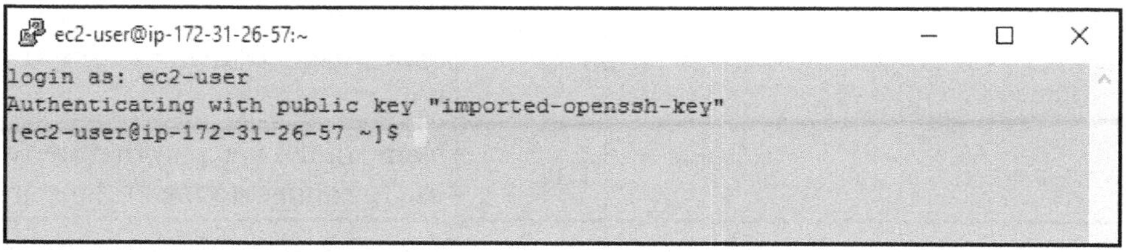

```
login as: ec2-user
Authenticating with public key "imported-openssh-key"
[ec2-user@ip-172-31-26-57 ~]$
```

Figure 3.22: Instance terminal

Once the login user is authenticated, you will see the **ec2-user** prompt.

AWS CLI

To execute the CLI script, open Command Prompt.

Launching an instance

Create a new EC2 instance:

```
aws ec2 run-instances ^
--image-id "ami-c998b6b2" ^
--instance-type "t2.micro" ^
--count 1 ^
```

```
--no-associate-public-ip-address ^
--key-name "aws-bootcamp" ^
--security-group-ids "sg-7c6ecf0f" ^
--user-data file://userData.txt
```

The following is the user data script used in run-instances:

userData.txt

```
echo "Your Shell Script"
```

The following are the options that can be used with run-instances:

Parameters	Optional	Descriptions
--image-id	False	ID of the AMI.
--instance-type	True	EC2 instance type.
--count	True	Number of EC2 instances to launch.
--associate-public-ip-address or --no-associate-public-ip-address	True	Whether the public IP address needs to be assigned to an EC2 instance or not.
--key-name	True	Name of the key pair that we will use to connect to the EC2 instance.
--security-group-ids	True	One or more security group IDs. We can provide multiple IDs as: sg-7c6ecf0f and sg-8c9ecf0f.
--user-data	True	Commands that will be executed while launching the EC2 instance.

For more parameters, go to
http://docs.aws.amazon.com/cli/latest/reference/ec2/run-instance
s.html.

AWS SDK - Java

To access the EC2 service, we need to create the AmazonEC2 object, as described in the key pair's AWS SDK - Java section.

Launching an instance

Create a new EC2 instance under your AWS account:

```
String imageId = "ami-c998b6b2";
 int minInstanceCount = 1;
 int maxInstanceCount = 1;
 String instanceId = runInstances(
        imageId,
        InstanceType.T2Micro,
        minInstanceCount,
        maxInstanceCount,
        groupName,
        keyPairName);
 ........
public String runInstances(
String amiImageId,
InstanceType instanceType,
 int minInstanceCount,
 int maxInstanceCount,
String securityGroupName,
String keyPairName) {
RunInstancesRequest runInstancesRequest =
 new RunInstancesRequest()
.withImageId(amiImageId)
.withInstanceType(instanceType)
.withKeyName(keyPairName)
.withSecurityGroups(securityGroupName)
.withMinCount(minInstanceCount)
.withMaxCount(maxInstanceCount);
RunInstancesResult runInstancesResult =
 amazonEC2.runInstances(
runInstancesRequest);
return runInstancesResult
.getReservation()
.getInstances()
.get(0)
.getInstanceId();
}
```

AWS CloudFormation

To create the EC2 instance, we need to use the AWS::EC2::Instance type:

```
"EC2Instance": {
    "Type": "AWS::EC2::Instance",
```

```
    "Properties": {
        "InstanceType": "t2.micro",
        "SecurityGroups": [{
            "Ref": "AWSBootcampSecurityGroup"
}],
        "KeyName": "aws-bootcamp",
        "ImageId": "ami-c998b6b2",
        "UserData": {
            "Fn::Base64": {
                "Fn::Join": [
"n", [
"#!/bin/bash",
"yum install httpd -y",
"service httpd start"
]
]
}
        }
    }
}
```

Elastic Load Balancer

Elastic Load Balancer (ELB) is a service that distributes user requests to multiple EC2 instances. By distributing the load, we ensure that our EC2 instances are properly utilized and share the same amount of load between different instances, so that no single instance is over-utilized or under-utilized. We can attach an EC2 instance to the load balancer as and when required. The ELB health check feature monitors the EC2 instance to check that application is up and running so that it can route requests. If the health check fails, ELB marks the EC2 instance as out-of-service so those new requests are not routed to those instances.

For high-availability applications, ELB can be associated with the Auto Scaling group, which can attach a new instance in the event of heavy traffic or remove the instance in the event of failure or low traffic. The auto-scaling group registers the new instance to be added in ELB or is used to remove any instance from ELB.

There are three types of load balancers available:

- **Application load balancer** :This is widely used when we want to apply some rules to route the request to a destination over HTTP and HTTPS.
- **Network load balancer**: This is commonly used for distributing TCP requests. It can scale up to millions of requests per second.

- **Classic load balancer:** This is the most common and preferred load balancer among the three. It is used with EC2 instances to distribute the traffic.

In this chapter, we will create a classic load balancer.

AWS Management Console

Go to AWS EC2 Management Console at `https://console.aws.amazon.com/ec2/home`.

Creating a load balancer

Create a classic load balancer:

1. Click **Load Balancers** under **LOAD BALANCING** on the left menu.
2. Click **Create Load Balancer**.
3. Select **Load Balancer Type**:

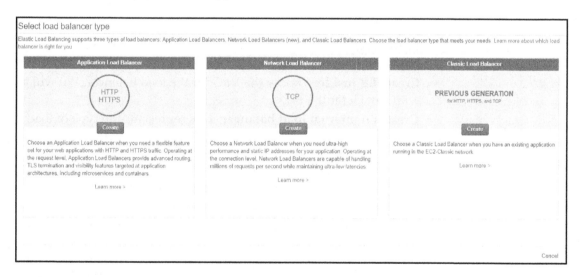

Figure 3.23: Selecting the load balancer type

Click on **Create** under **Classic Load Balancer**.

4. Define the load balancer:

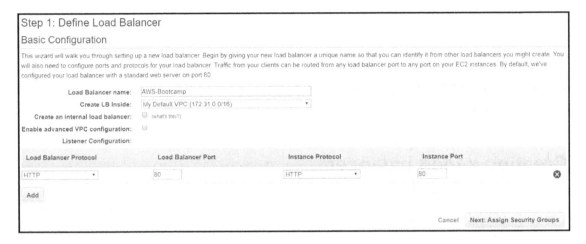

Figure 3.24: Defining the load balancer

Here, we will provide the following details:

- **Load Balancer Name**: A friendly name to represent your application.
- **Create LB inside**: Choose the VPC for the load balancer. We will go with **My Default VPC**.
- **Create an internal load balancer**: This represents the type of load balancer we want to create. We will keep the checkbox unchecked so that the load balancer will be accessed via the internet.
- **Enable advanced VPC configuration**: Enabling advanced VPC configuration will allow us to select the subnets that will provide us with higher availability for our load balancer.
- **Listener Configuration**: This allows us to configure multiple listeners for connection requests. The listener takes a frontend protocol and the port of the load balancer, and a backend protocol and the port of the EC2 instance for connections. We will keep the default listener configuration.

Click **Next: Assign Security Groups**.

5. Assign the **Security Groups**:

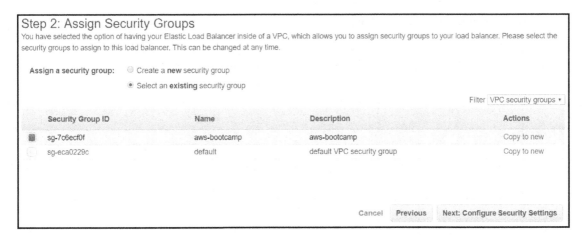

Figure 3.25: Assigning the security groups

We can assign multiple security groups that act as a firewall to allow access to our load balancer. We will select the **aws-bootcamp** security group.

Click **Next: Configure Security Settings**.

6. Configure the **Security Settings**:

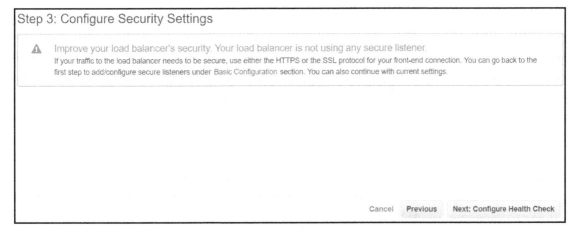

Figure 3.26: Configuring the security settings

There are no changes here, as we are not using a secure listener. Click **Next: Configure Health Check**.

7. Configure the **Health Check**:

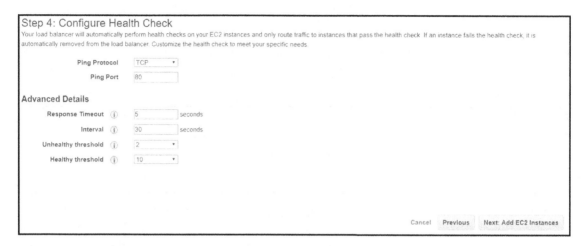

Figure 3.27: Configuring the health check

Here, we need to provide the following details:

- **Ping Protocol**: Protocol on which your backend instance application is running
- **Ping Port**: Port on which your backend instance application is running
- **Ping Path**: Path which will be invoke by the load balancer to ensure your application is up and running
- **Response Timeout**: This denotes the time to wait for a response from the application for a health check request
- **Interval**: This denotes the interval time between health check requests
- **Unhealthy threshold**: This denotes a consecutive health check request count to declare the EC2 instance as unhealthy
- **Healthy threshold**: This denotes a consecutive health check request count to declare the EC2 instance as healthy so that the load balancer can route traffic to this instance

Click **Next: Add EC2 Instances.**

8. Add the **EC2 Instances**:

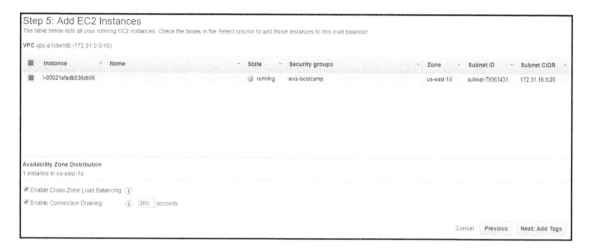

Figure 3.28: Adding the EC2 instances

Here, select the EC2 instances you want to add under this load balancer.

 Make sure your application is up and running on port 80. For our example, we have installed and started the `httpd` server on the EC2 instance.

Also, select the **Enable Cross-Zone Load Balancing** checkbox to allow requests to route across multiple backend instances in all availability zones and the **Enable Connection Draining** checkbox with 300 seconds to allow existing traffic to continue flowing.

Enabling **Connection Draining** will also ensure that traffic is not redirected to de-registered or unhealthy instances. It also ensures that requests in the process are completed while instances are getting de-registered or are unhealthy.

Click **Next: Add Tags**.

9. Add the **Tags**:

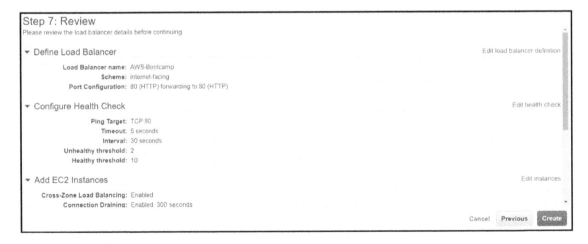

Figure 3.29: Adding the tags

Here, add the tags that can be used to identify your application's load balancer or adding certain metadata. Click **Review and Create**.

10. **Review** the details:

Figure 3.30: Reviewing the load balancer details

Review the configuration and click **Create**.

11. Check the **Load Balancer Creation Status**:

Figure 3.31: Load balancer creation status

It takes some time to create the load balancer. Once created, click **Close**.

12. Check the list of load balancers:

Figure 3.32: List of load balancers

Here, you can see that the new load balancer has been created. The instance registration under the load balancer takes some time. Copy the **DNS name** value and open it in the browser:

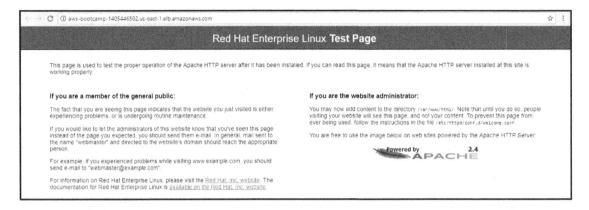

Figure 3.33: Load balancer DNS name

Here, you can see that the load balancer has routed your request to your application running on the registered EC2 instance.

AWS CLI

To execute the CLI script, open Command Prompt.

Creating a load balancer

Create a classic load balancer:

```
aws elb create-load-balancer ^
--load-balancer-name "AWS-Bootcamp" ^
--listeners
"Protocol=HTTP,LoadBalancerPort=80,InstanceProtocol=HTTP,InstancePort=80" ^
--availability-zones "us-east-1d" ^
--security-groups "sg-7c6ecf0f" ^
--tags "Key=Name,Value=AWS-Bootcamp"
```

The following are the options that can be used with `create-load-balancer`:

Parameters	Optional	Descriptions
`--load-balancer-name`	False	Friendly name for the load balancer name which identifies the application.
`--listeners`	False	Listeners configuration for the frontend (client to load balancer) and backend (load balancer to EC2 instance) for connection requests.
`--availability-zones`	True	One or more availability zones for the load balancer.
`--subnets`	True	Subnet ID to which the load balancer will be attached under VPC.
`--security-groups`	True	Security group ID to attach to the load balancer.
`--scheme`	True	This identifies the type of load balancer. By default the load balancer is internet facing. To create load balancer for internal VPC access only, we need to specify the value as internal.
`--tags`	True	One or more tags can be assigned to the load balancer.

Creating load balancer listeners

Create a listener under the load balancer:

```
aws elb create-load-balancer-listeners ^
--load-balancer-name "AWS-Bootcamp" ^
--listeners
"Protocol=HTTP,LoadBalancerPort=80,InstanceProtocol=HTTP,InstancePort=80"
```

The following are the options that can be used to create load balancer listeners:

Parameters	Optional	Descriptions
`--load-balancer-name`	False	Load balancer name to which the listener needs to be attached
`--listeners`	False	Listeners configuration for frontend (client to load balancer) and backend (load balancer to EC2 instance) for connection requests.

Configuring a health check

Configure the health check:

```
aws elb configure-health-check ^
--load-balancer-name "AWS-Bootcamp" ^
--health-check
"Target=TCP:80,Interval=30,Timeout=5,UnhealthyThreshold=2,HealthyThreshold=
2"
```

The following are the options that can be used to configure the health check:

Parameters	Optional	Descriptions
`--load-balancer-name`	False	Load balancer name to configure the health check.
`--health-check`	False	Health check parameters.

Registering an instance

Register an EC2 instance with the load balancer:

```
aws elb register-instances-with-load-balancer ^
--load-balancer-name "AWS-Bootcamp" ^
--instances "i-00021afadb836cb96"
```

The following are the options that can be used with `register-instances-with-load-balancer`:

Parameters	Optional	Descriptions
`--load-balancer-name`	False	Load balancer name to which the instance needs to be attached.
`--instances`	False	One or more EC2 instance IDs separated by a space like this: `i-00021afadb836cb96 i-00021afadb836cb97`

AWS SDK - Java

To access the Elastic Load Balancer service, we need to create the `AmazonElasticLoadBalancing` object:

```
AmazonElasticLoadBalancing elbClient =
    AmazonElasticLoadBalancingClientBuilder
                .standard()
    //          .withClientConfiguration(getClientConfiguration())
                .withCredentials(getCredentials())
                .withRegion(Regions.US_EAST_1)
                .build();
```

The `ClientConfiguration` and `AWSCredentialsProvider` objects are created in the same way as we did in `Chapter 2`, *Configuring IAM*.

Creating a load balancer

Create a classic load balancer:

```
String availabilityZone = "us-east-1d";
  String loadBalancerName = "AWS-Bootcamp";
 String dnsName = createLoadBalancer(
        loadBalancerName,
        Arrays.asList(groupId),
        Arrays.asList(availabilityZone));
 ........
 public String createLoadBalancer(
String loadBalancerName,
List<String> securityGroups,
List<String> availabilityZones) {
String protocol = "HTTP";
```

```
 int loadBalancerPort = 80;
 int instancePort = 80;
Listener httpListener =
 new Listener()
.withProtocol(protocol)
.withLoadBalancerPort(loadBalancerPort)
.withInstancePort(instancePort);
CreateLoadBalancerRequest createLoadBalancerRequest =
 new CreateLoadBalancerRequest()
.withLoadBalancerName(loadBalancerName)
.withListeners(httpListener)
.withSecurityGroups(securityGroups)
.withAvailabilityZones(availabilityZones);
CreateLoadBalancerResult createLoadBalancerResult =
 elbClient.createLoadBalancer(
createLoadBalancerRequest);
return createLoadBalancerResult.getDNSName();
}
```

Creating load balancer listeners

Create a listener under the load balancer:

```
String loadBalancerProtocol = "HTTP";
 String instanceProtocol = "HTTP";
 Integer instancePort = 80;
 Integer loadBalancerPort = 80;
 createLoadBalancerListeners(
         loadBalancerName,
         loadBalancerProtocol,
         instanceProtocol,
         loadBalancerPort,
         instancePort);
 ........
 public void createLoadBalancerListeners(
String loadBalancerName,
String loadBalancerProtocol,
String instanceProtocol,
Integer instancePort,
Integer loadBalancerPort) {
Listener listener = createListener(
loadBalancerProtocol,
instanceProtocol,
instancePort,
loadBalancerPort);
CreateLoadBalancerListenersRequest request =
```

```
new CreateLoadBalancerListenersRequest()
.withLoadBalancerName(loadBalancerName)
.withListeners(Arrays.asList(listener));
CreateLoadBalancerListenersResult result =
 elbClient.createLoadBalancerListeners(request);
}
private Listener createListener(
String loadBalancerProtocol,
String instanceProtocol,
Integer instancePort,
Integer loadBalancerPort) {
Listener listener = new Listener()
.withInstanceProtocol(instanceProtocol)
.withProtocol(loadBalancerProtocol)
.withInstancePort(instancePort)
.withLoadBalancerPort(loadBalancerPort);
return listener;
}
```

Configuring a health check

Configure the health check:

```
int healthyThreshold = 2;
 int unhealthyThreshold = 2;
 int interval = 30;
 String target = "TCP:80";
 int timeout = 5;
 configureHealthCheck(
         loadBalancerName,
         healthyThreshold,
         unhealthyThreshold,
         interval,
         target,
         timeout);
 .......
public void configureHealthCheck(
String loadBalancerName,
 int healthyThreshold,
 int unhealthyThreshold,
 int interval,
String target,
 int timeout) {
HealthCheck healthCheck = createHealthCheck(
healthyThreshold,
unhealthyThreshold,
```

```
interval,
target,
timeout);
ConfigureHealthCheckRequest configureHealthCheckRequest =
 new ConfigureHealthCheckRequest()
.withHealthCheck(healthCheck)
.withLoadBalancerName(loadBalancerName);
ConfigureHealthCheckResult configureHealthCheckResult =
 elbClient.configureHealthCheck(
configureHealthCheckRequest);
}
private HealthCheck createHealthCheck(
 int healthyThreshold,
 int unhealthyThreshold,
 int interval,
String target,
 int timeout) {
HealthCheck healthCheck = new HealthCheck()
.withHealthyThreshold(healthyThreshold)
.withInterval(interval)
.withTarget(target)
.withTimeout(timeout)
.withUnhealthyThreshold(unhealthyThreshold);
return healthCheck;
}
```

Registering a instance

Register an EC2 instance with the load balancer:

```
registerInstancesWithLoadBalancer(
        loadBalancerName,
        Arrays.asList(instanceId));
........
public void registerInstancesWithLoadBalancer(
String loadBalancerName,
List<String> instanceIds) {
List<Instance> elbInstanceList =
getELBInstanceList(instanceIds);
RegisterInstancesWithLoadBalancerRequest request =
 new RegisterInstancesWithLoadBalancerRequest()
.withLoadBalancerName(loadBalancerName)
.withInstances(elbInstanceList);
RegisterInstancesWithLoadBalancerResult result =
 elbClient.registerInstancesWithLoadBalancer(request);
}
```

```java
private List<Instance> getELBInstanceList(
List<String> instanceIds) {
List<Instance> instanceList = new ArrayList<>();
if(instanceIds!=null && !instanceIds.isEmpty()) {
 for(String instanceId: instanceIds){
instanceList.add(new Instance()
.withInstanceId(instanceId));
}
}
return instanceList;
}
```

AWS CloudFormation

To create the Elastic Load Balancer, we need to use the
`AWS::ElasticLoadBalancing::LoadBalancer` type:

```json
"ElasticLoadBalancer": {
    "Type": "AWS::ElasticLoadBalancing::LoadBalancer",
    "Properties": {
        "Tags" : [
{
                "Key": "Name",
                "Value": "AWS-Bootcamp"
}
],
        "HealthCheck": {
            "HealthyThreshold": 2,
            "Interval": 30,
            "Target": "TCP:80",
            "Timeout": 5,
            "UnhealthyThreshold": 2
},
        "Listeners": [{
            "InstancePort": 80,
            "PolicyNames": [],
            "LoadBalancerPort": 80,
            "Protocol": "HTTP",
            "InstanceProtocol": "HTTP"
}],
        "SecurityGroups": [{
            "Fn::GetAtt": ["AWSBootcampSecurityGroup", "GroupId"]
}],
        "ConnectionSettings": {
            "IdleTimeout": 600
},
```

```
        "Scheme": "internet-facing",
        "AvailabilityZones": [
"us-east-1d"
],
        "Instances" : [{
            "Ref" : "EC2Instance"
}]
}
  }
```

Auto Scaling groups

Auto Scaling is used to manage EC2 instances, whereby a number of instances can be
created for our application based on traffic. Auto Scaling helps to keep a group of healthy
instances for applications to run. Based on the Auto Scaling configuration, we can add more
instances. An Auto Scaling event can be triggered from CloudWatch monitoring, where it
measures the metrics configured and if it achieves its threshold limit, it triggers an event to
the Auto Scaling group.

AWS Management Console

Go to AWS EC2 Management Console at `https://console.aws.amazon.com/ec2/home`.

Creating an Auto Scaling group

Create an Auto Scaling group, which will launch scalable instances:

1. Click **Launch Configuration** under **Auto Scaling** on the left menu.
2. Click **Create Auto Scaling Group**.
3. Create the **Auto Scaling Group**:

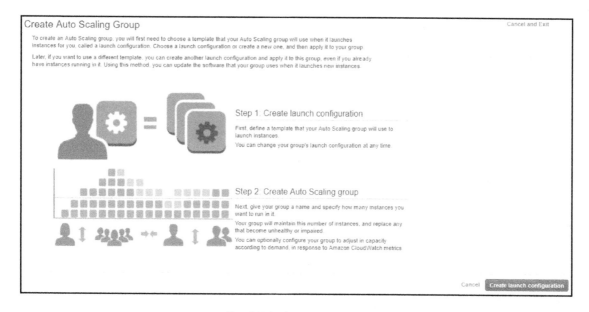

Figure 3.34: Creating the Auto Scaling group

Click **Create launch configuration**.

4. Select an AMI:

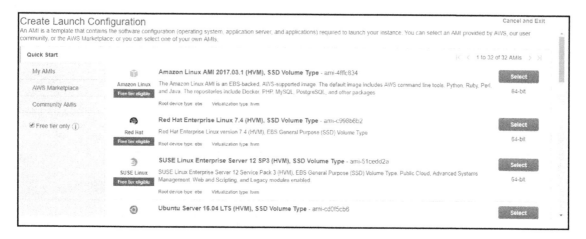

Figure 3.35: Selecting an AMI for the launch configuration

Here we need to select the AMI for our EC2 instance. We will select the **Red Hat Enterprise Linux 7.4 (HVM), SSD Volume Type** and click **Select**.

5. Select the instance type:

Filter by:	All instance types ⌄	Current generation ⌄	Show/Hide Columns				
Currently selected: t2.micro (Variable ECUs, 1 vCPUs, 2.5 GHz, Intel Xeon Family, 1 GiB memory, EBS only)						

	Family	Type ⌄	vCPUs ⓘ ⌄	Memory (GiB) ⌄	Instance Storage (GB) ⓘ ⌄	EBS-Optimized Available ⓘ	Network Performance ⓘ ⌄
☐	General purpose	t2.nano	1	0.5	EBS only	-	Low to Moderate
■	General purpose	t2.micro Free tier eligible	1	1	EBS only	-	Low to Moderate
☐	General purpose	t2.small	1	2	EBS only	-	Low to Moderate
☐	General purpose	t2.medium	2	4	EBS only	-	Low to Moderate
☐	General purpose	t2.large	2	8	EBS only	-	Low to Moderate
☐	General purpose	t2.xlarge	4	16	EBS only	-	Moderate

Cancel   Previous   **Next: Configure details**

Figure 3.36: Selecting the instance type for the launch configuration

Here, we will select the EC2 instance type. We will select the **t2.micro** instance type and click **Next: Configure details**.

6. Configure the details:

Create Launch Configuration

Name ⓘ	AWS-Bootcamp
Purchasing option ⓘ	☐ Request Spot Instances
IAM role ⓘ	None ▾
Monitoring ⓘ	☐ Enable CloudWatch detailed monitoring Learn more

▸ Advanced Details

💬 Later, if you want to use a different launch configuration, you can create a new one and apply it to any Auto Scaling group. Existing launch configurations cannot be edited.

Cancel   Previous   **Skip to review**   Next: Add Storage

Figure 3.37: Configuring the details for the launch configuration

Here, we will provide the following details:

- **Name**: Provide the launch configuration name

- **Purchasing option**: Decide whether we want a spot instance or an on-demand instance
- **IAM role**: IAM role that needs to be attached to the EC2 instance
- **Monitoring**: Decide whether we need CloudWatch monitoring for our EC2 instances that are launched

We also have optional advanced details:

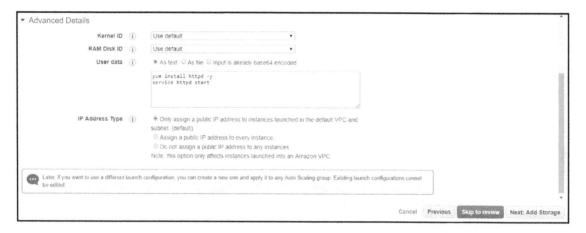

Figure 3.38: Advanced details for the launch configuration

Here, we will provide the following details:

- **Kernel ID**: We need to select the Kernel ID thWe need to select the Kernel ID that will be used by EC2 instances. This Kernel ID helps our EC2 instances to get updated with security fixes, patches, and new functionalities.
- **RAM Disk ID**: We need to select the RAM Disk ID, which contains drivers that help the selected Kernel to work.
- **User data**: User data is the script that will be executed while bootstrapping the EC2 instance.
- **IP Address Type**: This denotes whether a public IP address needs to be assigned to the EC2 instance or not.

Once the configuration has been done, click **Next: Add Storage**.

7. Add the storage:

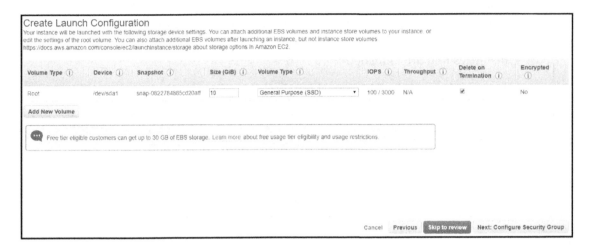

Figure 3.39: Adding the storage for the launch configuration

Here, we can attach the volume to our EC2 instances. So based on the storage configuration, our new scaled-in EC2 instance will be launched with the requisite volume. Click **Next: Configure Security Group**.

8. Configure the security group:

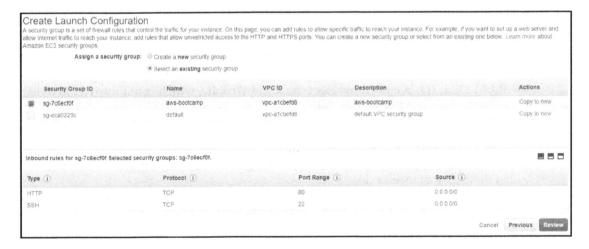

Figure 3.40: Security group for the launch configuration

Here, we will attach one or more security groups that will be attached to EC2 instances. Click **Review**.

9. Review the launch configuration:

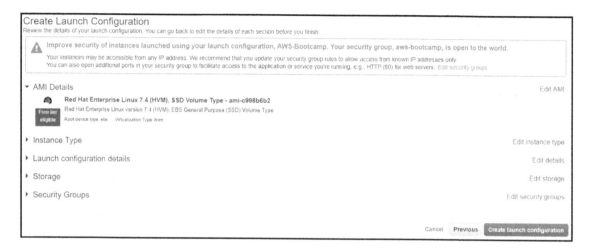

Figure 3.41: Reviewing the launch configuration

Review the launch configuration and if all looks good, click **Create launch configuration**.

10. Select the key pair:

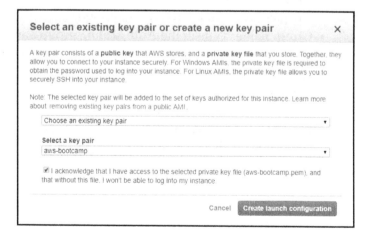

Figure 3.42: Selecting the key pair for the launch configuration

This is an important step. Assigning a key pair for the launch configuration will allow us to log in to EC2 instances. Select the key pair, **aws-bootcamp**, and click **Create launch configuration**. This will create the launch configuration and the user will be redirected to create the Auto Scaling Configuration screen.

11. Configure the Auto Scaling group:

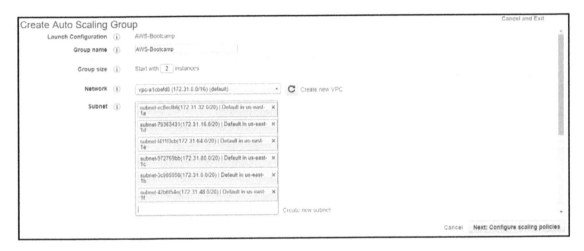

Figure 3.43: Auto Scaling group configuration

Here, we will provide the following details:

- **Launch Configuration**: This field will be pre-populated as we have navigate from the launch configuration.
- **Group name**: Type in the Auto Scaling group name.
- **Group Size**: The desired capacity of the EC2 instances.
- **Network**: VPC under which EC2 instances needs to be created.
- **Subnet**: This will allow us to define a range of IP addresses that differentiate from other EC2 resources. If you need your instance to be available publicly over the internet, use public subnets, and if you need private access within VPC, use private subnets.

Also, we can optionally configure advanced details:

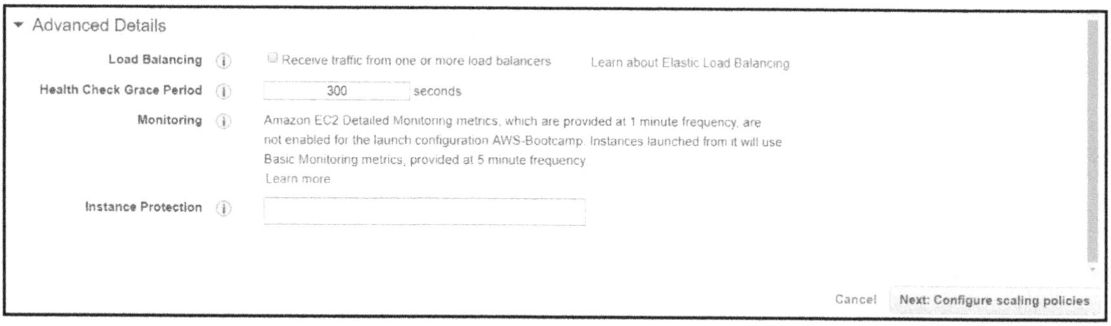

Figure 3.44: Advanced details for Auto Scaling group

We will provide the following details:

- **Load Balancing**: Enabling this will allow us to listen from single or multiple load balancers.
- **Health Check Grace Period**: Time period for which the Auto Scaling process should wait for an instance health check. This configuration is important, as newly scaled instances may take some time to boot so set the parameter value accordingly.
- **Monitoring**: Detailed monitoring metrics are provided for your EC2 instances. Enabling this may incur more charges.
- **Instance Protection**: Setting the value as **Protect From Scale In** will protect instances from termination.

Once the configuration has been done, click **Next: Configure scaling policies**.

12. Configure the scaling policies:

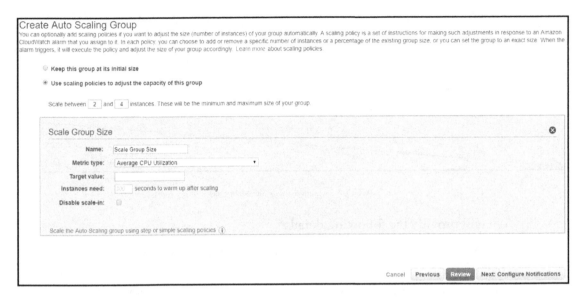

Figure 3.45: Scaling policies

Here, we have the option to define either **Keep this group at its initial size** or **Use scaling policies to adjust the capacity of this group**. We will go with the second option. Set the minimum and maximum instances that can grow dynamically.

We can either configure **Scale Group Size** or we can define Increase and Decrease Group Size. We will configure Increase and Decrease Group Size. To do this click the **Scale the Auto Scaling group using step or simple scaling policies** link, which will allow us to configure Increase and Decrease Group Size:

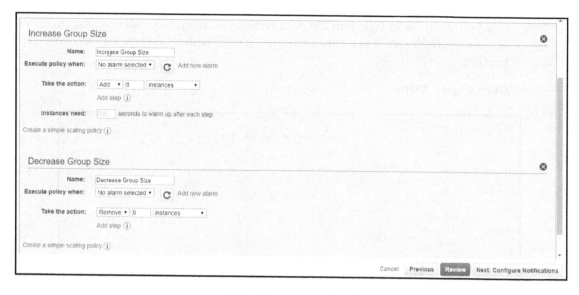

Figure 3.46: Scale using simple scaling policies

Provide the name for your Increase Group Size.

If you already have an alarm created on the EC2 instance, select it; otherwise, click **Add new alarm** under **Increase Group Size**:

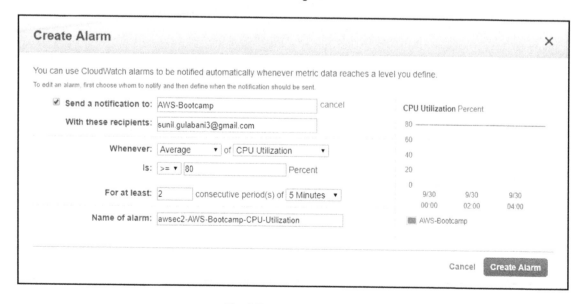

Figure 3.47: Alarm for Increase Group Size

Configure the alarm based on the parameters you want the instance to scale into. For our example, we will create an alarm on CPU utilization when it reaches to 80 percent.

Click **Create Alarm**:

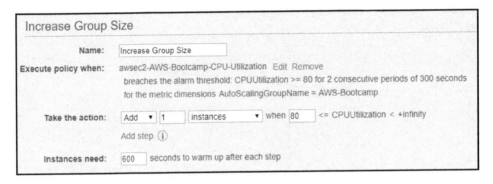

Figure 3.48: Increase Group Size

Configure an action to **Add** an instance and a time for your instance to warm up.

Next, configure **Decrease Group Size**. Provide a name for your Decrease Group Size. Then, click **Add new alarm** under **Decrease Group Size**:

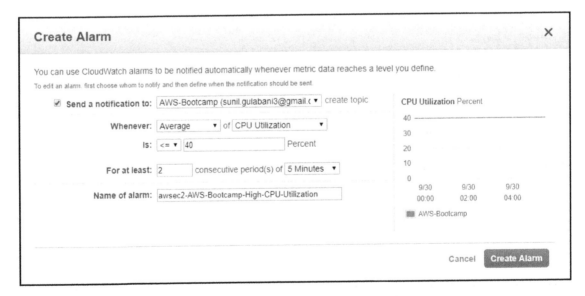

Figure 3.49: Alarm for Decrease Group Size

Configure the alarm based on the parameters you want the instance to scale-out. For our example, we will create an alarm on the CPU utilization when it reaches to 40 percent.

Click **Create Alarm**:

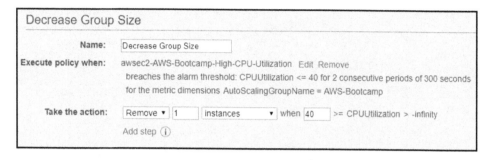

Figure 3.50: Decrease Group Size

Configure an action to **Remove** an instance and click **Next: Configure Notifications**.

13. Configure the notifications:

Figure 3.51: Configuring the notifications

Here, we can configure whether we need notifications when instances launch, terminate, fail to launch, or fail to terminate. Click **Next: Configure Tags**.

14. Configure the tags:

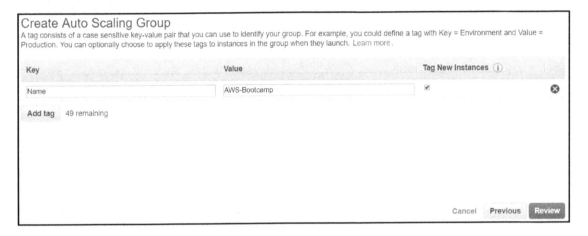

Figure 3.52: Configuring the tags

Here, we will add tags as key-value pairs. Selecting the **Tag New Instances** checkbox will copy the tags to newly created EC2 instances.

Once done, click **Review**.

15. Review the Auto Scaling group:

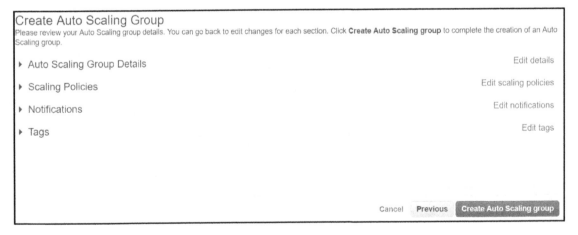

Figure 3.53: Reviewing the Auto Scaling group

Review the Auto Scaling group configuration and then click **Create Auto Scaling Group**.

16. Check the Auto Scaling group creation status:

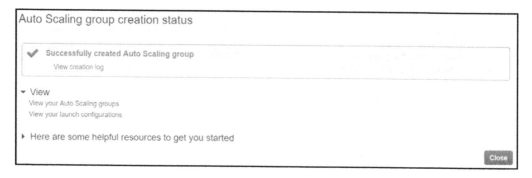

Figure 3.54: Auto Scaling group creation status

This shows the status of our Auto Scaling group. Click **Close** and this will navigate to the Auto Scaling Group screen:

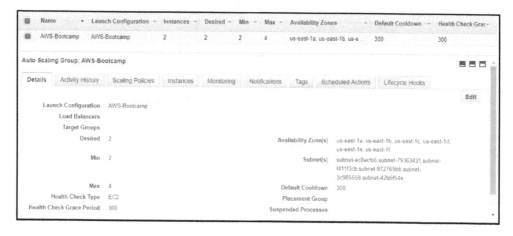

Figure 3.55: Auto Scaling group listing

Here, we can see that our Auto Scaling group has been created and also it has launched two EC2 instances.

AWS CLI

To execute the CLI script, open Command Prompt.

Creating a launch configuration

Create the launch configuration that can be used in the Auto Scaling group:

```
aws autoscaling create-launch-configuration ^
--launch-configuration-name "AWS-Bootcamp" ^
--image-id "ami-c998b6b2" ^
--key-name "aws-bootcamp" ^
--security-groups "sg-7c6ecf0f" ^
--instance-type "t2.micro" ^
--associate-public-ip-address ^
--block-device-mappings "[{"DeviceName":
"/dev/sda1","Ebs":{"VolumeSize":10}}]"
```

The following are the options that can be used with `create-launch-configuration`:

Parameters	Optional	Descriptions
`--launch-configuration-name`	False	Friendly name for the launch configuration.
`--image-id`	True	**Amazon Machine Image (AMI) ID.**
`--key-name`	True	Name of the key pair.
`--security-groups`	True	Security groups that need to be attached to instances. We can provide more than one security group: `sg-7c6ecf0f sg-7c6ecf0e sg-7c6ecf0d`
`--classic-link-vpc-id`	True	Classic-linked enabled VPC ID. This is used only if we launch EC2-classic instances.
`--classic-link-vpc-security-groups`	True	Security groups that need to be attached to EC2-classic instances. We can provide more than one security group: `sg-7c6ecf0f sg-7c6ecf0e sg-7c6ecf0d`.

`--user-data`	True	User data is the script that will be executed while bootstrapping the EC2 instance.
`--instance-id`	True	EC2 instance ID from which the configuration can be copied.
`--instance-type`	True	EC2 instance type. This option is used when we don't provide `--instance-id`.
`--kernel-id`	True	Kernel ID that is associated with Amazon Machine Image.
`--ramdisk-id`	True	Ram Disk ID that is associated with Amazon Machine Image.
`--block-device-mappings`	True	We can provide multiple block device mappings that need to be attached to EC2 instances.
`--instance-monitoring`	True	This option is used for enabling detailed EC2 monitoring. We can provide a value for this option: `Enabled=true` or `Enabled=false`
`--spot-price`	True	Maximum hourly spot price for EC2 instances.
`--iam-instance-profile`	True	Instance profile ARN that needs to be attached to E2 instances.
`--ebs-optimized` or `--no-ebs-optimized`	True	This denotes whether an instance is optimized for Amazon EBS I/O. By default, EBS is not optimized.
`--associate-public-ip-address` or `--no-associate-public-ip-address`	True	This denotes whether an instance needs to assign a public IP address or only a private IP address needs to be assigned.

`--placement-tenancy`	True	Defines the tenancy of the instance. Valid values can be: • `default` • `dedicated` If we provide a dedicated value, instances run on single-tenant hardware and can only be used under VPC.

Creating an Auto Scaling group

Create an Aauto Scaling group:

```
aws autoscaling create-auto-scaling-group ^
--auto-scaling-group-name "AWS-Bootcamp" ^
--launch-configuration-name "AWS-Bootcamp" ^
--desired-capacity 2 ^
--min-size 2 ^
--max-size 4 ^
--default-cooldown 300 ^
--vpc-zone-identifier "subnet-ec8ecfb6,subnet-3c985558,subnet-972769bb"
^
--health-check-type EC2 ^
--health-check-grace-period 300 ^
--no-new-instances-protected-from-scale-in ^
--tags Key=Name,Value=AWS-Bootcamp,PropagateAtLaunch=true
```

The following are the options that can be used with `create-auto-scaling-group`:

Parameters	Optional	Descriptions
`--auto-scaling-group-name`	False	Auto Scaling group name.
`--launch-configuration-name`	True	Launch configuration name, which will be used to launch EC2 instances.
`--instance-id`	True	EC2 Instance ID from which the launch configuration can be created.
`--min-size`	False	Minimum count of EC2 instances.
`--max-size`	False	Maximum count of EC2 instances.

`--desired-capacity`	True	Number of EC2 instances to be running. The desired capacity can be greater than or equal to the minimum size and less than or equal to the maximum size. If we don't provide the desired capacity, the minimum size is considered as the desired capacity.
`--default-cooldown`	True	Time period for Auto Scaling activity to start after the last activity is completed.
`--availability-zones`	True	Availability zones for EC2 instances to be created. We can provide multiple availability zone as: `us-east-1a us-east-1b us-east-1c` We can avoid this parameter if we specify the `--vpc-zone-identifier` option.
`--load-balancer-names`	True	Classic load balancer's name. We can provide multiple load balancer names as: `elb-1 elb-2 elb-3`
`--target-group-arns`	True	Target group **Amazon Resource Names (ARNs)**. We can use this to define application load balancers. We can provide multiple target group ARNs as: `target-group-1 target-group-2 target-group-3`
`--health-check-type`	True	Type of health check. Valid values can be: • `EC2` (default) • `ELB`
`--health-check-grace-period`	True	Time period for which Auto Scaling waits for checking the health status of an EC2 instance to get it fully in service.
`--placement-group`	True	Placement group under which EC2 instances will be launched.
`--vpc-zone-identifier`	True	Multiple subnet IDs that will be used to assign IP addresses for EC2 instances.

		Multiple termination policies used to select instances to terminate. Valid values can be: • OldestInstance • NewestInstance • OldestLaunchConfiguration • ClosestToNextInstanceHour • Default We can provide multiple values as: Default OldestInstance NewestInstance
`--termination-policies`	True	

`--new-instances-protected-from-scale-in`
or
`--no-new-instances-protected-from-scale-in`
	True	This denotes whether new instances are protected from termination.

`--lifecycle-hook-specification-list`	True	Life cycle hooks allow us to perform some actions while pausing Auto Scaling group launches or terminating them.
`--tags`	True	Multiple tags can be assigned to the Auto Scaling group and we can also copy them on EC2 instances launched by the Auto Scaling group.

Creating a scaling policy

Create a simple scaling policy for scale-in under the Auto Scaling group:

```
aws autoscaling put-scaling-policy ^
--auto-scaling-group-name "AWS-Bootcamp" ^
--policy-name "Increase Group Size" ^
--policy-type "SimpleScaling" ^
--adjustment-type "ChangeInCapacity" ^
--scaling-adjustment 1 ^
--cooldown 300
```

The following are the options that can be used with put-scaling-policy:

Parameters	Optional	Descriptions
`--auto-scaling-group-name`	False	Auto-scaling group name under which the scaling policy will be created.
`--policy-name`	False	Policy name that represents your scaling policy.

`--policy-type`	True	Scaling policy type. Valid values are: • `SimpleScaling` (default) • `StepScaling` • `TargetTrackingScaling`
`--adjustment-type`	True	Adjustment type used with the SimpleScaling and StepScaling policy type. Valid values are: • `ChangeInCapacity` • `ExactCapacity` • `PercentChangeInCapacity`
`--min-adjustment-magnitude`	True	Minimum number of instances to scale.
`--scaling-adjustment`	True	Number of instances to either scale in or scale out. This is used with the policy type SimpleScaling only.
`--cooldown`	True	Time period for Auto Scaling activity to start after the last activity is completed. If we don't provide this option, the Auto Scaling group's default value is considered.
`--metric-aggregation-type`	True	CloudWatch aggregation type used with the StepScaling policy type. Valid values are: • `Minimum` • `Maximum` • `Average`
`--step-adjustments`	True	Multiple adjustments configuration which can be chosen based on the size of alarm breach. We can provide values: • `MetricIntervalLowerBound=50, MetricIntervalUpperBound=60, ScalingAdjustment=1` • `MetricIntervalLowerBound=60, MetricIntervalUpperBound=80, ScalingAdjustment=2`

`--estimated-instance-warmup`	True	Estimated time for which an EC2 instance can start to contribute to CloudWatch metrics. This is used with the policy types StepScaling or `TargetTrackingScaling`. If this option is not provided, then the default value will be the same as the cooldown period.
`--target-tracking-configuration`	True	Specifies the target tracking policy. This is used with the `TargetTrackingScaling` policy type only.

Next, attach a CloudWatch alarm to scale-in the policy:

```
aws cloudwatch put-metric-alarm ^
--alarm-name "IncreaseGroupSize-AWS-Bootcamp" ^
--alarm-description "Alarm for Increase Group Size" ^
--actions-enabled ^
--dimensions Name=AutoScalingGroupName,Value=AWS-Bootcamp ^
--namespace "AWS/EC2" ^
--metric-name "CPUUtilization" ^
--statistic "Average" ^
--comparison-operator "GreaterThanOrEqualToThreshold" ^
--threshold 80.0 ^
--unit "Percent" ^
--evaluation-periods 2 ^
--period 300 ^
--alarm-actions "arn:aws:autoscaling:us-
east-1:1234567890:scalingPolicy:f92ad81a-32ed-4dac-
adc3-95c6eafeebec:autoScalingGroupName/AWS-Bootcamp:policyName/Increase
Group Size"
```

Now we will create a simple scaling policy for scale-out under the Auto Scaling group:

```
aws autoscaling put-scaling-policy ^
--auto-scaling-group-name "AWS-Bootcamp" ^
--policy-name "Decrease Group Size" ^
--policy-type "SimpleScaling" ^
--adjustment-type "ChangeInCapacity" ^
--scaling-adjustment -1 ^
--cooldown 300
```

Next, attach a CloudWatch alarm to scale-out the policy:

```
aws cloudwatch put-metric-alarm ^
--alarm-name "DecreaseGroupSize-AWS-Bootcamp" ^
--alarm-description "Alarm for Decrease Group Size" ^
--actions-enabled ^
--dimensions Name=AutoScalingGroupName,Value=AWS-Bootcamp ^
--namespace "AWS/EC2" ^
--metric-name "CPUUtilization" ^
--statistic "Average" ^
--comparison-operator "LessThanOrEqualToThreshold" ^
--threshold 40.0 ^
--unit "Percent" ^
--evaluation-periods 2 ^
--period 300 ^
--alarm-actions "arn:aws:autoscaling:us-
east-1:1234567890:scalingPolicy:524e5c2a-837f-47d3-8b48-88291d6c6db3:autoSc
alingGroupName/AWS-Bootcamp:policyName/Decrease Group Size"
```

AWS SDK - Java

To access the Elastic Load Balancer service and CloudWatch service, we need to create the `AmazonAutoScaling` and `AmazonCloudWatch` object:

```
AmazonAutoScaling autoScaling = AmazonAutoScalingClientBuilder
                .standard()
 //             .withClientConfiguration(getClientConfiguration())
                .withCredentials(getCredentials())
                .withRegion(Regions.US_EAST_1)
                .build();

AmazonCloudWatch cloudWatch = AmazonCloudWatchClientBuilder
                .standard()
 //             .withClientConfiguration(getClientConfiguration())
                .withCredentials(getCredentials())
                .withRegion(Regions.US_EAST_1)
                .build();
```

The `ClientConfiguration` and `AWSCredentialsProvider` objects are created in the same way as we did in Chapter 2, *Configure IAM.*

Creating a launch configuration

Create the launch configuration that can be used in the Auto Scaling group:

```
String launchConfigurationName = "AWS-Bootcamp";
String imageId = "ami-c998b6b2";
String instanceType = InstanceType.T2Micro.toString();
String spotPrice = null;
String iamInstanceProfile = null;
boolean instanceMonitoringEnabled = false;
String kernelId = null;
String ramDiskId = null;
String userData = null;
boolean associatePublicIpAddress = true;
List<String> securityGroups = Arrays.asList("sg-7c6ecf0f");
String keyPairName = "aws-bootcamp";
String blockDeviceName = "/dev/sda1";
Integer volumeSize = 10;

createLaunchConfiguration(
        launchConfigurationName,
        imageId,
        instanceType,
        spotPrice,
        iamInstanceProfile,
        instanceMonitoringEnabled,
        kernelId,
        ramDiskId,
        userData,
        associatePublicIpAddress,
        securityGroups,
        keyPairName,
        blockDeviceName,
        volumeSize
);
........
public void createLaunchConfiguration(
String launchConfigurationName,
String imageId,
String instanceType,
String spotPrice,
String iamInstanceProfile,
boolean instanceMonitoringEnabled,
String kernelId,
String ramDiskId,
String userData,
boolean associatePublicIpAddress,
```

```
List<String> securityGroups,
String keyPairName,
String blockDeviceName,
Integer volumeSize
) {
InstanceMonitoring instanceMonitoring =
 new InstanceMonitoring()
.withEnabled(instanceMonitoringEnabled);
BlockDeviceMapping blockDeviceMapping =
createBlockDeviceMapping(blockDeviceName, volumeSize);
CreateLaunchConfigurationRequest request =
 new CreateLaunchConfigurationRequest()
.withLaunchConfigurationName(launchConfigurationName)
.withImageId(imageId)
.withInstanceType(instanceType)
.withIamInstanceProfile(iamInstanceProfile)
.withInstanceMonitoring(instanceMonitoring)
.withAssociatePublicIpAddress(
associatePublicIpAddress)
.withBlockDeviceMappings(blockDeviceMapping)
.withSecurityGroups(securityGroups)
.withKeyName(keyPairName);
if(!StringUtils.isNullOrEmpty(spotPrice)) {
request.setSpotPrice(spotPrice);
}
if(!StringUtils.isNullOrEmpty(kernelId)) {
request.setKernelId(kernelId);
}
if(!StringUtils.isNullOrEmpty(ramDiskId)) {
request.setRamdiskId(ramDiskId);
}
if(!StringUtils.isNullOrEmpty(userData)) {
request.setUserData(userData);
}
CreateLaunchConfigurationResult result =
 autoScaling.createLaunchConfiguration(request);
}
private BlockDeviceMapping createBlockDeviceMapping(
String blockDeviceName,
Integer volumeSize) {
Ebs ebs = new Ebs()
.withVolumeSize(volumeSize);
BlockDeviceMapping blockDeviceMapping =
 new BlockDeviceMapping()
.withDeviceName(blockDeviceName)
.withEbs(ebs);
return blockDeviceMapping;
}
```

Creating an Auto Scaling group

Create an Auto Scaling group:

```
String autoScalingGroupName = "AWS-Bootcamp";
 Integer minimumSize = 2;
String vpcZoneIdentified = "subnet-
ec8ecfb6,subnet-3c985558,subnet-972769bb";
List<String> loadBalancerNames = null;
Integer healthCheckGracePeriod = 300;
boolean instanceProtected = false;
Integer maximumSize = 4;
 createAutoScalingGroup(
        autoScalingGroupName,
        launchConfigurationName,
        minimumSize,
        vpcZoneIdentified,
        loadBalancerNames,
        healthCheckGracePeriod,
        instanceProtected,
        maximumSize);
........
public void createAutoScalingGroup(
String autoScalingGroupName,
String launchConfigurationName,
Integer minimumSize,
String vpcZoneIdentified,
List<String> loadBalancerNames,
Integer healthCheckGracePeriod,
 boolean instanceProtected,
Integer maximumSize) {
CreateAutoScalingGroupRequest
createAutoScalingGroupRequest =
 new CreateAutoScalingGroupRequest()
.withLaunchConfigurationName(launchConfigurationName)
.withAutoScalingGroupName(autoScalingGroupName)
.withDesiredCapacity(minimumSize)
.withVPCZoneIdentifier(vpcZoneIdentified)
.withHealthCheckGracePeriod(healthCheckGracePeriod)
.withNewInstancesProtectedFromScaleIn(
instanceProtected)
.withMinSize(minimumSize)
.withMaxSize(maximumSize);
if(!CollectionUtils.isNullOrEmpty(loadBalancerNames)) {
createAutoScalingGroupRequest
.setLoadBalancerNames(loadBalancerNames);
}
```

```
CreateAutoScalingGroupResult
createAutoScalingGroupResult =
 autoScaling.createAutoScalingGroup(
createAutoScalingGroupRequest);
}
```

Creating a Scaling Policy

Create a simple scaling policy for scale-in under the Auto Scaling group:

```
String scaleInPolicyName = "Increase Group Size";
 Integer scaleInAdjustment = 1;
Integer scaleInCoolDown = 300;
String scaleInPolicyARN = putScalingPolicy(
        autoScalingGroupName,
        scaleInPolicyName,
        scaleInAdjustment,
        scaleInCoolDown);
........
public String putScalingPolicy(
String asgName,
String policyName,
Integer scalingAdjustment,
Integer coolDown) {
PutScalingPolicyRequest putScalingPolicyRequest =
 new PutScalingPolicyRequest()
.withAutoScalingGroupName(asgName)
.withPolicyName(policyName)
.withPolicyType("SimpleScaling")
.withAdjustmentType("ChangeInCapacity")
.withScalingAdjustment(scalingAdjustment)
.withCooldown(coolDown);
PutScalingPolicyResult putScalingPolicyResult =
 autoScaling.putScalingPolicy(
putScalingPolicyRequest);
return putScalingPolicyResult.getPolicyARN();
}
```

Next, attach a CloudWatch alarm to scale-in the policy:

```
String scaleInAlarmName = "IncreaseGroupSize-AWS-Bootcamp";
  String scaleInDimensionName = "AutoScalingGroupName";
String scaleInDimensionValue = autoScalingGroupName;
String scaleInNamespace = "AWS/EC2";
String scaleInMetricName = "CPUUtilization";
Statistic scaleInStatistic = Statistic.Average;
ComparisonOperator scaleInComparisonOperator =
```

```
        ComparisonOperator.GreaterThanOrEqualToThreshold;
Double scaleInThreshold = 80.0;
String scaleInUnit = "Percent";
Integer scaleInEvaluationPeriod = 2;
Integer scaleInPeriod = 300;
putMetricAlarm(scaleInAlarmName,
        scaleInPolicyARN,
        scaleInDimensionName,
        scaleInDimensionValue,
        scaleInNamespace,
        scaleInMetricName,
        scaleInStatistic,
        scaleInComparisonOperator,
        scaleInThreshold,
        scaleInUnit,
        scaleInEvaluationPeriod,
        scaleInPeriod);
........
public void putMetricAlarm(
String alarmName,
String alarmActionsARN,
String dimensionName,
String dimensionValue,
String namespace,
String metricName,
Statistic statistic,
ComparisonOperator comparisonOperator,
Double threshold,
String unit,
Integer evaluationPeriod,
Integer period) {
Dimension dimension = createDimension(
dimensionName, dimensionValue);
PutMetricAlarmRequest putMetricAlarmRequest =
 new PutMetricAlarmRequest()
.withAlarmName(alarmName)
.withActionsEnabled(true)
.withAlarmActions(alarmActionsARN)
.withDimensions(dimension)
.withNamespace(namespace)
.withMetricName(metricName)
.withStatistic(statistic)
.withComparisonOperator(comparisonOperator)
.withThreshold(threshold)
```

```
.withUnit(unit)
.withEvaluationPeriods(evaluationPeriod)
.withPeriod(period);
PutMetricAlarmResult putMetricAlarmResult =
 cloudWatch.putMetricAlarm(
putMetricAlarmRequest);
}
private Dimension createDimension(
String dimensionName,
String dimensionValue) {
Dimension dimension = new Dimension()
.withName(dimensionName)
.withValue(dimensionValue);
return dimension;
}
```

Now we will create a simple scaling policy for scale-out under the Auto Scaling group:

```
String scaleOutPolicyName = "Decrease Group Size";
 Integer scaleOutAdjustment = -1;
  Integer scaleOutCoolDown = 300;
 String scaleOutPolicyARN = putScalingPolicy(
        autoScalingGroupName,
        scaleOutPolicyName,
        scaleOutAdjustment,
        scaleOutCoolDown);
```

Next, attach a CloudWatch alarm to scale-out the policy:

```
String scaleOutAlarmName = "DecreaseGroupSize-AWS-Bootcamp";
String scaleOutDimensionName = "AutoScalingGroupName";
String scaleOutDimensionValue = autoScalingGroupName;
String scaleOutNamespace = "AWS/EC2";
String scaleOutMetricName = "CPUUtilization";
Statistic scaleOutStatistic = Statistic.Average;
ComparisonOperator scaleOutComparisonOperator =
        ComparisonOperator.LessThanOrEqualToThreshold;
Double scaleOutThreshold = 40.0;
String scaleOutUnit = "Percent";
Integer scaleOutEvaluationPeriod = 2;
Integer scaleOutPeriod = 300;
 putMetricAlarm(scaleOutAlarmName,
        scaleOutPolicyARN,
        scaleOutDimensionName,
        scaleOutDimensionValue,
        scaleOutNamespace,
        scaleOutMetricName,
        scaleOutStatistic,
```

```
            scaleOutComparisonOperator,
            scaleOutThreshold,
            scaleOutUnit,
            scaleOutEvaluationPeriod,
            scaleOutPeriod);
```

AWS CloudFormation

To create the launch configuration, we need to use the
`AWS::AutoScaling::LaunchConfiguration` type:

```
    "LaunchConfiguration": {
        "Type": "AWS::AutoScaling::LaunchConfiguration",
        "Properties": {
            "UserData": {
                "Fn::Base64": {
                    "Fn::Join": [
    "n",
    [
    "#!/bin/bash",
    "yum install httpd -y",
    "service httpd start"
    ]
    ]
    }
    },
            "ImageId": "ami-c998b6b2",
            "KeyName": "aws-bootcamp",
            "SecurityGroups": [
    {
                    "Ref": "AWSBootcampSecurityGroup"
    }
    ],
            "IamInstanceProfile": {
                "Ref": "RootInstanceProfile"
    },
            "InstanceType": "t2.micro"
    }
     }
```

To create the Auto Scaling group, we need to use the
`AWS::AutoScaling::AutoScalingGroup` type:

```
    "AutoScalingGroup": {
        "Type": "AWS::AutoScaling::AutoScalingGroup",
        "Properties": {
```

```
            "LoadBalancerNames": [{
                "Ref": "ElasticLoadBalancer"
}],
            "MinSize": "2",
            "LaunchConfigurationName": {
                "Ref": "LaunchConfiguration"
},
            "AvailabilityZones": [{
                "Fn::Select": [
0, {
                        "Fn::GetAZs": {
                            "Ref": "AWS::Region"
}
}
]
}, {
                "Fn::Select": [
1, {
                        "Fn::GetAZs": {
                            "Ref": "AWS::Region"
}
}
]
}],
            "DesiredCapacity": "2",
            "Tags" : [
{
                    "Key": "Name",
                    "Value": "aws-bootcamp",
                    "PropagateAtLaunch": true
}
],
            "MaxSize": "4",
            "TerminationPolicies": [
"OldestInstance"
],
            "HealthCheckGracePeriod": "600",
            "HealthCheckType": "EC2"
},
        "UpdatePolicy": {
            "AutoScalingRollingUpdate": {
            "PauseTime": "PT1M",
            "MaxBatchSize": 1,
            "MinInstancesInService": 2
}
    }
}
```

To create the scaling policy for scale-up, we need to use the
`AWS::AutoScaling::ScalingPolicy` type:

```
"ScaleUpPolicy": {
    "Type": "AWS::AutoScaling::ScalingPolicy",
    "Properties": {
        "ScalingAdjustment": "1",
        "Cooldown": 300,
        "AutoScalingGroupName": {
            "Ref": "AutoScalingGroup"
},
        "AdjustmentType": "ChangeInCapacity"
}
  }
```

To create a CloudWatch alarm that will trigger the scaling policy for scale-up, we need to
use the `AWS::CloudWatch::Alarm` type:

```
"CPUAlarmHigh": {
    "Type": "AWS::CloudWatch::Alarm",
    "Properties": {
        "EvaluationPeriods": 2,
        "Dimensions": [{
            "Name": "AutoScalingGroupName",
            "Value": {
                "Ref": "AutoScalingGroup"
}
}],
        "AlarmActions": [{
            "Ref": "ScaleUpPolicy"
}],
        "AlarmDescription": "High CPU Utilization",
        "Namespace": "AWS/EC2",
        "Period": 300,
        "ComparisonOperator": "GreaterThanOrEqualToThreshold",
        "Statistic": "Average",
        "Threshold": "80",
        "Unit": "Percent",
        "MetricName": "CPUUtilization"
    }
  }
```

To create the scaling policy for scale-down, we need to use the
`AWS::AutoScaling::ScalingPolicy` **type**:

```
"ScaleDownPolicy": {
    "Type": "AWS::AutoScaling::ScalingPolicy",
    "Properties": {
        "ScalingAdjustment": "-1",
        "Cooldown": 300,
        "AutoScalingGroupName": {
            "Ref": "AutoScalingGroup"
},
        "AdjustmentType": "ChangeInCapacity"
    }
    }
```

To create a CloudWatch alarm that will trigger the scaling policy for scale-down, we need to
use the `AWS::CloudWatch::Alarm` **type**:

```
"CPUAlarmLow": {
    "Type": "AWS::CloudWatch::Alarm",
    "Properties": {
        "EvaluationPeriods": 2,
        "Dimensions": [{
            "Name": "AutoScalingGroupName",
            "Value": {
                "Ref": "AutoScalingGroup"
}
}],
        "AlarmActions": [{
            "Ref": "ScaleDownPolicy"
}],
        "AlarmDescription": "Low CPU Utilization",
        "Namespace": "AWS/EC2",
        "Period": 300,
        "ComparisonOperator": "LessThanOrEqualToThreshold",
        "Statistic": "Average",
        "Threshold": "40",
        "Unit": "Percent",
        "MetricName": "CPUUtilization"
    }
    }
```

Elastic Block Storage

Amazon Elastic Block Storage (**Amazon EBS**) is a durable block storage volume that can be used with EC2 instances. EBS offers reliable high performance that enables the applications to run efficiently. We can scale the EBS volume up and down within minutes by paying a low price for the volume we use. EBS handles fault tolerance by replicating the volume in availability zones. EBS also provides the option to take a snapshot of the EBS volume which can be stored on Amazon S3 periodically. This snapshot can be used as a baseline for new volume or can be used for backup and restore purposes. EBS offers a wide range of volumes which are efficient in different use cases. We can choose wisely which type of EBS volume is suitable for our application or software. The following are the volume types:

- General Purpose SSD (gp2)
- Provisioned IOPS SSD (io1)
- Throughput Optimized HDD (st1)
- Cold HDD (sc1)
- Magnetic (standard)

Summary

In this chapter, we have covered the most important service, Amazon EC2, which helps us to run our application on the server. Also, we covered how we can balance the load between multiple EC2 instances and auto scale the server based on the CPU utilization. We can choose any metrics to auto scale our EC2 instances. These Auto Scaling groups also help us to handle fault tolerance of EC2 instances and scale up and down accordingly. In the next chapter, we will be learning about the **Simple Storage Service** (**S3**), which is used to store any type of files and can be accessed over HTTP.

4
Storing Files on S3

Amazon **Simple Storage Service (S3)** is a web storage service accessed via the HTTP protocol using a web service interface. It is used to store/retrieve files centrally over the internet, which helps developers to create applications that are highly scalable, efficient, secured, and inexpensive. S3 offers unlimited storage, so developers need not worry about disk space issues.

In this chapter, we will cover the following topics:

- Bucket
- Objects
- Static website hosting

Amazon S3 is also an online object storage service accessed over the internet that allows us to add, read, and delete files. The following are the interfaces that are supported, using which we can store and get files from S3:

- REST web service
- SOAP web service
- BitTorrent

Amazon S3 allows us to store any kinds of files (called as objects) in a secure manner. We can control the access of the files that are getting uploaded to S3. Amazon S3 offers multiple storage classes, which helps to lower the costs of storing the files. For example, if we want to store a file that is not being used frequently, we can store that file with Standard-IA (Infrequent Access) so that S3 treats that file to be stored on the infrequent access store. Amazon S3 offers unlimited storage space, so we don't need to worry about the storage capacity. We don't need to deal with how the data is getting stored and retrieved; Amazon S3 does it for you. We are just dealing with the key associated with the object (file).

Amazon S3 allows us to store the application data, backups, and archived data. It charges users based on the amount of data stored and bandwidth used to transfer the data. So it becomes inexpensive for users to use such services, which have the ability to scale and become secure without investing in storage infrastructure management. Though Amazon S3 guarantees a server uptime of 99.9 percent, there are 0.01 percent chances of failure. So, for that, Amazon S3 comes with the configuration to replicate your data across multiple regions so that if your source region is down, you can get the same data from another region where the data is replicated. For end users, the entire process is seamless; Amazon S3 replicates the data in the background. Replicating the data might incur more charges as data is getting stored in multiple regions.

Amazon S3 treats any kind of file as an object. For storing objects, we need to create the S3 bucket. A single bucket can have any number of objects. We can either provide access permissions on the bucket or individual objects. We can also make objects publicly or privately accessible. Amazon S3 can also be integrated with cloud-based applications or on-premises applications or other AWS resources such as Amazon **Elastic Compute Cloud (EC2)**, Amazon **Elastic Block Storage (EBS)**, Amazon Glacier, and Amazon Lambda.

It also provides static website hosting, where we can deploy our website and map a domain name. It's easy and cost-efficient to host a website by uploading the HTML pages and enabling the static website hosting configuration. Apart from this, we can also redirect the HTTP request coming through S3 to another HTTP/S URL.

Bucket

Bucket is a logical structure under which we can store the data such as photos, videos, documents, and audio files. We need to provide unique bucket names across the globe irrespective of different AWS accounts and AWS regions.

Amazon allows us to store unlimited data in the bucket. There is a limit for bucket creation which is 100. This limit can be increased by raising a request to Amazon.

A bucket can be created in any of the AWS regions. Choosing a region for the bucket is very much important as this helps us to optimize latency to transfer data from S3 to clients.

To create a bucket, we need to provide a unique name and choose a region. If we don't provide the region, it will be created in the US East (Northern Virginia) region. Region-specific endpoints are allocated in S3. The endpoint for the US East (Northern Virginia) region will be: s3.amazonaws.com.

And if we choose another region, then the endpoint will be: `s3-<region>.amazonaws.com` or `s3.<region>.amazonaws.com`.

For example, if we choose the Asia Pacific (Mumbai) region for bucket, then the endpoint looks like this: `s3.ap-south-1.amazonaws.com` or `s3-ap-south-1.amazonaws.com`.

 For bucket naming conventions refer to `http://docs.aws.amazon.com/AmazonS3/latest/dev/BucketRestrictions.html`.

AWS Management Console

Go to AWS S3 Management Console at `https://console.aws.amazon.com/s3/home`:

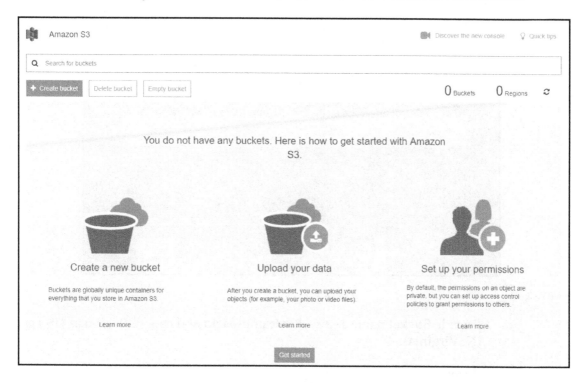

Figure 4.1: S3 Home Page

Creating a bucket

Create a new bucket under your AWS account:

1. Click on the **Create bucket** button:

Figure 4.2: Create bucket

Provide **Bucket name** as **aws-bootcamp-packt** and choose **Region** as **US East (N. Virginia)**.

If you don't need to set the bucket properties and permissions, you can click on **Create**. Otherwise, click on **Next**.

2. Set the bucket properties:

Figure 4.3: Set bucket properties

Here we can set the bucket properties as follows:

- **Versioning**: Enabling this will help to store multiple versions of the object
- **Server access logging**: It enables the logging on the bucket level
- **Tags**: This helps us to manage and track the cost based on the tag values
- **Object-level logging**: This enables logging for an object using the AWS CloudTrail

Click on **Next**.

3. Set permissions as follows:

Figure 4.4: Set bucket permissions

Here, we can define who can access the bucket and its objects. Setting permissions at bucket level are considered resource-based access policies. By default, Amazon S3 bucket has private access. Only the bucket owner can have access to bucket.

We will keep the default permissions and click on **Next**.

4. Review the create bucket details and click on **Create bucket:**

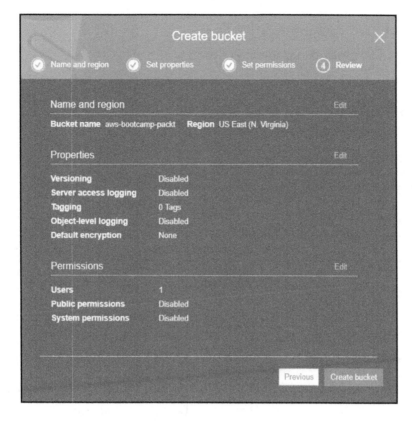

Figure 4.5: Review create bucket

This will create the bucket and we can view the newly created bucket:

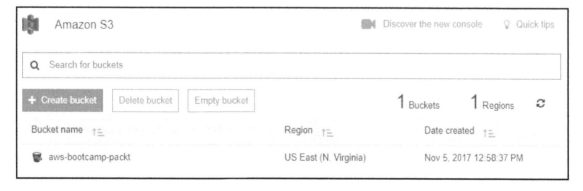

Figure 4.6: Bucket Listing

AWS CLI

To execute the CLI script, open Command Prompt.

Creating a bucket

Create a new bucket under your AWS account:

```
aws s3api create-bucket
--bucket "aws-bootcamp-packt"
--create-bucket-configuration LocationConstraint=ap-south-1
```

The following are the options which can be used with `create-bucket`:

Parameters	Optional	Description
`--bucket`	False	This is a friendly name for the bucket.
`--acl`	True	This is the canned **Access Control Limit** (**ACL**) that will be applicable to the bucket. The following are the valid values: • `private` • `public-read` • `public-read-write` • `authenticated-read`
`--create-bucket-configuration`	True	Using this, we can set the region of the bucket. With this option, we need to specify the region as follows: `LocationConstraint=<region-name>`
`--grant-full-control`	True	This will grant read, write, read ACP, and write ACP permissions.
`--grant-read`	True	This will grant read permissions to list the objects.
`--grant-read-acp`	True	This will grant read permissions to read the bucket ACL.
`--grant-write`	True	This will grant create, overwrite, and delete the object's permissions.

--grant-write-acp	True	This will grant write bucket ACL permissions.

AWS SDK (Java)

To access the S3 service, we need to create the `AmazonS3` object as follows:

```
AmazonS3 amazonS3 = AmazonS3ClientBuilder
                .standard()
  //            .withClientConfiguration(getClientConfiguration())
                .withCredentials(getCredentials())
                .withRegion(Regions.US_EAST_1)
                .build();
```

`ClientConfiguration` and `AWSCredentialsProvider` objects are created in the same way as we mentioned in `Chapter 2`, *Configuring IAM*.

Creating a bucket

Create a new bucket under your AWS account:

```
createBucket("aws-bootcamp-packt", Region.US_Standard);
........
public void createBucket(
        String bucketName,
        Region region) {
    CreateBucketRequest createBucketRequest =
            new CreateBucketRequest(bucketName, region);

    Bucket bucket =
            amazonS3.createBucket(createBucketRequest);
}
```

To grant the access, we have methods under the CreateBucketRequest class to set Access Control List and Canned ACL.

AWS Cloud Formation

To create a bucket, we need to use the `AWS::S3::Bucket` type:

```
"AWSBootcampPacktS3Bucket": {
"Type" : "AWS::S3::Bucket",
```

```
"DeletionPolicy": "Retain",
"Properties" : {
"AccessControl" : "BucketOwnerFullControl",
"BucketName" : "aws-bootcamp-packt",
"Tags" : [{
"Key" : "Chapter",
"Value" : "4"
}],
"VersioningConfiguration": {
"Status" : "Suspended"
}
    }
 }
```

Here, we also mentioned `DeletionPolicy` as `Retain`. This means if we delete the cloud formation stack, this S3 bucket should be retained as it may contain important information.

Objects

Amazon S3 allows us to store data in the form of objects inside the bucket. It stores objects in key-value form, where the object is assigned with a unique key and the value is the object. S3 doesn't restrict to store the amount of data on the bucket. The size of the objects can be up to 5 terabytes. Each object is assigned a URL, which can be accessed via the HTTP or HTTPS protocol. We can manage the access control list at the object level also.

Amazon S3 stores objects in a flat structure. It doesn't have any hierarchical structure where we can group objects under the bucket. But Amazon S3 Management Console provides support for displaying objects under folders and nested subfolders. Amazon Management Console distinguishes the folders with / in the object's key name. For example, if we provide the object key as `PACKT/chapter4.txt`, then it will show `PACKT` as the folder and below that `chapter4.txt` as the object.

Each S3 object contains the following:

- **Data**: This is the actual object
- **Key**: These are unique to an object under the bucket
- **Metadata**: The following are the types of metadata that can be assigned to an object:
  - **System metadata**: Amazon S3 creates metadata on its own such as creation time, last modified date, and content length.

- **User-defined metadata**: We can also create custom metadata, which can be used for our purposes. User-defined metadata keys should have a prefix such as `x-amz-meta-` in order to distinguish it from system metadata.

AWS Management Console

Go to the AWS S3 Management Console at `https://console.aws.amazon.com/s3/home`.

Creating a folder

Create a folder under your bucket:

1. Click on the **aws-bootcamp-packt** bucket under which the folder needs to be created:

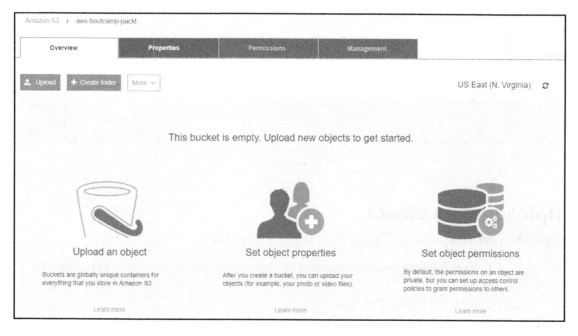

Figure 4.7: Bucket Details

2. Click on the **Create folder** button:

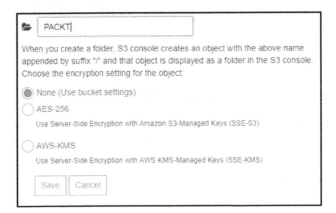

Figure 4.8: Create Folder

Provide the folder name as PACKT and select the encryption setting as per your needs. We will keep the encryption setting as **None**. Click on **Save**:

Figure 4.9: Folder Created

Uploading an object

Upload an object with a specified key name in your bucket:

1. Click on the **aws-bootcamp-packt** bucket under which you want to upload the object.
2. Click on the **Upload** button:

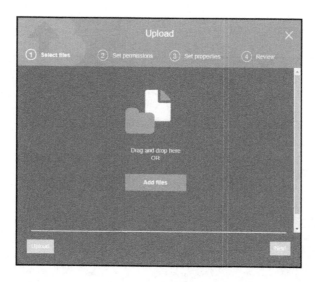

Figure 4.10: Upload Object

3. Click on **Add files** or you can drag and drop your files:

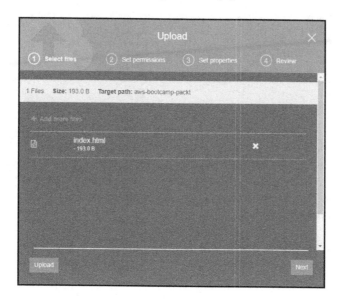

Figure 4.11: Add files

Click on **Upload** to directly add files to bucket or you can click on **Next** to set permissions and properties for the files. We will click on **Next** to set permissions and properties.

4. Set permissions:

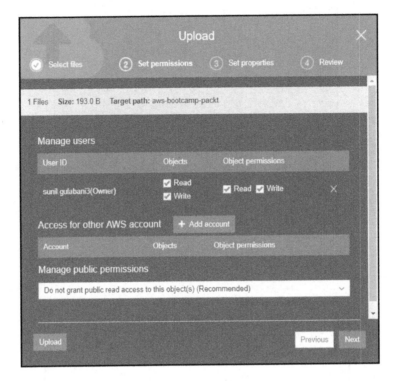

Figure 4.12: Set Permissions

Here, we can set permissions for the files, which are being uploaded so that specified users or AWS accounts have access to these files. We can also make the files available to the public for read access. It is not recommended to grant read access to the public as it may be misused and you may get charged more. It is recommended to grant access to your website or to authenticated users.

It is not recommended to grant public access to the object.

Click on **Next.**

5. Set Properties: Here, we can set the Storage class, Encryption technique, Metadata, and Tag:

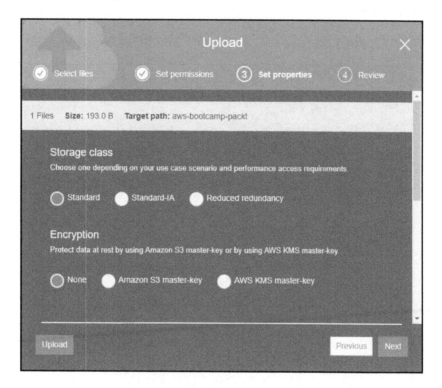

Figure 4.13: Set Properties – 1

Under the Storage Class we have the following properties:

- **Standard**: This storage class is used to achieve high durability, availability, and performance object storage for frequently accessed objects.
- **Standard-IA**: This storage class is used to access infrequent objects. It provides a feature of rapid access, when needed, with an associated fee for retrieval.
- **Reduced redundancy**: This storage class allows us to store data, which is noncritical and is reproducible if the data is lost. Amazon maintains a lower level of redundancy in this type of storage than in the Standard Storage class.

Under Encryption, we have the following properties:

- **None**: There is no encryption technique to be implemented

- **Amazon S3 master-key**: Amazon S3 manages the data key and master key
- **AWS KMS master-key**: Amazon S3 manages the data key and the client manages the master key

In order to take a look at more properties, refer to the following screenshot:

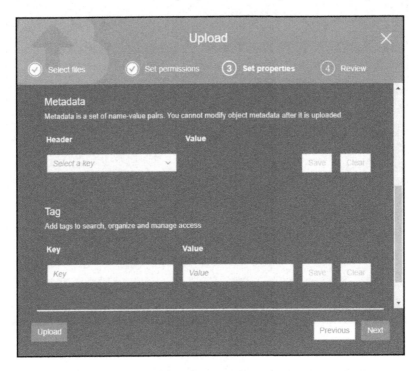

Figure 4.14: Set Properties – 2

Under Metadata, we can set the object's metadata such as Cache-Control, Cache-Disposition, Content-Encoding, Content-Language, Content-Type, Expires, Website-Redirect-Location, and custom metadata such as x-amz-meta-.

Under Tag, we can add tags which can be used for cost-based tagging or for identifying the project to which this object belongs.

Click on **Next.**

6. Review: Review the files, permissions, and properties:

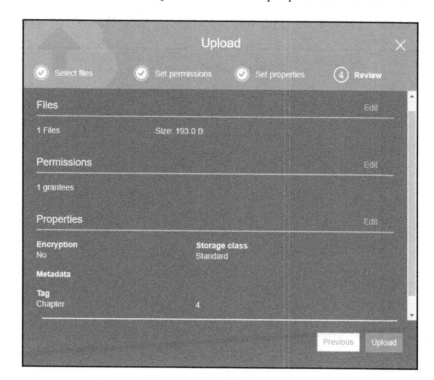

Figure 4.15: Review Upload Object

Click on **Upload.**

7. Object Listing: The object has been uploaded under our bucket:

Figure 4-16: Object Uploaded

In a similar way, we can upload objects inside the folder.

Getting an object

To get or download an object, select the object and click on the **Download** button:

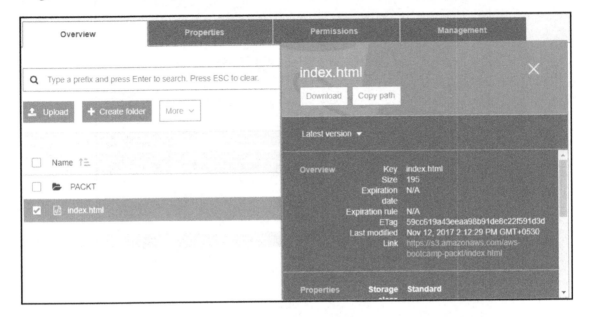

Figure 4.17: Download Object

This will download the object to your local machine.

AWS CLI

To execute the CLI script, open Command Prompt.

Creating a folder

Create a folder under your bucket:

```
aws s3api put-object
--bucket "aws-bootcamp-packt"
--key "PACKT/"
```

The following are the options, which can be used with `put-object`:

Parameters	Optional	Description
`--bucket`	False	This is a friendly name of the bucket.
`--key`	False	This is a friendly key name using which the object (folder) will be identified. To create the folder, the key should be suffixed by / and to create the object with the folder, the folder name should be delimited by / in the key name. Consider the following example: Folder Key: `PACKT/` Object Key: `PACKT/chapter4.txt`

It is important to append / as the suffix in the key, so that Amazon S3 Management Console can identify it as a folder. Though Amazon S3 doesn't have a folder structure, it is just a logical structure so that S3 client tools such as Amazon Management Console and S3 Browser can be seen in a folder structure.

Uploading an object

Upload an object with a specified key name in your bucket:

```
aws s3api put-object ^
--bucket "aws-bootcamp-packt" ^
--key "PACKT/index.html" ^
--body index.html ^
--tagging Chapter=4
```

We mentioned the key as `PACKT/index.html`, where `PACKT` is the upload object inside the folder.

The following are the options that can be used with `put-object`:

Parameters	Optional	Description
`--bucket`	False	This is the name of the bucket.
`--key`	False	This is a friendly key name using which the object will be identified. To create a folder, the key should be suffixed by / and to create the object with the folder, the folder name should be delimited by / in the key name. Consider the following example: Folder Key: `PACKT/` Object Key: `PACKT/chapter4.txt`
`--acl`	True	This is the canned ACL that needs to be applied on the object. The following are the valid values: • `private` • `public-read` • `public-read-write` • `authenticated-read` • `aws-exec-read` • `bucket-owner-read` • `bucket-owner-full-control`
`--body`	True	This is the object's data given as BLOB.
`--cache-control`	True	This is the caching behavior for an object to be used in the request and reply chain.
`--content-disposition`	True	This specifies the presentational information for the object.
`--content-encoding`	True	This specifies the encoding technique implemented on the object.
`--content-language`	True	This is the object's language.
`--content-length`	True	This is the length of the object in bytes.
`--content-md5`	True	Based on 64-encoded 128-bit MD5 digest of an object.
`--content-type`	True	This is the content type of the object.

`--expires`	True	This is the date and time after which the object should not be cached.
`--grant-full-control`	True	This provides `READ`, `READ_ACP`, and `WRITE_ACP` permissions to the grantee to access objects.
`--grant-read`	True	This provides `READ` permissions on the object data and its metadata.
`--grant-read-acp`	True	This provides `READ_ACP` permissions on the object's ACL.
`--grant-write-acp`	True	This provides `WRITE_ACP` permissions on the object's ACL.
`--metadata`	True	This is used to attach metadata to an object.
`--server-side-encryption`	True	This defines which algorithm to use for server-side encryption. The following are the valid values: • `AES256` • `aws:kms`
`--storage-class`	True	This defines the storage class of an object. The following are the valid values: • `STANDARD` • `STANDARD_IA` • `REDUCED_REDUNDANCY`
`--website-redirect-location`	True	This is used when we have configured bucket as a website. By defining this, we can redirect the request to another object or to an external URL.
`--sse-customer-algorithm`	True	This defines the encryption algorithm.
`--sse-customer-key`	True	This defines the encryption key to be used by Amazon S3 to encrypt the data.
`--sse-customer-key-md5`	True	This defines the 128-bit MD5 digest of the encryption key to ensure the encryption key was transmitted to Amazon S3 server without error.

`--ssekms-key-id`	True	This defines the KMS ID using which the object will be encrypted.
`--request-payer`	True	This defines that the requester needs to pay for the access to the object. The following is the valid value here: • `Requester`
`--tagging`	True	This includes tags that can be defined in key-value form.

Getting an object

Download an object and store it to a file:

```
aws s3api get-object ^
--bucket "aws-bootcamp-packt" ^
--key "PACKT/index.html" "packt-index.html"
```

The following are the options that can be used with get-object:

Parameters	Optional	Description
`--bucket`	False	This is the bucket name.
`--key`	False	This is the key name of the S3 object.
`--if-match`	True	This returns the object only when the value specified matches the object's ETag.
`--if-modified-since`	True	This returns the object only when the object has been modified after the mentioned date.
`--if-none-match`	True	This returns the object only when the value specified doesn't match to the object's ETag.
`--if-unmodified-since`	True	This returns the object only when the object has not been modified since the mentioned date.
`--range`	True	This downloads the range bytes of an object.

`--response-cache-control`	True	This sets the Cache-Control header of the response.
`--response-content-disposition`	True	This sets the Content-Disposition header of the response.
`--response-content-encoding`	True	This sets the Content-Encoding header of the response.
`--response-content-language`	True	This sets the Content-Language header of the response.
`--response-content-type`	True	This sets the Content-Type header of the response.
`--response-expires`	True	This sets the Expires header of the response.
`--version-id`	True	This gets the specific version ID of an object.
`--sse-customer-algorithm`	True	This is the customer algorithm that is used for encryption-decryption of the object's data.
`--sse-customer-key`	True	This is the customer-provided encryption key for Amazon S3.
`--sse-customer-key-md5`	True	This is the 128-bit MD5 digest of the encryption key
`--request-payer`	True	This defines that requester confirms that he will be charged for this GET operation. The following is the valid value here: Requestor
`--part-number`	True	This is the part number of an object.
`Outfile`	False	This is the filename of an object, which will be downloaded.

AWS SDK (Java)

AWS SDK (Java) provides multiple implementations to upload and get the object. We will demonstrate one of the implementations next:

Creating a folder

Create a folder under your bucket:

```
String folderName = "PACKT";


createFolder(bucketName, folderName);

........

public void createFolder(
        String bucketName,
        String folderName) {
    ObjectMetadata metadata = new ObjectMetadata();

    metadata.setContentLength(0);

    InputStream emptyContent =
            new ByteArrayInputStream(new byte[0]);

    PutObjectRequest putObjectRequest =
            new PutObjectRequest(
                    bucketName, folderName + "/",
                    emptyContent, metadata);

    PutObjectResult putObjectResult =
            amazonS3.putObject(putObjectRequest);

}
```

Here, we created an empty content of length 0 and appended / as the suffix to the folder name. This will create an empty object, which will be treated as a folder by Amazon S3 Management Console.

Uploading an object

Upload an object with the specified key name in your bucket:

```
File file = new File("index.html");

String keyName = "PACKT/index.html";


putObject(bucketName, keyName, file);

........

public void putObject(
        String bucketName,
        String keyName,
        File file) throws IOException {

    PutObjectRequest putObjectRequest =
            new PutObjectRequest(bucketName, keyName, file);

    PutObjectResult putObjectResult =
            amazonS3.putObject(putObjectRequest);
}
```

Getting an Object

Download an object and store it to a file:

```
String keyName = "PACKT/index.html";

 String downloadedFileName = "packt-index.html";


getObject(bucketName, keyName, downloadedFileName);

........

public void getObject(
        String bucketName,
        String keyName,
        String downloadedFileName) throws IOException {

    S3Object s3Object = amazonS3.getObject(
            new GetObjectRequest(bucketName, keyName));
```

```
InputStream inputStream = s3Object.getObjectContent();

String objectData = IOUtils.toString(inputStream);


Path path = Paths.get(downloadedFileName);

Files.write(path, objectData.getBytes());
inputStream.close();
}
```

This code snippet downloads the object from Amazon S3 and stores it on your machine with the filename `packt-index.html`.

Static Website Hosting

Amazon S3 allows us to host a static website. Static HTML pages can be deployed on S3 and using the scripting language (such as JavaScript) we can make it a dynamic website. For hosting, we need to configure the bucket website configuration and map our domain name to redirect the request to the Amazon S3 bucket.

Let's see how we can host a static website on Amazon S3.

AWS Management Console

Let's see how to host a static website on Amazon S3:

1. Create the S3 bucket and grant public access: Create a bucket with the name `www.blog.tweakings3.com` and grant **Public** permissions so that anonymous users can access the HTML files:

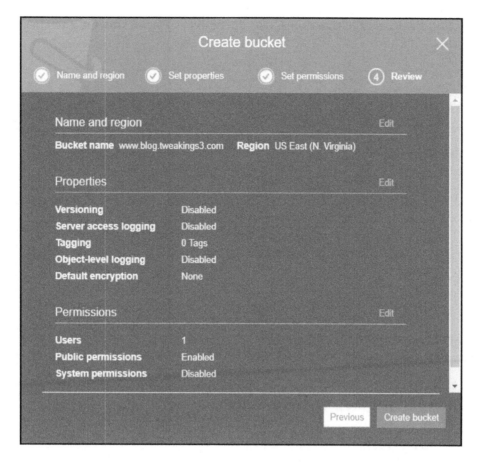

Figure 4.18: Create Bucket (www.blog.tweakings3.com)

2. Upload the HTML file: Upload `index.html` file to bucket
   `www.blog.tweakings3.com`.

3. Edit the **Bucket** permission: Go to the Bucket's **Permission** tab and click on **Bucket Policy**.

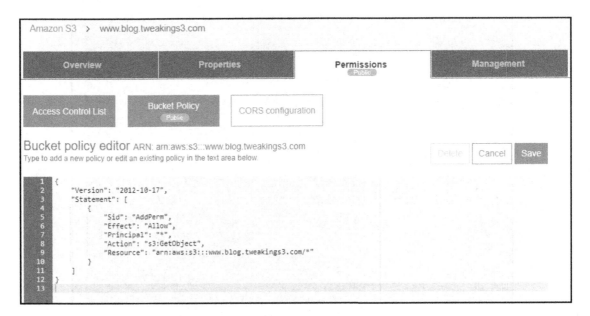

Figure 4.19: Bucket Policy

Add the following policy and click on **Save**:

```
{
    "Version": "2012-10-17",
    "Statement": [{
        "Sid": "AddPerm",
        "Effect": "Allow",
        "Principal": "*",
        "Action": "s3:GetObject",
        "Resource": "arn:aws:s3:::www.blog.tweakings3.com/*"
    }]
}
```

This will prompt you with a warning, **This bucket has public access**. Ignore this warning as we want to provide public access to this bucket, and then click on **Save**.

4. Configure **Static website hosting** Properties: Go to the bucket's properties tab and click on **Static website hosting**:

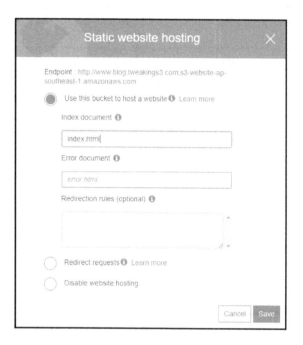

Figure 4.20: Static Website Hosting Configuration

We will choose the **Use this bucket to host a website** option as this contains the configuration for home page and error page settings. Provide the home page HTML filename and an error page HTML filename. We can also configure the redirection rules for redirecting the request to the specific content.

Click on **Save**.

5. Create S3 bucket and redirect the request

    Create a bucket with the name `blog.tweakings3.com` and configure the static
    website hosting properties as shown in the following screenshot:

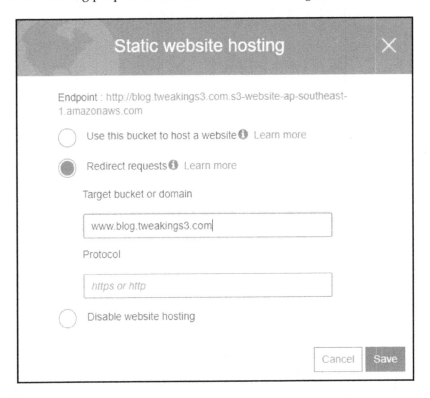

Figure 4.21: Static Website Hosting Configuration for Redirecting Request

Whenever we get a request for this URL `blog.tweakings3.com`, it should
redirect the request to the `www.blog.tweakings3.com` bucket. With this
configuration, we ensure that `blog.tweakings3.com` and
`www.blog.tweakings3.com` work for the request.

Click on **Save**.

6. Configure the Hosted Zone:Here, we will map our domain name with the S3 bucket so that we can serve the static website. For this, you need a domain name and a hosted zone created. We already have a domain name **tweakings3.com** purchased from Amazon Route53.

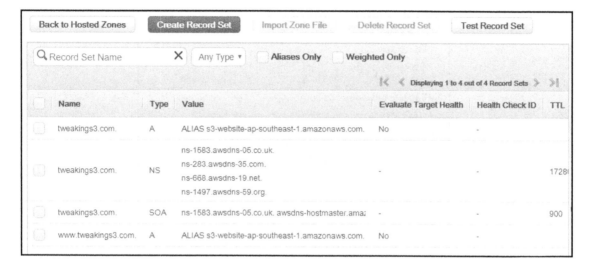

Name	Type	Value	Evaluate Target Health	Health Check ID	TTL
tweakings3.com.	A	ALIAS s3-website-ap-southeast-1.amazonaws.com.	No	-	
tweakings3.com.	NS	ns-1583.awsdns-05.co.uk. ns-283.awsdns-35.com. ns-668.awsdns-19.net. ns-1497.awsdns-59.org.	-	-	1728(
tweakings3.com.	SOA	ns-1583.awsdns-05.co.uk. awsdns-hostmaster.ama;	-	-	900
www.tweakings3.com.	A	ALIAS s3-website-ap-southeast-1.amazonaws.com.	No	-	

Figure 4.22: Existing Hosted Zone

AWS Route53 is a **Domain Name System (DNS)** web service, which translates and routes domain name requests to the respective IP address. For more details on Route53, visit `https://aws.amazon.com/route53/`.

We will create one subdomain and redirect our request to the bucket.

Click on **Create Record Set**:

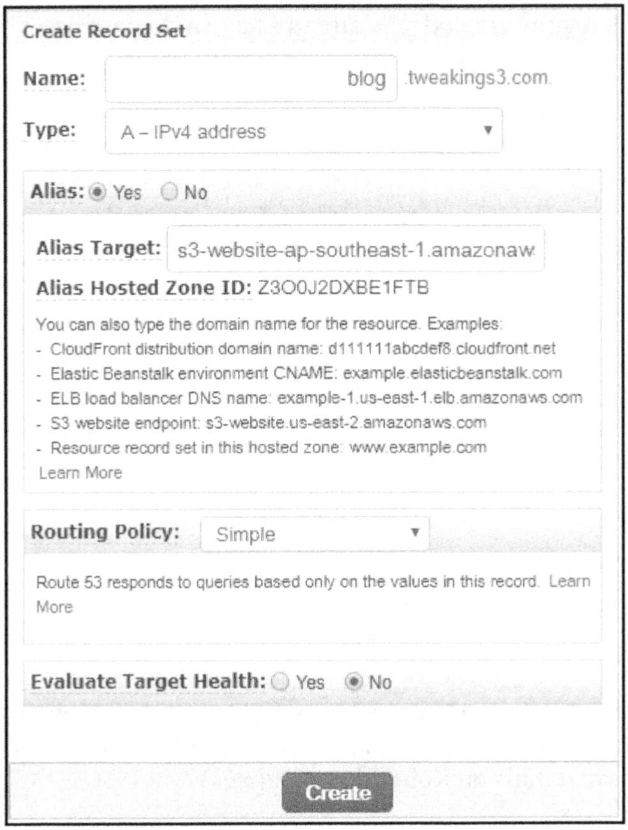

Figure 4.23: Record Set for blog.tweakings3.com

Provide the name as **blog** and set the **Alias** option to **Yes**. Here, we can provide **Alias Target** as **s3-website-ap-southeast-1.amazonaws.com**, which means the request will be redirected to the following:

```
http://blog.tweakings3.com.s3-website-ap-southeast-1.amazonaws.com
```

Create another Record Set with the name **www.blog** and set the Alias option to **Yes** and **Alias Target** as the same S3 URL **s3-website-ap-southeast-1.amazonaws.com**. So this record set states that it will redirect **www.blog.tweakings3.com** to the following:

```
http://www.blog.tweakings3.com.s3-website-ap-southeast-1.amazonaws.com
```

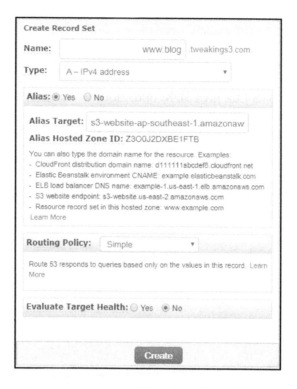

Figure 4.24: Record Set for www.blog.tweakings3.com

7. Test the URL: Try executing the following URLs:

http://www.blog.tweakings3.com/ or http://blog.tweakings3.com/

Figure 4.25: Test URL

 It may take some time to map the DNS name to the Amazon S3 Bucket.

Summary

In this chapter, we have covered how to create an Amazon S3 bucket, upload objects, and host a static website. We covered the bucket creation and uploading objects using the Management Console, AWS CLI, Java SDK, and Cloud Formation Script. We can configure the permissions as per our application needs. It is important not to grant public access over the bucket and object to anonymous users. This may incur heavy charges if the URL is being used by some other users or application. We also covered how to configure the Hosted Zone for hosting a static website on Amazon S3.

In the next chapter, we will be learning about the **Relational Database Service (RDS)**, which is used to create database instances and clusters.

5
Managing RDS

Amazon **Relational Database Service (RDS)** is a cloud database service that is easy to set up, operate, and scale. Amazon RDS helps to reduce database administrative tasks such as version upgrade, backups, restoration, and software patching. It is cost efficient and we can automate the scaling of the database size and hardware.

In this chapter, we will cover the following topics:

- Supported databases
- DB instances

Amazon RDS offers managed service for database engines, management, and administration. Amazon RDS is exposed over a web service interface where we can easily create and manage databases. The Amazon RDS managed service ensures that the user gets fast performance, security for database access, scalability, and high availability. With this, we don't need to deal with database infrastructure management, backup strategies, software patching, or any other database administrative tasks, so that the user can focus on the application life cycle. Amazon RDS offers a wide range of database engines such as:

- Amazon Aurora
- MariaDB
- Oracle
- MySQL
- PostgreSQL
- Microsoft SQL server

Amazon RDS allows us to configure the database server to have fault tolerance and high availability using Multi-AZ deployment (within the same region). When we configure Multi-AZ deployment, it automatically replicates the primary database to the secondary databases within a few milliseconds. In the case of primary database failure, any of the secondary databases is switched to primary and Amazon RDS looks to recover the failed primary database.

Amazon RDS also allows us to take snapshots at configured time intervals so that in case of disaster recovery, we can restore the database at a certain point-in-time copy. Apart from this, we can also encrypt the database volume for security purpose with the default **Key Management Service (KMS)** key or the customer's KMS key. So, in case the database volume is even hacked, the intruder won't be able to decrypt the database volume without the encryption key. Encryption strategy is also transparent at application level. The application doesn't need to know what and how the encryption is being done at database level. We can also encrypt the database backups, read replicas, and database snapshots.

Users can also avail the database migration service from Amazon to switch from on-premise database or from other database service providers to Amazon RDS databases.

Supported databases

Amazon RDS supports the database engines that we will elaborate on shortly.

Amazon Aurora

Amazon Aurora is a fully managed relational database engine provided by Amazon Web Services. As Aurora offers MySQL and PostgreSQL database compatibility, we can use our existing code, client tools, applications, and database drivers as is. Aurora comes with all the features, which are provided by MySQL and PostgreSQL database, and additionally it caters to cost-effectiveness and performance efficiency, which are provided by commercial database engines. Database migration becomes easier and seamless due to compatibility without making any changes for datatypes or data conversions.

MariaDB

MariaDB is a fully managed service provided by Amazon. MariaDB was being forked from MySQL, so all the features of MySQL are incorporated with additional features of MariaDB. It is being developed by MySQL developers and is being managed by the open source community. MariaDB is also a preferred choice, where we need to build HIPAA compliant applications. On top of MariaDB features, Amazon RDS adds support for parallel replication and thread pooling for MariaDB DB instances. Amazon RDS MariaDB supports XtraDB and Aria storage engines.

For more information on HIPAA compliance, see
https://aws.amazon.com/compliance/hipaa-compliance/.

Oracle

Oracle database is a commercial database provided by Oracle. Amazon RDS offers Oracle database to create database instances. We can set-up, scale, and operate Oracle database deployment within minutes. We don't need to care about installing the database or creating infrastructure for the database. Amazon RDS provides the following two licensing models:

- **License included**: Amazon manages the license procurement of the Oracle database for you and charges you accordingly. So it becomes more convenient for users to focus on creating the database instead of provisioning the licensing part.
- **Bring-Your-Own-License (BYOL)**: Under BYOL, the user needs to provide existing Oracle database license or purchase the license directly from Oracle. This is useful when you have already purchased the Oracle database license.

MySQL

Amazon RDS offers MySQL database engine. The user has the flexibility to choose the MySQL version offered by Amazon RDS. Amazon RDS provides easy interfaces and APIs to set up, scale, and operate in minutes. MySQL is a popular database used worldwide. Amazon RDS offers MySQL database engine under the free usage tier with some limitations like we can create database instances without Multi-AZ deployments. Later, we will have our first-hand experience of MySQL and get started with Amazon RDS.

PostgreSQL

PostgreSQL is a popular open source and **Object Relational Database Management System (ORDBMS)**. It is a preferred choice among start-ups, enterprises, geospatial applications, and so on. It has capability to handle heavy load for small to large internet facing applications. Amazon RDS offers support for PostgreSQL database engine, where we can eradicate the complex installation process and set-up, scale, and operate in a couple of minutes.

Microsoft SQL Server

Microsoft SQL Server is a commercial database offered by Amazon RDS. The user has the flexibility to choose the edition and version of the database and can easily switch between them. Amazon RDS provides the following two licensing models:

- **License included**: Amazon manages the license procurement of the database on behalf of you and charges you accordingly. So, it becomes more convenient for the user to focus on creating the database instead of provisioning the licensing part.
- **License Mobility through Software Assurance** or **BYOL**: Under this model, the user will be providing the existing database license or purchase the license directly from Microsoft and provide it to Amazon RDS. This is useful when you have already purchased the Microsoft database license.

DB instance

Database instances is a central part of the Amazon RDS. We can provision the DB instances, which deploys any of the supported database engines. The user can create multiple databases (schemas) in the DB instance.

We need to provide a unique identifier to the DB instance. This identifier needs to be unique across the AWS region for our account. Also, while creating the DB instance, we need to choose the database engine. Different database engines have different configuration parameters. We can either provide the configuration parameters at the time of creation or after it is being created. We also need to choose the DB instance class, which is important as it defines the computation and memory capacity of the DB instance.

For more details on the DB instance class, refer to `http://docs.aws.amazon.com/AmazonRDS/latest/UserGuide/Concepts.DBInstanceClass.html`.

We also need to allocate the DB instance storage capacity, where RDS will store our data. DB instance storage can also be encrypted using KMS for security measures. Using KMS only, we can decrypt the storage volume data. This encryption mechanism is transparent to the application and users as they are carried out at storage level. Amazon offers the following three storage types:

- Magnetic

- General purpose (SSD)
- Provisioned IOPS (PIOPS)

Each storage type differs in performance and cost. So we have control over what performance we want to cater from our DB instance.

Let's get started with creating DB instances using different ways.

AWS Management Console

The AWS Management Console allows us to create and manage the AWS services in an easy way. For our demonstration, we will be creating the MySQL DB instance.

Creating a security group

Create a security group, which will be attached to the DB instance so that a specific port is accessible. Security groups can be created in the same manner as described in Chapter 3, *Building Servers Using EC2.*

As we will be creating MySQL DB instance, we need to open the MySQL default port 3306 in the security group. The following is the security group that will be created:

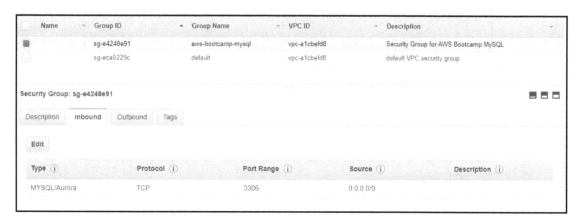

Figure 5.1: Security group

We created the security group under our default VPC as this VPC will be used for the DB instance also.

Creating a DB instance

Go to the AWS RDS Management Console
(`https://console.aws.amazon.com/rds/home#dbinstances`), and follow these steps :

1. Click on the **Launch DB Instance**.
2. **Choose the DB engine**: Here, we need to select the DB engine from the databases supported by Amazon RDS:

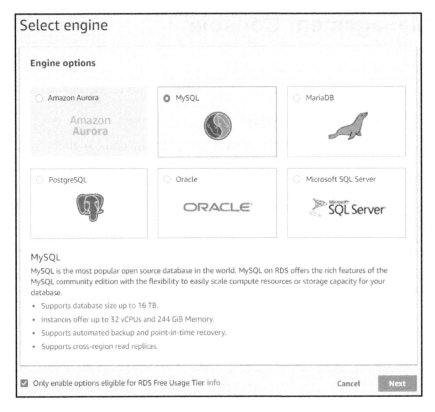

Figure 5.2: Select DB engine

We will choose the **MySQL** DB engine option, enable the checkbox for **Only enable options eligible for RDS Free Usage Tie**r so that we don't make any configurations that may incur charges, and then click on **Next**.

3. **Specific DB details**: Here, we need to provide instance specifications and settings such as database identifier, database username, and password:

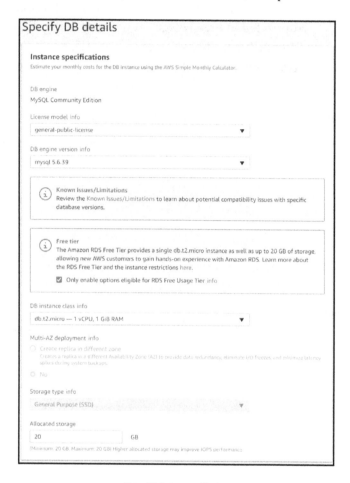

Figure 5.3: Instance specifications

Provide instance specification details such as:

- **License model**: Choose the default **general-public-license.**
- **DB engine version**: Choose the version for which we want to create the database.
- **DB instance class**: Choose the class that defines the memory and CPU configuration for your DB instance. We will go with `db.t2.micro` as it comes under the **Free Tier.**

- **Multi-AZ deployment**: If we select **Yes**, then it will enable Multi-AZ deployment, which will create a standby replica of DB instance in another Availability Zone. **Multi-AZ deployment** is not supported in **Free Usage Tier**, so it is being disabled.
- **Storage type**: Choose `General Purpose`.
- **Allocated storage**: Allocate the storage size. We will go with the minimum storage size required, which is `20 GB`.

Next, we need to configure **Settings** details:

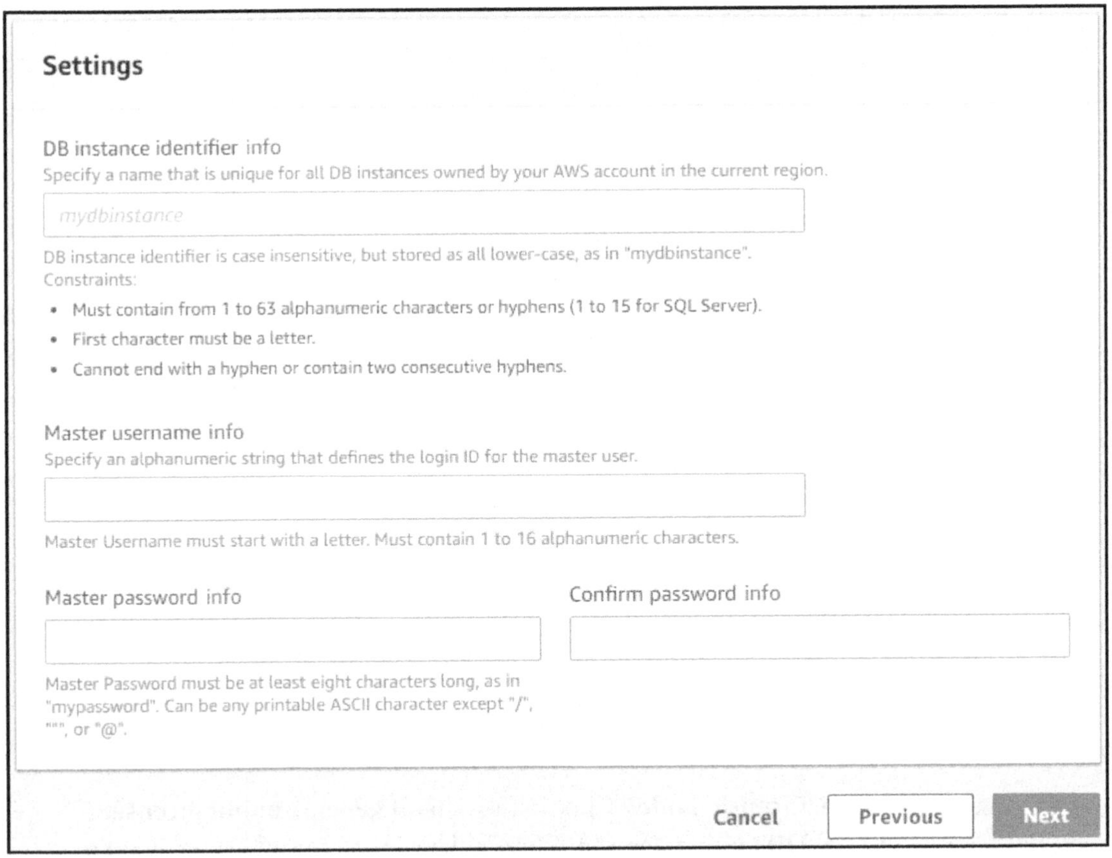

Settings

DB instance identifier info
Specify a name that is unique for all DB instances owned by your AWS account in the current region.

> mydbinstance

DB instance identifier is case insensitive, but stored as all lower-case, as in "mydbinstance".
Constraints:
- Must contain from 1 to 63 alphanumeric characters or hyphens (1 to 15 for SQL Server).
- First character must be a letter.
- Cannot end with a hyphen or contain two consecutive hyphens.

Master username info
Specify an alphanumeric string that defines the login ID for the master user.

Master Username must start with a letter. Must contain 1 to 16 alphanumeric characters.

Master password info   **Confirm password** info

Master Password must be at least eight characters long, as in "mypassword". Can be any printable ASCII character except "/", """, or "@".

Cancel   Previous   Next

Figure 5.4: Settings

Provide **Settings** details as follows:

- **DB instance identifier**: Type in the identifier with which your DB instance will be identified
- **Master username**: Type in your database master username
- **Master password**: Type in your database master password
- **Confirm password**: Once again type in your database master password

Click on **Next**.

4. **Configure advanced settings**: Under advance settings, we need to provide **Network & Security**:

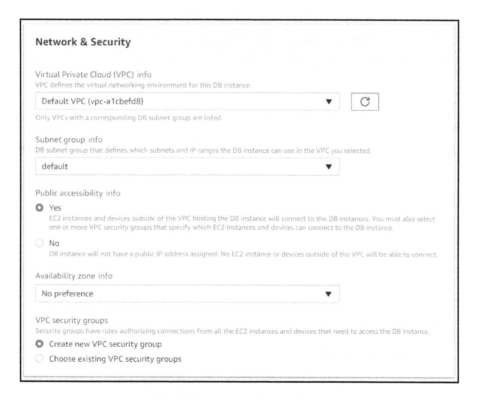

Figure 5.5: Advanced settings – Network and Security

Provide **Network & Security** details as follows:

- **Virtual Private Cloud (VPC)**: Choose the **Default VPC**.
- **Subnet group**: Choose the default **Subnet Group** that defines the subnets and IP ranges for accessibility.
- **Public accessibility**: This flag defines whether outside VPC access is allowed. If we select **No**, it is only accessible within VPC and no public IP address will be assigned.
- **Availability zone**: We can provide our preference for the Availability Zone.
- **VPC security groups**: Choose the **security group**, which will expose the endpoint and ports to the IP addresses.

Next we need to configure **Database options**:

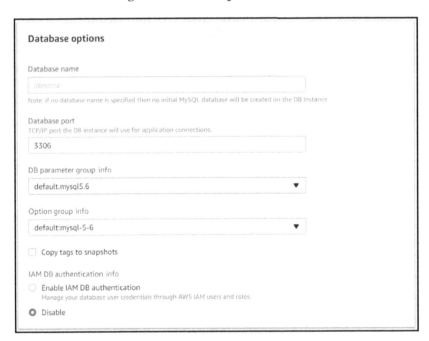

Figure 5.6: Advanced settings – database options

Provide **Database option** details as follows:

- **Database name**: Type in `awsbootcamp` as `dbname`. This will create a database under your DB instance.
- **Database port**: Type in your choice of port or keep the database default port `3306`.
- **DB parameter group**: This defines the database parameter group, which contains the database parameter configuration.
- **Option group**: We can enable any additional functionality such as Memcached support on MySQL, Oracle, or Microsoft SQL Server encryption.
- **Copy tags to snapshots**: This flag defines whether tags need to be copied to Snapshots so that it becomes easier for us to identify which snapshot belongs to which DB instance.
- **Enable IAM DB authentication**: This flag defines whether the database users are managed by IAM users and roles

Next we need to configure **Encryption** settings:

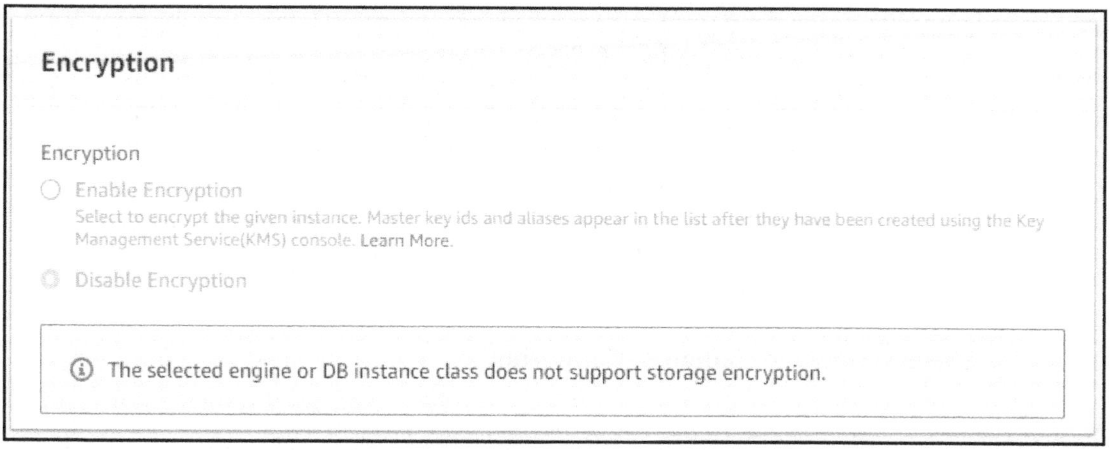

Encryption

Encryption

○ Enable Encryption
Select to encrypt the given instance. Master key ids and aliases appear in the list after they have been created using the Key Management Service(KMS) console. Learn More.

○ Disable Encryption

ⓘ The selected engine or DB instance class does not support storage encryption.

Figure 5.7: Advance Settings – Encryption

Enabling the encryption option will enable encryption of the database instance and snapshots. Only certain type of DB instance classes support storage encryption.

5. The next step is to configure **Backup**:

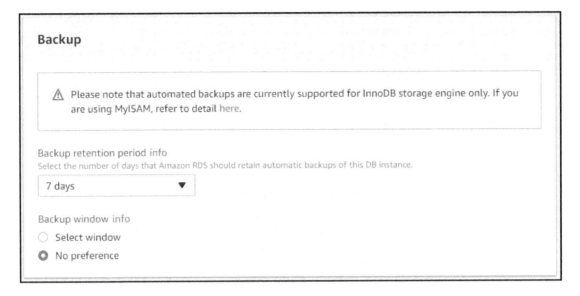

Figure 5.8: Advance Settings – Backup

Provide **Backup** details as follows:

- **Backup retention period**: This defines the number of days automated backup needs to be retained. If we provide value as 0, it means no backup needs to be taken.
- **Backup window**: This allows us to provide a time window during which the backup will be taken if the backup retention period is greater than 0.

6. The next step is to configure **Monitoring**:

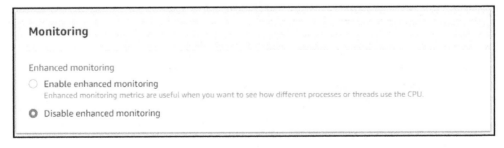

Figure 5.9: Advance Settings – Monitoring

Enabling the enhanced monitoring option will help in enhanced monitoring of our DB instance.

7. Next, we need to configure **Log exports**:

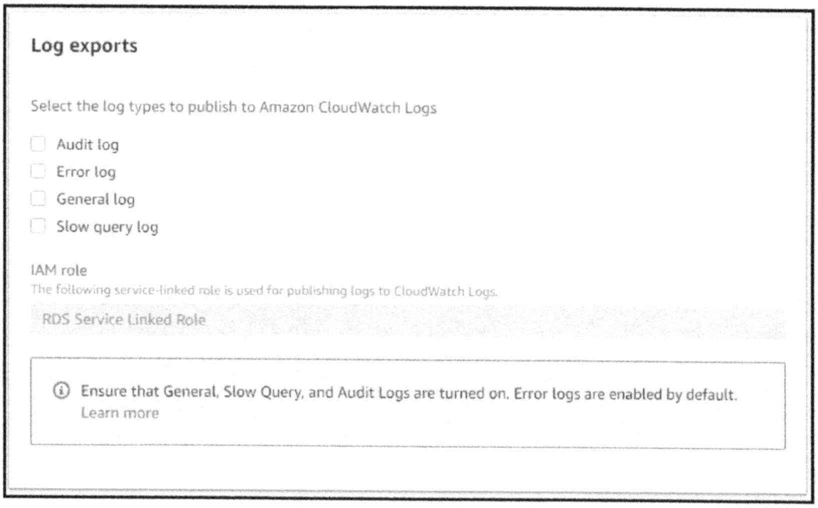

Log exports

Select the log types to publish to Amazon CloudWatch Logs

☐ Audit log
☐ Error log
☐ General log
☐ Slow query log

IAM role
The following service-linked role is used for publishing logs to CloudWatch Logs.

RDS Service Linked Role

ⓘ Ensure that General, Slow Query, and Audit Logs are turned on. Error logs are enabled by default.
   Learn more

Figure 5.10: Advance Settings – Log exports

Select the check boxes for which logs you want to publish to Amazon CloudWatch Logs. Publishing to CloudWatch Logs help us to store and monitor the logs in an efficient manner. We can also create metrics from the logs and create alarm based on these metrics so that we can take certain actions.

8. Next we need to configure the **Maintenance** setting:

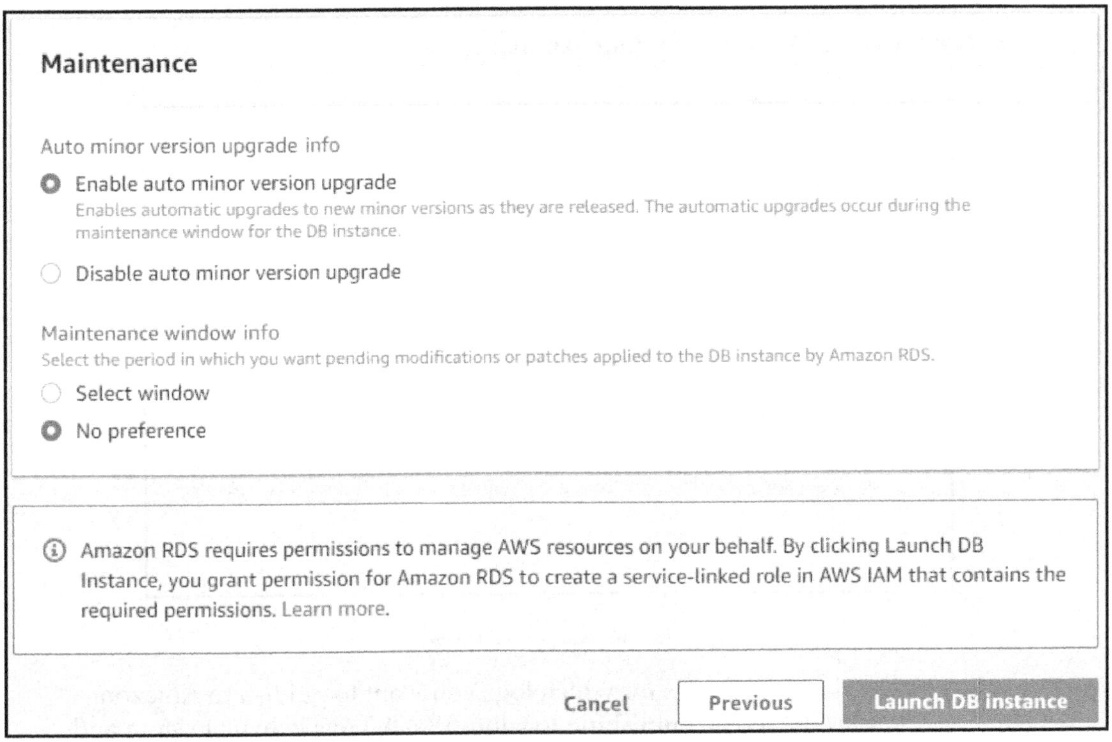

Maintenance

Auto minor version upgrade info

◉ Enable auto minor version upgrade
Enables automatic upgrades to new minor versions as they are released. The automatic upgrades occur during the maintenance window for the DB instance.

○ Disable auto minor version upgrade

Maintenance window info
Select the period in which you want pending modifications or patches applied to the DB instance by Amazon RDS.

○ Select window
◉ No preference

ⓘ Amazon RDS requires permissions to manage AWS resources on your behalf. By clicking Launch DB Instance, you grant permission for Amazon RDS to create a service-linked role in AWS IAM that contains the required permissions. Learn more.

Cancel   Previous   **Launch DB instance**

Figure 5.11: Advance Settings – Log exports

Provide **Maintenance** details as follows:

- **Enable auto minor version upgrade**: This defines whether database minor version upgrades should be automatically applied or not during the maintenance window
- **Maintenance window**: This time window is for database maintenance activity that will be done by Amazon RDS

Once all the configuration is done, click on **Launch DB instance**: This will start the process for launching our DB instance:

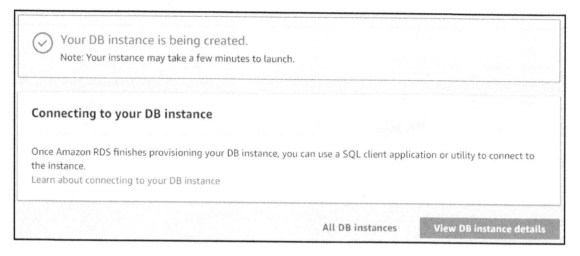

Figure 5.12: DB instance created

9. Click on **View DB instance details** to view the database instances:

Figure 5.13: View DB instances

Here, we can see that our new database instance is created. We can get the database endpoint from the details view of our database instance and can connect to the database and operate on it.

Testing the database connection

Let's test the database connection using the MySQL workbench client:

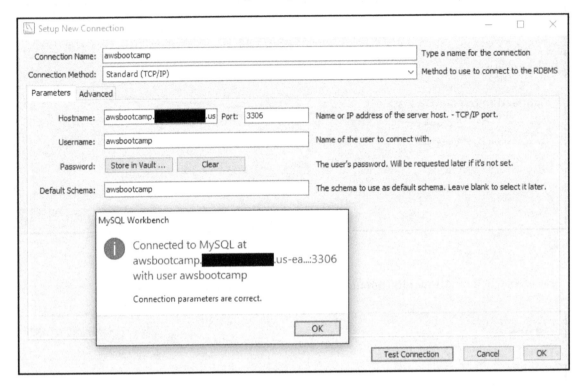

Figure 5.14: Test database connection

We provided the following inputs:

- **Connection name**: Type in a user friendly name, which identifies your database
- **Connection method**: Select standard TCP/IP
- **Hostname**: Type in the DB instance endpoint
- **Port**: Type in the DB instance port
- **Username**: Type in the DB instance username
- **Password**: Type in the DB instance password
- **Default schema**: Type in the default schema of the DB instance

Click on **Test Connection**. This should prompt for successful connection to the database.

AWS CLI

To execute the CLI script, open Command Prompt.

Creating a DB instance

Create a new DB instance under your AWS account using the following code:

```
aws rds create-db-instance ^
--db-instance-identifier "AWSBootcamp" ^
--db-instance-class "db.t2.micro" ^
--engine "MySQL" ^
--no-multi-az ^
--master-username "awsbootcamp" ^
--master-user-password "abcd12345" ^
--db-name "awsbootcampdb" ^
--storage-type "gp2" ^
--allocated-storage "20" ^
--publicly-accessible ^
--backup-retention-period "0" ^
--vpc-security-group-ids "sg-e4248e91"
```

The following are the options, which can be used with `create-db-instance`:

Parameters	Optional	Descriptions
`--engine`	False	This is the database engine that needs to be used for creating the DB instance. The valid values are as follows: • `aurora` • `aurora-postgresql` • `mariadb` • `mysql` • `oracle-ee` • `oracle-se2` • `oracle-se1` • `oracle-se` • `postgres` • `sqlserver-ee` • `sqlserver-se` • `sqlserver-ex` • `sqlserver-web`
`--license-model`	True	This is the license model of the database that needs to be used. The following are the valid values: • `license-included` • `bring-your-own-license` • `general-public-license`

`--engine-version`	True	This is the database engine version.
`--db-instance-class`	False	This is the DB instance class, which defines the compute and memory capacity of the instance.
`--multi-azor--no-multi-az`	True	This denotes whether `multi-az` is enabled or not. If we set `multi-az` to true, then we won't be able to provide the availability zone option.
`--storage-type`	True	This denotes the storage type of the DB instance. The following are the valid values: • `standard` • `gp2` • `io1`
`--allocated-storage`	True	This is the DB instance storage size in gigabytes.
`--db-instance-identifier`	False	This denotes the DB instance identifier.
`--master-username`	True	This is the name of the master username.
`--master-user-password`	True	This is the password for the master user.
`--db-subnet-group-name`	True	This is the DB subnet group to be attached to the DB instance.
`--publicly-accessibleor--no-publicly-accessible`	True	This denotes whether the database will be publicly accessible or not.
`--availability-zone`	True	This is the EC2 availability zone in which the DB instance will be created.
`--vpc-security-group-ids`	True	This is the list of EC2 security group IDs to be attached to the DB instance.
`--db-name`	True	This is the database name, which will be created when the DB instance is created. If we don't specify the DB name, then no database will be created under the DB instance.
`--port`	True	This is the port of the database instance to which we can connect.
`--db-parameter-group-name`	True	This is the DB parameter group name, which will be attached to the DB instance.

`--option-group-name`	True	This is the option group name, which will be attached to the DB instance.
`--copy-tags-to-snapshotor--no-copy-tags-to-snapshot`	True	This denotes whether tags need to be copied to snapshots from the DB instance.
`--enable-iam-database-authenticationor--no-enable-iam-database-authentication`	True	This denotes whether the database can be accessed using the IAM.
`--storage-encryptedor--no-storage-encrypted`	True	This specifies storage needs to be encrypted.
`--backup-retention-period`	True	This denotes the number of days automated backups need to be retained. If we provide the value as 0, automated backups will be disabled.
`--preferred-backup-window`	True	This denotes the time range during which automated backups can be taken.
`--enable-performance-insightsor--no-enable-performance-insights`	True	This enables or disables the performance insights of the DB instance.
`--auto-minor-version-upgradeor--no-auto-minor-version-upgrade`	True	This denotes whether minor version upgrade needs to be applied automatically or not.
`--preferred-maintenance-window`	True	This denotes the time range during which autoversion upgrade will be applied.
`--db-security-groups`	True	This is the list of DB security groups to be attached to the DB instance.
`--iops`	True	This is the amount of provisioned IOPS to be allocated to the DB instance.
`--character-set-name`	True	This is the CharacterSet to be applied on the DB instance.
`--tags`	True	This is how we can tag the DB instance in the key-value pair.
`--db-cluster-identifier`	True	This is the DB cluster identifier under which the DB instance will be associated.
`--tde-credential-arn`	True	This is the ARN of the key store.
`--tde-credential-password`	True	This is the password for the TDE credentials ARN.
`--kms-key-id`	True	This is the KMS Key Identifier for encryption of the DB instance.

--domain	True	This denotes the Active Directory Domain under which the DB instance will be created.
--monitoring-interval	True	This is the interval in seconds between points when enhanced monitoring metrics are collected.
--monitoring-role-arn	True	This is the IAM Role ARN, which provides access to RDS to send metrics to cloudwatch logs.
--domain-iam-role-name	True	This is the IAM Role ARN, which provides access to RDS to call APIs to the directory service.
--promotion-tier	True	This denotes the order in which an Aurora replica needs to make primary instance when a failure occurs of the existing primary instance.
--timezone	True	This denotes the timezone of the DB instance.
--performance-insights-kms-key-id	True	This is the AWSKMS Key Identifier for encryption of the performance insights data.

AWS SDK – Java

To access RDS service, we need to create the AmazonRDS object as follows:

```
AmazonRDS amazonRDS = AmazonRDSClientBuilder
    .standard()
    .withClientConfiguration(getClientConfiguration())
    .withCredentials(getCredentials())
    .withRegion(Regions.US_EAST_1)
    .build();
```

ClientConfiguration and AWSCredentialsProvider objects are created same as we mentioned in Chapter 2, *Configuring IAM*.

Creating a DB instance

We need to create a new DB instance under the AWS account using the following code:

```
String securityGroupId = "sg-e4248e91";
String rdsInstanceName = "AWSBootcamp";
String dbInstanceClass = "db.t2.micro";
String dbEngine = "MySQL";
booleanmultiAZEnabled = false;
String masterUsername = "awsbootcamp";
String masterPassword = "abcd12345";
String dbName = "awsbootcampdb";
String storageType = "gp2"; // standard, gp2, io1
Integer storageCapacity = 20;
createDBInstance(
    rdsInstanceName,
    dbInstanceClass,
    dbEngine,
    multiAZEnabled,
    masterUsername,
    masterPassword,
    dbName,
    storageType,
    storageCapacity,
    Arrays.asList(securityGroupId));
.........
public void createDBInstance(
    String rdsInstanceName,
    String dbInstanceClass,
    String dbEngine,
    boolean multiAZEnabled,
    String masterUsername,
    String masterPassword,
    String dbName,
    String storageType,
    int storageCapacityInGB,
    List<String>dbSecurityGroups) {
    CreateDBInstanceRequestcreateDBInstanceRequest =
        new CreateDBInstanceRequest()
                    .withDBInstanceIdentifier(rdsInstanceName)
                    .withDBInstanceClass(dbInstanceClass)
                    .withEngine(dbEngine)
                    .withMultiAZ(multiAZEnabled)
                    .withMasterUsername(masterUsername)
                    .withMasterUserPassword(masterPassword)
                    .withDBName(dbName)
                    .withStorageType(storageType)
```

```
                          .withAllocatedStorage(storageCapacityInGB)
                          .withPubliclyAccessible(true)
                          .withBackupRetentionPeriod(0)
                          .withVpcSecurityGroupIds(dbSecurityGroups);
        DBInstancedbInstance =
                amazonRDS.createDBInstance(
                        createDBInstanceRequest);
    }
```

We will be using the same security group, which we created in the *AWS Management Console* section.

AWS CloudFormation

To create the DB instance, we need to use the `AWS::RDS::DBInstance` type:

```
"AWSBootcampDBInstance": {
    "Type": "AWS::RDS::DBInstance",
    "Properties": {
        "DBInstanceClass": "db.t2.micro",
        "DBInstanceIdentifier": "awsbootcamp",
        "Engine": "MySQL",
        "MultiAZ": false,
        "MasterUsername": "awsbootcamp",
        "MasterUserPassword": "abcd12345",
        "DBName": "awsbootcampdb",
        "StorageType": "gp2",
        "AllocatedStorage": "20",
        "PubliclyAccessible": true,
        "BackupRetentionPeriod": "0",
        "VPCSecurityGroups": [
                "sg-e4248e91"
        ]
    }
}
```

Here, we used the same security group ID (`sg-e4248e91`), which we created earlier to expose the MySQL port `3306`.

Summary

In this chapter, we learned about Amazon RDS and its supported database engines as Amazon Aurora, PostgreSQL, MySQL, MariaDB, Oracle, and Microsoft SQL Server. Amazon RDS is a managed service, which helps the user to easily create and operate the database infrastructure. We can provide a secured access using the database supported user management and also configure IAM to access the database. We have an option to create the DB instance with Multi-AZ enabled, which will help us to configure highly available database for production workload. Also, we can set-up the automated backup and version upgrades by defining a specific time in which you don't have much workload on the database. Also, Amazon RDS provides us the option to create the DB cluster which will contain one or more DB instances. DB cluster helps us to handle fault tolerance by switching the replica instance to the primary instance.

In Chapter 6, *Implementing DynamoDB – NoSQL Database,* we will see how we can use the Amazon DynamoDB, NoSQL database. We will see how to create tables and operations such as create, retrieve, update, and delete on Amazon DynamoDB.

6
Implementing DynamoDB – NoSQL Database

Traditionally, IT companies were dependent on **Relational Database Management Systems (RDBMSs)** for storing their application data. A huge amount of data is being stored every day in databases, which are usually structured in nature. In the past, RDBMS were the default choice for client-server applications so that applications could store data by following the **Atomic, Consistent, Isolated, and Durable (ACID)** property. RDBMS follows the ACID properties for database transactions. Looking at today's application needs, the speed and nature of data is changing over time. So, to support the unstructured or dynamic data, RDBMS needs to be cost effective, reliable, durable, and scalable. RDBMS also needs to maintain the relationships between tables and overheads of joins for **Create, Retrieve, Update, and Delete (CRUD)** operations. So, to handle those challenges, **Not Only SQL (NoSQL)** came in to the picture. NoSQL can handle unstructured data efficiently with low cost. The amount and nature of data is leading IT companies to switch to NoSQL from RDBMS. The following are the advantages of NoSQL:

- Unstructured data
- Cost-effective
- Dynamic schema
- High scalability
- Distributed computing
- No relationship

In this chapter, we will cover the following topics:

- Basic concepts
- DynamoDB tables
- CRUD operations

Amazon DynamoDB is a fully managed NoSQL database service which meets user expectations regarding performance. DynamoDB handles such cumbersome tasks as handling distributed databases, replication, software patching, hardware procurement, and so on. We just need to deal with the DynamoDB tables and the rest is all handled by Amazon. DynamoDB also allows us to configure the read and write throughput capacity so that, based on the application needs, we can improve the performance. Also, we can change the configuration for read and write throughput capacity without downtime. DynamoDB also provides support for auto scaling read and write capacity. This is helpful when our application grows and the configured capacity is not able to handle the new incoming traffic. Amazon CloudWatch monitors the capacity at regular intervals and, if needed, modifies the throughput capacity up or down. Auto scaling is applicable for DynamoDB tables and secondary indexes. DynamoDB doesn't restrict us to store a specific amount of data. Instead, we can store any amount of data seamlessly and without any configuration changes for storage. DynamoDB supports the key-value data model. Each row is called items and columns are called attributes. While creating a DynamoDB table, it is mandatory to provide the primary key attribute names so that the item can be uniquely stored in the database. As DynamoDB is a NoSQL database, it is schema-less so we can add as many attributes as we want under each item on-the-fly. It is not mandatory to have the same column definition for all the rows. Different rows may have different columns. DynamoDB also provides support for secondary indexes (global and local) to fetch the items. Secondary indexes are useful if we want our application to have search capability on different columns other than the table's primary key columns. DynamoDB also provides streams to capture the modified data via events. DynamoDB streams need to be enabled so that we can get the data modification events. We can create a trigger on AWS Lambda to listen to the DynamoDB stream which will get a stream record and AWS Lambda can then process the event. Consider a scenario where we want to perform some action, such as sending a notification when a certain column's value is added to the DynamoDB table. In this case, we can set a trigger that will send a new record event to AWS Lambda and it will check for the respective value and if the condition is met it will send a notification.

Basic concepts

Let's look at the basic concepts of DynamoDB.

Tables

DynamoDB stores data in tables. A table contains multiple rows which are known as **items**. DynamoDB is not restricted to storing an amount of data in one table. While creating the DynamoDB table, we need to provide primary key attribute(s), which will identify the items uniquely:

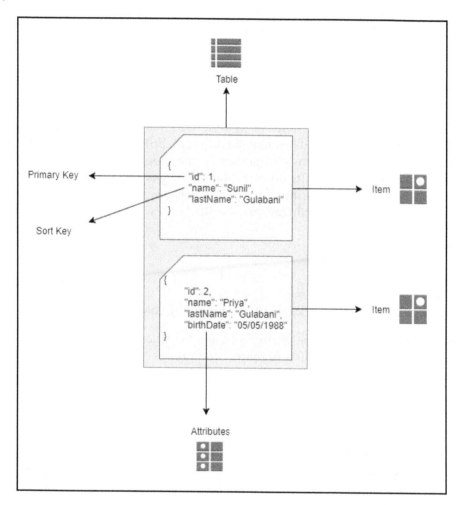

Figure 6.1: Basic concepts

Items

Items are similar to relational database table rows or tuples. We can store any amount of items in one table. A table can contain only unique (single or composite) primary keys of each item. If the new item contains the same primary keys that are already present in a table, it will override the item with the new one. In the preceding sample table, we can see that two items are created in the table. The maximum size of a single item can be up to 400 KB, which includes all the attributes (columns).

Attributes

Attributes are similar to database columns or fields that hold the data. DynamoDB doesn't have a fixed schema where all the items need to have the same attributes. Some items may have certain attributes and some items may be different. But it is recommended to have similar attributes for different items so that they define a logical entity. We can assign scalar and non-scalar data types to the attributes. Scalar data types can contain a string, number, or binary. We can have nested attributes up to 32 levels deep. In the preceding sample table, we can see that **lastName** and **birthDate** are the attributes whereas **id** and **name** are the primary keys.

Data types

DynamoDB data types can be divided into the following categories:

- **Scalar types**: Scalar types represent a single value; that is, the attribute can't have nested values, such as lists or maps. Scalar types can be any of the following:
  - string
  - number
  - binary
  - Boolean
  - null.
- **Document types**: Document types represent a complex structure similar to a JSON document. Document types consist of lists and maps and can be nested up to 32 levels deep.
- **Set types**: Set types allow us to store the attribute value in sets, which can be a Number Set, String Set, or Binary Set. A single attribute can only contain the same type of data values in a set. Each attribute value in a set should be unique. Also, we can't store empty sets.

Each data type has its limitations of storing values. For more information, please visit `http://docs.aws.amazon.com/amazondynamodb/latest/ developerguide/HowItWorks.NamingRulesDataTypes.html`

Primary keys

A primary key is used to identify the item uniquely. We need to provide the primary key while creating the table. Other attributes can be added later, as DynamoDB is schema-less. DynamoDB allow us to create primary keys in two ways:

- **Partition key**: When we create a primary key using the single attribute, it is known as a partition key. DynamoDB takes the partition key attribute value and creates a hash value. Using the generated hash value, a partition is decided where the item will be stored. So, using a single primary key, we can't have the same primary key value for two items.

- **Partition key and sort key**: When we create a primary key using two attributes, it is known as a partition key and sort key. This is also referred to as a composite primary key. DynamoDB takes the partition key attribute value and creates a hash value. Using the generated hash value, a partition is decided where the item will be stored. Items are then sorted based on the sort key attribute value and stored. So using this composite primary key, a partition key can be the same for multiple items, but a combination of a partition key and sort key needs to be unique. In the preceding sample table, we have *id* as the partition key and *name* as the sort key.

Secondary indexes

Secondary indexes are used to query the data faster and more efficiently on non-primary key attributes of a table. Secondary indexes are formed from the base table and can have their own primary key and attributes, which have to be from the base table. As and when the application behavior changes, we may need to alter our query to efficiently fetch data from the database. So, in such scenarios, we can make use of secondary indexes on attributes which we are going to query for efficient performance. We can create secondary indexes in a table and use them along with query or scan operations. Secondary indexes can be associated with one table only. When we create a secondary index, the table is known as the **base table** from where data will be obtained. We can create our own schema for a secondary index that needs to be available when we query it.

As and when the base table is modified, associated secondary indexes are also updated so that we get the real-time data. Secondary indexes are of two types:

- **Global secondary index**: A global secondary index allows us to create an index on the base table with different partition keys and sort keys of the base table. It provides flexibility to the user to create an index any time with or after the table creation. As and when we want to alter our queries that rely on partition keys and sort keys, we can recreate the index to meet our requirement. Also a global secondary index has its own provisioned throughput, which means we can alter the capacity without affecting the base table's provisioned throughput.
- **Local secondary index**: A local secondary index allows us to create an index on the base table with the same partition key but with a different sort key. We cannot create a local secondary index after the table is created. While creating a local secondary key, we need to keep in mind that provisioned throughput capacity is being shared with the base table. So while calculating the base table's provisioned throughput, we may need to consider the throughput that is going to be consumed by the local secondary index.

Streams

DynamoDB Streams is similar to the relational database trigger applied on a DynamoDB table. Whenever any item is created, modified, or deleted from the table, the trigger will be invoked and this will be captured on DynamoDB Streams. We can configure an AWS Lambda trigger to process the stream events. Each event is represented by a stream record. Stream records are processed in the same manner as they are generated.

DynamoDB tables

Let's look at how to create a DynamoDB table.

AWS Management Console

The AWS Management Console allows us to easily create and manage the AWS services.

Creating a table

Go to AWS DynamoDB Management Console at `https://console.aws.amazon.com/dynamodb/home`:

1. Click on **Create table:**

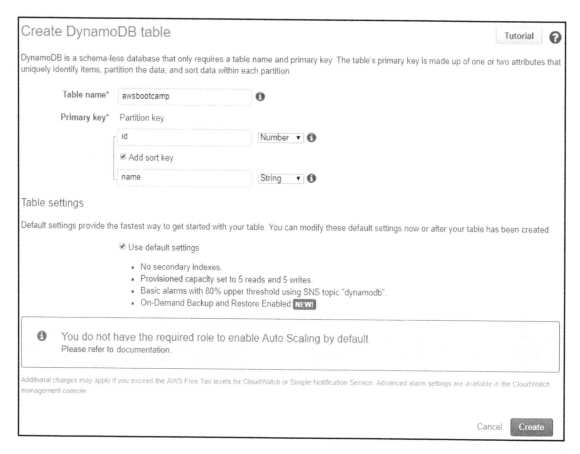

Figure 6.2: Creating a table

Provide the following details:

- **Table name**: Type in **awsbootcamp**.
- **Primary key**:
  - **Partition key**: Type in **id** and select **Number** as the data type
  - **Sort key**: Type in **name** and select **String** as the data type
- **Table settings**: If we want to change the default table settings, then uncheck **Use default settings** and configure the **Secondary indexes**, **Provisioned capacity**, and **Auto Scaling**. For our example, we will change the **Read capacity units** to 1 and the **Write capacity units** to 1:

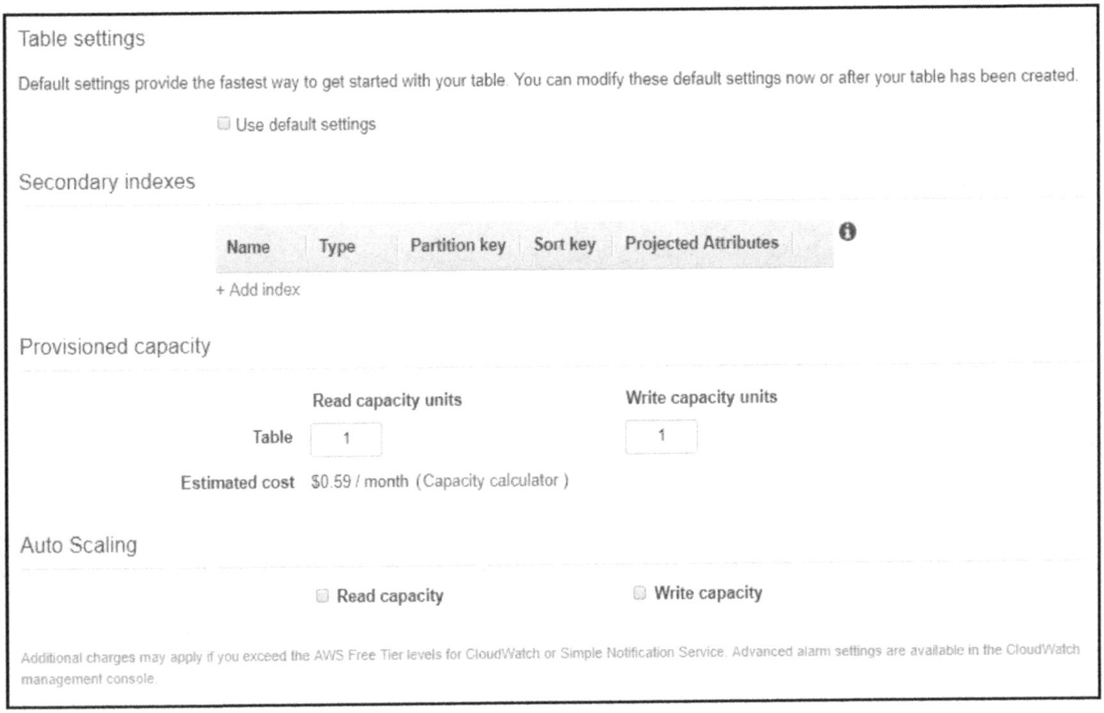

Table settings

Default settings provide the fastest way to get started with your table. You can modify these default settings now or after your table has been created.

☐ Use default settings

Secondary indexes

Name	Type	Partition key	Sort key	Projected Attributes	

+ Add index

Provisioned capacity

	Read capacity units	Write capacity units
Table	1	1

Estimated cost $0.59 / month (Capacity calculator)

Auto Scaling

☐ Read capacity   ☐ Write capacity

Additional charges may apply if you exceed the AWS Free Tier levels for CloudWatch or Simple Notification Service. Advanced alarm settings are available in the CloudWatch management console.

Figure 6.3: Table settings

2. Once the table configuration has been done, click **Create**. The table will be created, as shown in the following screenshot:

Figure 6.4: Table listing

Here, we can see the created table and on the right section, we can see the different tabs that show the table overview, items (data that is stored on table), CloudWatch metrics, alarms associated with the table, provisioned throughput, indexes, global tables, backups, triggers (if streams are enabled), access control, and tags.

AWS CLI

To execute the CLI script, open **Command Prompt**.

Creating a table

The following command will create a new table under your AWS account:

```
aws dynamodb create-table ^
--table-name "awsbootcamp" ^
--key-schema AttributeName=id,KeyType=HASH
AttributeName=name,KeyType=RANGE ^
    --attribute-definitions AttributeName=id,AttributeType=N
AttributeName=name,AttributeType=S ^
        --provisioned-throughput ReadCapacityUnits=1,WriteCapacityUnits=1
```

The following are the options that can be used when creating a table:

Parameters	Optional	Descriptions
`--table-name`	False	Table name should be unique in the region you are creating
`--key-schema`	False	Key schema contains the primary key attributes. The primary key contains only a partition key or partition key and sort key. We need to provide the Attribute Name and Key Type for the key schema. The format can be: `AttributeName=id,` `KeyType=HASH AttributeName=name,` `KeyType=RANGE.` For the partition key, the key type needs to be HASH and for the sort key, it needs to be RANGE.
`--attribute-definitions`	False	Attributes definitions are the schema format. Although it is not mandatory to provide the entire schema, we do need to provide the primary key attributes and its data types. The format can be in form of a list: `AttributeName=id,` `AttributeType=N AttributeName=name,` `AttributeType=SValid` values for attribute types are N (number), S (string), or B (binary)
`--provisioned-throughput`	False	We can provide the read and write capacity units through this property. The format can be: `ReadCapacityUnits=5,` `WriteCapacityUnits=5.` The values need to be of a long data type.

`--local-secondary-indexes`	True	We can define one or more local secondary indexes for a table. A maximum of five local secondary indexes can be created. The format can be:
		`IndexName=awsbootcampindex,`
		`KeySchema=[{AttributeName=id,KeyType=HASH},`
		`{AttributeName=name,KeyType=RANGE}],Projection=`
		`{ProjectionType=INCLUDE,NonKeyAttributes=`
		`[id,name,lastName,birthDate]}`
		Valid values for KeyType are:
		• `HASH`
		• `RANGE`
		Valid values for ProjectionType are:
		• `KEYS_ONLY`
		• `INCLUDE`
		• `ALL`

`--global-secondary-indexes`	True	We can define one or more global secondary indexes for a table. We can create a maximum of five global secondary indexes. The format can be:
		`IndexName=awsbootcampglobalindexes,KeySchema=`
		`AttributeName=name,KeyType=HASH},`
		`{AttributeName=lastName,KeyType=RANGE}],Projection=`
		`{ProjectionType=INCLUDE,NonKeyAttributes=`
		`[id,name,lastName,birthDate]},ProvisionedThroughput=`
		`{ReadCapacityUnits=1,WriteCapacityUnits=1}`
		Valid values for KeyType are:
		• `HASH`
		• `RANGE`
		Valid values for ProjectionType are:
		• `KEYS_ONLY`
		• `INCLUDE`
		• `ALL`

`--stream-specification`	True	We can enable the DynamoDB streams for specific events. The format can be: `StreamEnabled=true,` `StreamViewType=KEYS_ONLY`. Valid values for `StreamEnabled` are: • `true` • `false` (by default) Valid values for StreamViewType are: • `KEYS_ONLY` • `NEW_IMAGE` • `OLD_IMAGE` • `NEW_AND_OLD_IMAGES`

The following code will create a local secondary index while creating a table:

```
aws dynamodb create-table ^
--table-name "awsbootcamp" ^
--key-schema AttributeName=id,KeyType=HASH
AttributeName=name,KeyType=RANGE ^
    --attribute-definitions AttributeName=id,AttributeType=N
AttributeName=name,AttributeType=S ^
    --provisioned-throughput ReadCapacityUnits=1,WriteCapacityUnits=1 ^
    --local-secondary-indexes
IndexName=awsbootcampindex,KeySchema=[{AttributeName=id,KeyType=HASH},{Attr
ibuteName=name,KeyType=RANGE}],Projection={ProjectionType=ALL}
```

Here, we can see that the partition key and sort key of the table and local secondary indexes have to be same. The following code will create a global secondary index while creating a table:

```
aws dynamodb create-table ^
--table-name "awsbootcamp" ^
--key-schema AttributeName=id,KeyType=HASH
AttributeName=name,KeyType=RANGE ^
    --attribute-definitions AttributeName=id,AttributeType=N
AttributeName=name,AttributeType=S AttributeName=lastName,AttributeType=S ^
    --provisioned-throughput ReadCapacityUnits=1,WriteCapacityUnits=1 ^
    --global-secondary-indexes
IndexName=awsbootcampglobalindexes,KeySchema=[{AttributeName=name,KeyType=H
ASH},{AttributeName=lastName,KeyType=RANGE}],Projection={ProjectionType=INC
LUDE,NonKeyAttributes=[birthDate]},ProvisionedThroughput={ReadCapacityUnits
=1,WriteCapacityUnits=1}
```

Here, we can see that the partition key and sort key of the table and global secondary indexes are different.

AWS SDK - Java

To access DynamoDB services, we need to create the AmazonDynamoDB object as:

```
AmazonDynamoDB amazonDynamoDB = AmazonDynamoDBClientBuilder
            .standard()
            .withClientConfiguration(getClientConfiguration())
            .withCredentials(getCredentials())
            .withRegion(Regions.US_EAST_1)
            .build();

DynamoDB dynamoDB = new DynamoDB(amazonDynamoDB);
```

The `ClientConfiguration` and `AWSCredentialsProvider` objects are created in the same way as we did in `Chapter 2`, *Configure IAM*.

Create table

To create a DynamoDB table, we need to provide the table name, single or composite primary key, provisioned throughput, and stream enabled flag. If we enable the streams, we need to provide the Stream View type.

The following code snippet will create the DynamoDB table with the name as `awsbootcamp`, the primary key as numeric, the sort key as string, and streams as disabled:

```
public void createTable(
    String tableName,
    Long readCapacity, Long writeCapacity,
    String partitionKeyName, String partitionKeyType,
    String sortKeyName, String sortKeyType,
    boolean streamEnabled, StreamViewType streamViewType) {
    ProvisionedThroughput provisionedThroughput =
        createProvisionedThroughput(
            readCapacity, writeCapacity);
    List < KeySchemaElement > keySchemaElements =
        new ArrayList < > ();
    KeySchemaElement partitionKeySchemaElement =
        createKeySchemaElement(
            partitionKeyName, KeyType.HASH);
    keySchemaElements.add(partitionKeySchemaElement);
    List < AttributeDefinition > attributeDefinitions =
        new ArrayList < > ();
    AttributeDefinition partitionKeyAttrDef =
        createAttributeDefinition(
            partitionKeyName, partitionKeyType);
    attributeDefinitions.add(partitionKeyAttrDef);
    if (!StringUtils.isNullOrEmpty(sortKeyName)) {
        KeySchemaElement sortKeySchemaElement =
            createKeySchemaElement(
                sortKeyName, KeyType.RANGE);
        keySchemaElements.add(sortKeySchemaElement);
        AttributeDefinition sortKeyAttrDef =
            createAttributeDefinition(
                sortKeyName, sortKeyType);
        attributeDefinitions.add(sortKeyAttrDef);
    }
    StreamSpecification streamSpecification =
        createStreamSpecification(
            streamEnabled, streamViewType);
```

```
    CreateTableRequest request =
        new CreateTableRequest()
        .withTableName(tableName)
        .withProvisionedThroughput(provisionedThroughput)
        .withKeySchema(keySchemaElements)
        .withAttributeDefinitions(attributeDefinitions)
        .withStreamSpecification(
            streamSpecification);
    CreateTableResult result =
        amazonDynamoDB.createTable(request);
}
```

To create a DynamoDB stream, we can use the following code snippet while creating the table. StreamViewType can be any of the following:

- StreamViewType.NEW_IMAGE

- StreamViewType.OLD_IMAGE

- StreamViewType.NEW_AND_OLD_IMAGES

- StreamViewType.KEYS_ONLY

```
private StreamSpecification
createStreamSpecification(
    boolean streamEnabled,
    StreamViewType streamViewType) {
    StreamSpecification streamSpecification =
        new StreamSpecification()
        .withStreamEnabled(streamEnabled);
    if (streamEnabled) {
        streamSpecification.
        setStreamViewType(streamViewType);
    }
    return streamSpecification;
}
```

The following code snippet is used to create AttributeDefinition, KeySchemaElement, and provisionedthroughput objects while creating the table:

```
private AttributeDefinition
createAttributeDefinition(
        String attributeName,
        String attributeType) {
        return new AttributeDefinition()
        .withAttributeName(attributeName)
        .withAttributeType(attributeType);
}
```

```
private KeySchemaElement createKeySchemaElement(
    String attributeName,
    KeyType keyType) {
    return new KeySchemaElement()
        .withAttributeName(attributeName)
        .withKeyType(keyType);
}
```

AWS CloudFormation

To create a DynamoDB table, we need to use the `AWS::DynamoDB::Table` type:

```
"AWSBootcampDDB": {
    "Type": "AWS::DynamoDB::Table",
    "Properties": {
        "TableName": "awsbootcamp",
        "AttributeDefinitions": [{
                "AttributeName": "id",
                "AttributeType": "N"
            },
            {
                "AttributeName": "name",
                "AttributeType": "S"
            }
        ],
        "KeySchema": [{
                "AttributeName": "id",
                "KeyType": "HASH"
            },
            {
                "AttributeName": "name",
                "KeyType": "RANGE"
            }
        ],
        "ProvisionedThroughput": {
            "ReadCapacityUnits": 1,
            "WriteCapacityUnits": 1
        }
    }
}
```

The preceding script will create the DynamoDB table with a specified partition key and sort key and configure the read and write provisioned throughput capacity.

CRUD operations

We will learn about the Create, Retrieve, Update, and Delete operations on the DynamoDB table using the Java SDK.

Create item

We will put items into the `awsbootcamp` table that we created in the previous section.

- Using `AmazonDynamoDB`:

  Let's create an item using the `AmazonDynamoDB` object:

```
Map<String, AttributeValue> item = new HashMap<>();

item.put("id", new AttributeValue().withN("1"));

item.put("name", new AttributeValue().withS("Sunil"));

item.put("lastName", new AttributeValue().withS("Gulabani"));

createItem(tableName, item);

........

public void createItem(
        String tableName,
        Map<String, AttributeValue> item) {

    PutItemRequest request = new PutItemRequest()
            .withTableName(tableName)
            .withItem(item);

    PutItemResult result = amazonDynamoDB.putItem(request);
}
```

- Using `DynamoDB`:

  Let's create an item using the `DynamoDB` object:

```
Item item2 = new Item()
        .withPrimaryKey("id", 2, "name", "Priya")
        .withString("lastName", "Gulabani")
        .withString("birthDate", "05/05/1988");
```

```
createItem2(tableName, item2);

........

public void createItem2(String tableName, Item item) {

    Table table = dynamoDB.getTable(tableName);

    PutItemSpec spec = new PutItemSpec()
            .withItem(item);

    PutItemOutcome outcome = table.putItem(spec);
}
```

Get item

The following code snippet will get the items from the table based on the partition key and sort key. We can also use Get Item with a strong consistent read by enabling it. By setting the strong consistent read property to true, it might take time to return the last updated value.

- Using AmazonDynamoDB:

    Let's get a specific item using the AmazonDynamoDB object:

```
Map<String, AttributeValue> retrieveKey = new HashMap<>();

retrieveKey.put("id", new AttributeValue().withN("1"));

retrieveKey.put("name", new AttributeValue().withS("Sunil"));

retrieveItem(tableName, retrieveKey);

........

public void retrieveItem(
        String tableName,
        Map<String, AttributeValue> key) {

    GetItemRequest request =
    new GetItemRequest()
    .withTableName(tableName)
    .withKey(key)
    .withConsistentRead(true);
```

```
        GetItemResult result = amazonDynamoDB.getItem(request);
    }
```

- Using DynamoDB:

Let's get a specific item using the DynamoDB object:

```
retrieveItem2(
    tableName,
    "id", // partition key
    2, // partition key value
    "name", // sort key
    "Priya" // sort key value
);
........

public void retrieveItem2(
        String tableName,
        String hashKeyName,
        Integer hashKeyValue,
        String rangeKeyName,
        String rangeKeyValue) {

    Table table = dynamoDB.getTable(tableName);

    PrimaryKey primaryKey = new PrimaryKey(
            hashKeyName, hashKeyValue,
            rangeKeyName, rangeKeyValue);

    GetItemSpec spec = new GetItemSpec()
            .withPrimaryKey(primaryKey)
            .withConsistentRead(true);

    Item item = table.getItem(spec);
    }
```

Query items

The following code snippet will query the items from the table based on the partition key and sort key. We can make a query on the table or secondary indexes. We will be defining the keyConditionExpression for fetching data based on the primary key (partition key and sort key) and filter the data based on the non-primary key attribute (lastName) using FilterExpression.

- Using AmazonDynamoDB:

Let's query items using the AmazonDynamoDB object:

```
String keyConditionExpression
        = "#nameKey = :nameValue and #idKey = :idValue";

 String filterExpressionForQuery =
 "#lastNameKey = :lastNameValue";

 Map<String, String> expressionAttributesNames
        = new HashMap<>();

expressionAttributesNames.put("#idKey", "id");

expressionAttributesNames.put("#nameKey", "name");

expressionAttributesNames.put("#lastNameKey", "lastName");

 Map<String, AttributeValue> expressionAttributeValues =
 new HashMap<>();

expressionAttributeValues.put(":idValue",
new AttributeValue().withN("1"));

expressionAttributeValues.put(":nameValue",
new AttributeValue().withS("Sunil"));

expressionAttributeValues.put(":lastNameValue",
new AttributeValue().withS("Gulabani"));

queryTable(
        tableName,
        keyConditionExpression,
        filterExpressionForQuery,
        expressionAttributesNames,
        expressionAttributeValues);

........

public void queryTable(
        String tableName,
        String keyConditionExpression,
        String filterExpression,
        Map<String, String> expressionAttributesNames,
        Map<String, AttributeValue> expressionAttributeValues
        ) {

    QueryRequest request = new QueryRequest()
```

```
                    .withTableName(tableName)
                    .withKeyConditionExpression(keyConditionExpression)
                    .withFilterExpression(filterExpression)
                    .withExpressionAttributeNames(expressionAttributesNames)
                    .withExpressionAttributeValues(expressionAttributeValues);

        QueryResult result = amazonDynamoDB.query(request);
    }
```

- Using `DynamoDB`:

Let's query items using the `DynamoDB` object:

```
String keyConditionExpression2
        = "#idKey = :idValue and #nameKey = :nameValue";

String filterExpressionForQuery2 =
"#lastNameKey = :lastNameValue";

Map<String, String> nameMap = new HashMap<>();

nameMap.put("#idKey", "id");

nameMap.put("#nameKey", "name");

nameMap.put("#lastNameKey", "lastName");

Map<String, Object> valueMap = new ValueMap()
        .withNumber(":idValue", 2)
        .withString(":nameValue","Priya")
        .withString(":lastNameValue", "Gulabani");

queryTable2(tableName,
        keyConditionExpression2,
        filterExpressionForQuery2,
        nameMap,
        valueMap);

........

public void queryTable2(
        String tableName,
        String keyConditionExpression,
        String filterExpression,
        Map<String, String> nameMap,
        Map<String, Object> valueMap
    ) {
```

```
Table table = dynamoDB.getTable(tableName);

QuerySpec spec = new QuerySpec()
        .withKeyConditionExpression(keyConditionExpression)
        .withFilterExpression(filterExpression)
        .withNameMap(nameMap)
        .withValueMap(valueMap);

ItemCollection<QueryOutcome> itemCollection =
        table.query(spec);
}
```

The following points need to be considered while using a query:

- `FilterExpression` is applied after the query is processed and before the final result is returned. `FilterExpression` can only be applied on non-primary key attributes.
- The result returned by the query is by default sorted based on the sort key in ascending order. If we need to have a descending sort order, we need to set `ScanIndexForward` as `false`. If the data type of the sort key is a number, it will sort based on the numeric order. And if the data type is a string or binary, it will sort based on the UTF-8 bytes.
- A query can read items based on the limit property provided or a maximum of 1 MB of data and it then applies a filter expression on the query result. If `LastEvaluatedKey` is present in the result, we need to paginate the result set.

Scanning items

The following code snippet will scan the entire table and get the items based on the non-partition keys. Scanning the entire table is a costly operation. It should be only used when we want to query on non-primary key attributes.

We will scan the table `awsbootcamp` on the `lastName` attribute.

- Using `AmazonDynamoDB`:

Let's apply the scan filter using the AmazonDynamoDB object:

```java
String filterExpression = "lastName = :lastNameValue";

 Map<String, AttributeValue> expressionAttributeValues2 =
 new HashMap<>();

 expressionAttributeValues2.put(":lastNameValue",
new AttributeValue().withS("Gulabani"));

 scanTable(
        tableName,
        filterExpression,
        expressionAttributeValues2);

........

public void scanTable(
        String tableName,
        String filterExpression,
        Map<String, AttributeValue> expressionAttributeValues) {

    ScanRequest request = new ScanRequest()
            .withTableName(tableName)
            .withFilterExpression(filterExpression)
            .withExpressionAttributeValues(expressionAttributeValues);

    ScanResult result = amazonDynamoDB.scan(request);
 }
```

* Using DynamoDB:

Let's apply the scan filter using the DynamoDB object:

```java
ScanFilter scanFilter = new ScanFilter("lastName").eq("Gulabani");

scanTable2(tableName, scanFilter);

........

public void scanTable2(
        String tableName,
        ScanFilter... scanFilters) {

    Table table = dynamoDB.getTable(tableName);

    ScanSpec spec = new ScanSpec()
            .withScanFilters(scanFilters);
```

```
        ItemCollection<ScanOutcome> itemCollection = table.scan(spec);
    }
```

We can also use `FilterExpression` to scan the table instead of `ScanFilters`. The following code snippet will use `FilterExpression` on the `birthDate` attribute:

```
String filterExpression2 = "birthDate = :birthDate";

ValueMap valueMap2 = new ValueMap()
        .withString(":birthDate","05/05/1988");

scanTable2(tableName, filterExpression2, valueMap2);

........

public void scanTable2(
        String tableName,
        String filterExpression,
        ValueMap valueMap) {

    Table table = dynamoDB.getTable(tableName);

    ScanSpec spec = new ScanSpec()
            .withFilterExpression(filterExpression)
            .withValueMap(valueMap);

    ItemCollection<ScanOutcome> itemCollection = table.scan(spec);
    }
```

The following points need to be considered while using a scan:

- `FilterExpression` is applied after the table or index is scanned and before the final result is returned. Unlike a query, `FilterExpression` can be applied on the primary key and non-primary key attributes.
- A scan is a sequential execution. To use the parallel scan, we can implement it by providing the `Segment` and `Total Segment` properties.
- A scan can read items based on the limit property provided or a maximum of 1 MB of data and it then applies a filter expression on the query result. If `LastEvaluatedKey` is present in the result, we need to paginate the result set.
- Scan operations should be avoided on a large table or secondary index as it slows down the performance.

- Scan operations match every item based on the filter expression and thus this can use the entire provisioned read capacity when the table or secondary index is large. Thus we should create a table or secondary index in such a way that we can use the query operation instead of a scan.

Update item

The following code snippet will update an item.

- Using AmazonDynamoDB:

Let's update an item using the AmazonDynamoDB object:

```
Map < String, AttributeValue > updateKey =
    new HashMap < > ();

updateKey.put("id",
    new AttributeValue().withN("1"));
updateKey.put("name",
    new AttributeValue().withS("Sunil"));

Map < String, AttributeValueUpdate > itemToUpdate =
    new HashMap < > ();

AttributeValueUpdate lastNameValueUpdate =
    new AttributeValueUpdate()
    .withValue(new AttributeValue()
        .withS("G."))
    .withAction(AttributeAction.PUT);
itemToUpdate.put("lastName", lastNameValueUpdate);

AttributeValueUpdate birthDateValueUpdate =
    new AttributeValueUpdate()
    .withValue(new AttributeValue()
        .withS("26/08/1987"))
    .withAction(AttributeAction.PUT);
itemToUpdate.put("birthDate", birthDateValueUpdate);

updateItem(tableName, updateKey, itemToUpdate);
.........
public void updateItem(
    String tableName,
    Map < String, AttributeValue > key,
    Map < String, AttributeValueUpdate > itemToUpdate) {
    UpdateItemRequest request =
```

```
    new UpdateItemRequest()
    .withTableName(tableName)
    .withKey(key)
    .withAttributeUpdates(itemToUpdate);

UpdateItemResult result =
    amazonDynamoDB.updateItem(request);
}
```

- Using `DynamoDB`:

Let's update an item using the DynamoDB object:

```
List < AttributeUpdate > attrUpdate =
    new ArrayList < > ();

attrUpdate.add(
    new AttributeUpdate("lastName")
    .put("G."));

attrUpdate.add(
    new AttributeUpdate("birthDate")
    .put("05/05/1989"));

updateItem2(
    tableName,
    "id",
    2,
    "name",
    "Priya",
    attrUpdate);
........
public void updateItem2(
    String tableName,
    String hashKeyName,
    Integer hashKeyValue,
    String rangeKeyName,
    String rangeKeyValue,
    List < AttributeUpdate > attrUpdate) {
    Table table =
        dynamoDB.getTable(tableName);

    PrimaryKey primaryKey =
        new PrimaryKey(
            hashKeyName, hashKeyValue,
            rangeKeyName, rangeKeyValue);

    UpdateItemSpec spec =
```

```
        new UpdateItemSpec()
        .withPrimaryKey(primaryKey)
        .withAttributeUpdate(attrUpdate);

    UpdateItemOutcome outcome =
        table.updateItem(spec);
}
```

Delete item

The following code snippet will delete an item from the table based on the partition key and sort key.

- Using `AmazonDynamoDB`:

  Let's delete an item using the `AmazonDynamoDB` object:

```
Map < String, AttributeValue > deleteKey =
    new HashMap < > ();

deleteKey.put("id",
    new AttributeValue().withN("1"));

deleteKey.put("name",
    new AttributeValue().withS("Sunil"));

deleteItem(tableName, deleteKey);
........
public void deleteItem(
    String tableName,
    Map < String, AttributeValue > key) {
    DeleteItemRequest request =
        new DeleteItemRequest()
        .withTableName(tableName)
        .withKey(key);

    DeleteItemResult result =
        amazonDynamoDB.deleteItem(request);
}
```

- Using DynamoDB:

Let's delete an item using the DynamoDB object:

```
deleteItem2(
    tableName,
    "id",
    2,
    "name",
    "Priya");
........
public void deleteItem2(
    String tableName,
    String hashKeyName,
    Integer hashKeyValue,
    String rangeKeyName,
    String rangeKeyValue) {
    Table table =
        dynamoDB.getTable(tableName);

    PrimaryKey primaryKey =
        new PrimaryKey(
            hashKeyName, hashKeyValue,
            rangeKeyName, rangeKeyValue);

    DeleteItemSpec spec =
        new DeleteItemSpec()
        .withPrimaryKey(primaryKey);

    DeleteItemOutcome outcome =
        table.deleteItem(spec);
}
```

Summary

In this chapter, we learned about Amazon DynamoDB, NoSQL database. DynamoDB frees the user from handling the burden of managing the infrastructure, scaling the database, administrative tasks, and so on. DynamoDB automatically replicates our data on multiple availability zones so that the data is highly available. We saw different ways, such as AWS Management Console, AWS CLI, and AWS SDK - Java, to create DynamoDB tables and we also performed CRUD operations using the AWS SDK - Java. While retrieving the data from tables, it is important to choose between the query and scan operations. Scan operations are slow when you are scanning and filtering items on large tables. So to avoid such a situation where provisioned read throughput is utilized by a scan operation, create a table or secondary indexes where you can use the query operation. In the next chapter, we will see how we can use Amazon ElastiCache. ElastiCache supports Redis and Memcached caching servers. We will create the ElastiCache server using the AWS Management Console, AWS CLI, and AWS SDK - Java, and we will also use CRUD operations.

7
Implementing Caching Using ElastiCache

Over decades, applications have become a core part of business processes. All business processes are being automated in the form of applications. The data that is projected in an application needs to be accurate, reliable, and fast. Data retrieval in an application plays an important role in user experience and some applications need to adhere to the designated response time in a **Service Level Agreement (SLA)**. Data volume are growing day by day and database systems are not sufficient to achieve faster data retrieval. To achieve a faster response time, either your backend infrastructure needs to be strong or you need some caching mechanism where you retrieve data from a caching server and return the data faster. A caching server saves a lot of time in fetching the data from your data stores or third-party APIs. As some of the data doesn't change for small periods of time, we can cache the data and use it whenever we need to. It is important that we store only data that is being frequently used and discard other infrequently used data stored on the cache server. A caching mechanism can be implemented in different types of applications, such as web page caching, static file caching by browsers, HTTP caching, caching data on third-party caching servers, and so on. Caching is a cheap solution to read the data from the cache instead of reading data from a database. If we directly read data from a database where we have thousands of requests coming at the same time, our database will experience a connection bottleneck and there will be load on the database, which may cause a failure. So, to avoid such a situation, we can add a cache in between so that instead of hitting the database, we will get the data from the cache servers.

In this chapter, we will cover the following topics:

- ElastiCache – Memcached
- ElastiCache – Redis

To provide a caching service, Amazon offers ElastiCache which is a fully managed service. Amazon ElastiCache supports the Redis and Memcached caching servers. These caching servers provide in-memory data stores that help applications to achieve high throughput.

We can also scale the caching servers based on the application traffic. Amazon seamlessly manages installation, configuration, high availability, clustering, scaling, and server failover. We can use this caching service when we need high intensity read operations to serve the data. Adding the ElastiCache service to our application infrastructure for faster read operations helps us to reduce latency and achieve high throughput. ElastiCache comes with a cluster configuration, where we need to define the number of nodes we want for the caching server. The other administrative tasks, such as software patching, failover detection, recovery, and so on, are taken care of by Amazon. We also have detailed cluster node monitoring so that we can configure a CloudWatch alarm and take the necessary actions when any metrics cross their threshold values.

ElastiCache – Memcached

Memcached is an open source, distributed caching server used for achieving high performance. It stores data in RAM so that retrievals can be faster and more efficient. ElastiCache is compatible with the Memcached caching server, so the tools and API clients used with the existing Memcached servers are compatible with the ElastiCache Memcached server. For Memcached ElastiCache, we can create a cluster of nodes, where data can be distributed based on the hashing mechanism. The cache keys need to be different so that you can make use of multiple nodes.

 More details on Memcached can be found at `https://memcached.org/`.

Let's look at how we can create a Memcached ElastiCache cluster.

AWS Management Console

Go to the AWS ElastiCache Management Console at `https://console.aws.amazon.com/elasticache/home`

1. Click **Memcached** on the left-hand menu.
2. Click the **Create** button.
3. Provide the ElastiCache cluster details as follows:

    - **Cluster engine**: Select the **Memcached** option.
    - **Name**: Type in `aws-bootcamp`.

- **Engine version compatibility**: Choose the default version only. Currently, the default version is **1.4.34**.
- **Port**: Type in port `11211` port, which the Memcached server will be running.
- **Parameter group**: Choose the parameter group that suits you best. We will go with the default parameter group. It contains default configuration parameters for your caching server.
- **Node type**: Choose the node type that suits you best. This plays an important role for the ElastiCache cluster as it defines how much memory will be attached. For our example, we will select the **cache.t2.micro (0.5 GiB)** node type. The node type can also be changed after the cluster has been created.
- **Number of nodes**: Select **2,** which means that the cluster will be created with two Memcached nodes:

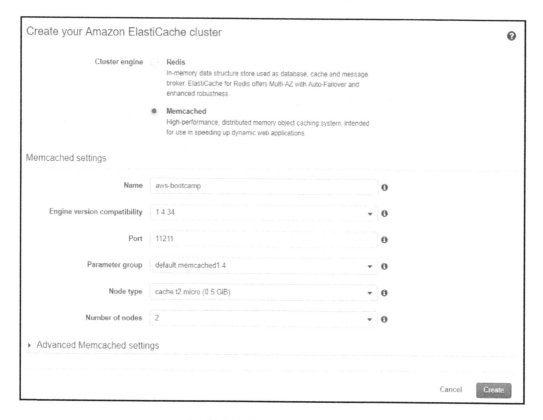

Figure 7.1: Creating the Memcached ElastiCache cluster

We can also configure the following **Advanced Memcached** settings:

- **Subnet group**: Choose an existing subnet group or create a new one. This helps to restrict access from outside VPC.
- **Preferred availability zone(s)**: Although it is not mandatory to provide **Preferred availability zone(s)**, it is important for managing failover in case one availability zone goes down. The number of preferred availability zones selected and the number of nodes to be created should match.
- **Security groups**: Choose the security group, which will allow you to access the cluster.
- **Maintenance window**: Choose a maintenance window during which maintenance activity, such as software patching or any cluster modification, can take place. If we don't provide a maintenance window, Amazon by default selects a particular time for this. The window should be selected at a time when your application does not have high traffic, so that the effect on your application is minimal.
- **Topic for SNS notification**: Select an SNS notification ARN to publish different cluster events. Cluster events can be configured so that clients that use these clusters can dynamically take actions, such as adding/removing nodes from client connections, scaling, snapshots, restoration completes or fails, and so on. For our example, we will select **Disable notifications**:

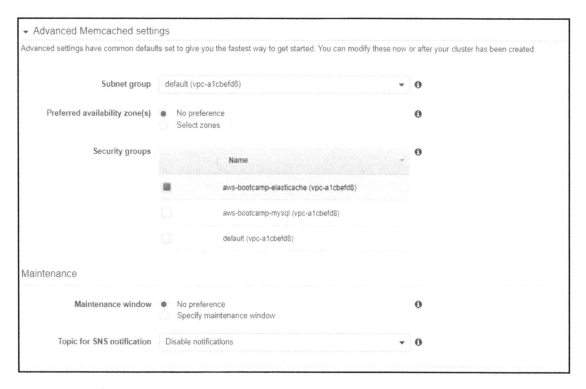

Figure 7.2: Creating a Memcached ElastiCache cluster - advanced settings

More details on ElastiCache events can be found
at https://docs.aws.amazon.com/AmazonElastiCache/latest/UserGuide
/ElastiCacheSNS.html.

Once the details have been provided, click **Create.** This will create the ElastiCache cluster. Creating the cluster may take some time, so the status will be **creating**. We need to wait until the status is **available**:

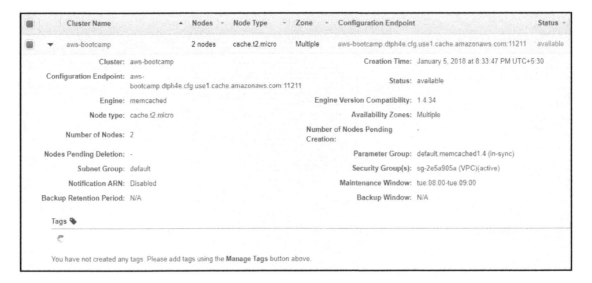

Figure 7.3: Memcached cluster listing

> **Configuration Endpoint** is used to connect to the cluster from Memcached clients.

AWS CLI

To execute the CLI script, open Command Prompt.

The following command will create a Memcached cluster with two nodes:

```
aws elasticache create-cache-cluster ^
--cache-cluster-id "aws-bootcamp" ^
--port "11211" ^
--engine "memcached" ^
--engine-version "1.4.34" ^
--cache-node-type "cache.t2.micro" ^
--num-cache-nodes 2 ^
--az-mode "single-az" ^
--security-group-ids "sg-2e5a905a"
```

The following are the options that can be used with `create-cache-cluster`:

Parameters	Optional	Descriptions
`--cache-cluster-id`	False	A friendly name (identifier) to assign to the cluster
`--port`	True	Port number on which the Memcached server will be running.
`--engine`	True	The engine name of which the cache cluster will be created. Valid values are:`memcached`, `redis`.
`--engine-version`	True	Defines the cache engine version number. To see the list of versions please refer to the following links: Memcached: `https://docs.aws.amazon.com/ AmazonElastiCache/latest/UserGuide/ SelectEngine.MemcachedVersions.html` Redis: `https://docs.aws.amazon.com/ AmazonElastiCache/latest/UserGuide/ SelectEngine.RedisVersions.html`
`--cache-node-type`	True	Defines the compute and memory capacity of the nodes in the cluster.
`--num-cache-nodes`	True	Number of nodes to be created in the cluster. Valid values are: **Memcached**: Between 1 to 20. If we want more the 20 nodes, we need to raise a request to Amazon to increase this limit. **Redis**: It has to be 1.
`--az-mode`	True	Defines the cluster nodes to be created in a single availability zone or multiple availability zones. This option is only valid for the Memcached engine. Valid values are: `single-az`, `cross-az`.
`--security-group-ids`	True	Defines one or more VPC security group ID to control access to the cluster. The format for specifying multiple security groups is:`sg-00001,sg-00002,sg-00003`.

`--replication-group-id`	True	The replication group ID under which this cluster will be attached. If this option is provided, this cluster becomes a read replica and if this option is not provided, this cluster works as a standalone cluster. This option is only valid for the Redis engine.
`--preferred-availability-zone`	True	Defines the availability zones for all the cluster nodes.
`--preferred-availability-zones`	True	Defines a list of availability zones for the cluster nodes. The number of nodes and preferred availability zones should be equal. This option is only valid for the Memcached engine. The format for specifying multiple availability zones is:`us-east1a,us-east1b`.
`--cache-parameter-group-name`	True	Defines the name of the parameter group which contains the configuration for the cache engine.
`--cache-subnet-group-name`	True	Defines the name of the subnet group in which the cluster will be created.
`--cache-security-group-names`	True	Defines the name of the security group when we want to create the cluster outside of VPC.

`--tags`	True	Tags can be assigned to the cluster for identifying the resource used for a project and the cost. The format for specifying tags is:
		`Key=chapter,Value=7,`
		`Key=author,Value=Sunil`

`--snapshot-arns`	True	Defines the Redis RDB snapshot file S3 ARN.
		The format for specifying multiple snapshot ARNs is:
		`arn:aws:s3:::BucketName/snapshot.rdb,`
		`arn:aws:s3:::BucketName/snapshot1.rdb`

`--preferred-maintenance-window`	True	Defines the weekly maintenance time window in which the cluster maintenance activity is performed. The format for specifying the maintenance window is: `ddd:hh24:mi-ddd:hh24:mi`. Valid values for `ddd` are: • `sun` • `mon` • `tue` • `wed` • `thu` • `fri` • `sat` Also `hh24` defines hours from 24 hours UTC and `mi` defines minutes. The minimum maintenance window should be 60 minutes.
`--notification-topic-arn`	True	Defines SNS ARN on which notifications will be sent for cluster events.
`--snapshot-retention-limit`	True	Defines the number of days automatic snapshots need to be retained. This option is only valid for the Redis engine.
`--snapshot-window`	True	Defines the daily time range for taking a cluster snapshot. This option is only valid for the Redis engine. The format for specifying the snapshot window is: `hh24:mi-hh24:mi`, where `hh24` defines hours from 24 hours UTC and `mi` defines minutes.
`--auth-token`	True	The password used while connecting to the Redis cache server when the `TransitEncryptionEnabled` property is set to `true` and the database configuration file has a `requirepass` line.

AWS SDK – Java

To access the ElastiCache service, we need to create the `AmazonElastiCache` object as:

```
AmazonElastiCache amazonElastiCache = AmazonElastiCacheClientBuilder
    .standard()
    .withClientConfiguration(getClientConfiguration())
```

```
        .withCredentials(getCredentials())
        .withRegion(Regions.US_EAST_1)
        .build();
```

The `ClientConfiguration` and `AWSCredentialsProvider` objects are created in the same way as we did in Chapter 2, *Configuring IAM*.

The following code snippet will create the Memcached ElastiCache cluster:

```
String cacheClusterId = "aws-bootcamp";

String memcachedEngine = "memcached";

String cacheNodeType = "cache.t2.micro";

Integer numCacheNodes = 2;

AZMode aZMode = AZMode.SingleAz;

int memcachePort = 11211;

String groupName = "aws-bootcamp-elasticache";

String groupDescription =
"Security Group for AWS Bootcamp Elasticache";

String cidr = "0.0.0.0/0";

Chapter3 chapter3 = new Chapter3();

String groupId = chapter3.createSecurityGroup(
    groupName, groupDescription);

chapter3.authorizeSecurityGroupIngress(
    groupName, memcachePort, cidr);

createCacheCluster(
    cacheClusterId,
    memcachedEngine,
    memcachePort,
    cacheNodeType,
    numCacheNodes,
    aZMode,
    groupId);

private void createCacheCluster(
        String cacheClusterId,
```

```
            String engine,
            int port,
            String cacheNodeType,
            Integer numCacheNodes,
            AZMode aZMode,
            String securityGroupId) {

    CreateCacheClusterRequest request =
            new CreateCacheClusterRequest()
                    .withCacheClusterId(cacheClusterId)
                    .withPort(port)
                    .withEngine(engine)
                    .withCacheNodeType(cacheNodeType)
                    .withNumCacheNodes(numCacheNodes)
                    .withAZMode(aZMode)
                    .withSecurityGroupIds(securityGroupId);

    CacheCluster cacheCluster =
            amazonElastiCache.createCacheCluster(request);

}
```

First, we will be creating the VPC security group to allow the Memcached port (`11211`). Once the security group has been created, we will create the cluster.

AWS CloudFormation

To create the Memcached ElastiCache cluster, first we need to create the security group using the `AWS::EC2::SecurityGroup` type:

```
"AWSBootcampSecurityGroupForMemcached": {
 "Type": "AWS::EC2::SecurityGroup",
 "Properties": {
  "GroupName": "aws-bootcamp-memcached-cache",
  "GroupDescription": "Enable access via port 11211",
  "SecurityGroupIngress": [{
   "IpProtocol": "tcp",
   "FromPort": "11211",
   "ToPort": "11211",
   "CidrIp": "0.0.0.0/0"
  }]
 }
}
```

To create the Memcached ElastiCache cluster, we need to use the
`AWS::ElastiCache::CacheCluster` type:

```
"AWSBootcampCacheClusterForMemcached": {
    "Type": "AWS::ElastiCache::CacheCluster",
    "Properties": {
        "ClusterName": "aws-bootcamp-m",
        "Port": "11211",
        "Engine": "memcached",
        "CacheNodeType": "cache.t2.micro",
        "NumCacheNodes": "2",
        "AZMode": "single-az",
        "VpcSecurityGroupIds": [{
            "Fn::GetAtt": [
                "AWSBootcampSecurityGroupForMemcached", "GroupId"
            ]
        }],
        "Tags": [{
            "Key": "name",
            "Value": "awsbootcamp-memcached"
        }]
    },
    "DependsOn": [
        "AWSBootcampSecurityGroupForMemcached"
    ]
}
```

ElastiCache – Redis

Redis is an open source and distributed in-memory caching server. **Redis** is an abbreviation of **RE**mote **DI**rectory **S**erver. It is one of the most popular in-memory key-value data stores. Redis provides such functionalities as caching, pub/sub, session management, and leaderboards.

Amazon provides a fully managed service for Redis and provides a customer managed Redis server on an EC2 instance. Using AWS ElastiCache for Redis, users will be free from the burden of managing administrative tasks such as installing, configuring, software patching, version upgrading, and so on. Redis also provides support for replication, where we can have a master/slave server and data will be asynchronously replicated on multiple slave servers. Using the replication feature, Redis can handle failover of the primary server by making the slave server the primary server.

More details can be found at `https://redis.io/`.

AWS Management Console

Go to AWS ElastiCache Management Console at
`https://console.aws.amazon.com/elasticache/home`.

Creating Redis (cluster mode disabled) ElastiCache server

Let's create the Redis ElastiCache server with cluster mode disabled:

1. Click **Redis** on the left navigation menu.
2. Click the **Create** button.
3. Provide the following Redis ElastiCache details:

    - **Cluster engine**: Select the **Redis** option.
    - **Cluster Mode enabled**: Keep it unchecked.
    - **Name**: Type in `aws-bootcamp-redis`.
    - **Description**: Type in `AWS Bootcamp redis server`.
    - **Engine version compatibility**: Choose the default version only. Currently, the default version is **3.2.10**.
    - **Port**: Type in port `6379`, on which the Redis server will be running.
    - **Parameter group**: Choose the default parameter group, **default.redis3.2**.
    - **Node type**: Select the **cache.t2.micro (0.5 GiB)** node type.

- **Number of replicas**: Type in **2,** which means that the cluster will be created with two Redis replicas. So a total of three nodes will be created; one acts as the primary node and the other two act as read replicas. If you don't want read replicas, select **None**:

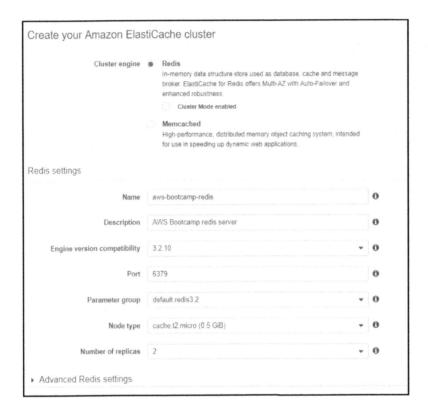

Figure 7.4: Creatimg Redis ElastiCache (cluster disabled)

We can also configure the following **Advanced Redis settings**:

- **Multi-AZ with Auto-Failover**: Enabling this option will create cluster nodes in multiple availability zones. In the event of primary node failures, user requests can be served using the read replica node. This feature is only available with Redis (3.2.4 or higher version) cluster mode enabled on T2 instances.
- **Subnet group**: Choose an existing subnet group or create a new one in which the Redis server will be running under your Amazon VPC. Creating one under a specific VPC will restrict access from outside the VPC.

- **Preferred availability zone(s)**: Although it is not mandatory to provide **Preferred availability zone(s),** it is important for managing the failover in case one availability zone goes down. The preferred availability zone should be equal to the number of nodes we want to create.
- **Security groups**: Choose the security group that will allow you to access the cluster.
- **Encryption at-rest**: Selecting this option will enable the encryption of data on the disk.
- **Encryption in-transit**: Selecting this option will enable the encryption of data on the wire. This feature is only allowed on the replication group when the data is moved from the primary server to the read replica, or between the application and replication group.
- **Seed RDB file S3 location**: Provide the RDB S3 location which contains the backup file to be restored on new servers.
- **Enable automatic backups**: Enabling this will automatically take backups daily.
- **Maintenance window**: Choose a maintenance window where maintenance activities, such as software patching or any cluster modification, can take place. If we don't provide a maintenance window, Amazon by default selects a particular time for this. The window should be selected for a time when your application does not have high traffic, so that your application has minimal effect.
- **Topic for SNS notification**: Select an SNS notification ARN to publish different cluster events. Cluster events can be configured so that clients that use these clusters can dynamically take actions, such as adding/removing nodes from client connections, scaling, snapshots, restoration completes or fails, and so on. For our example, we will select **Disable notifications**:

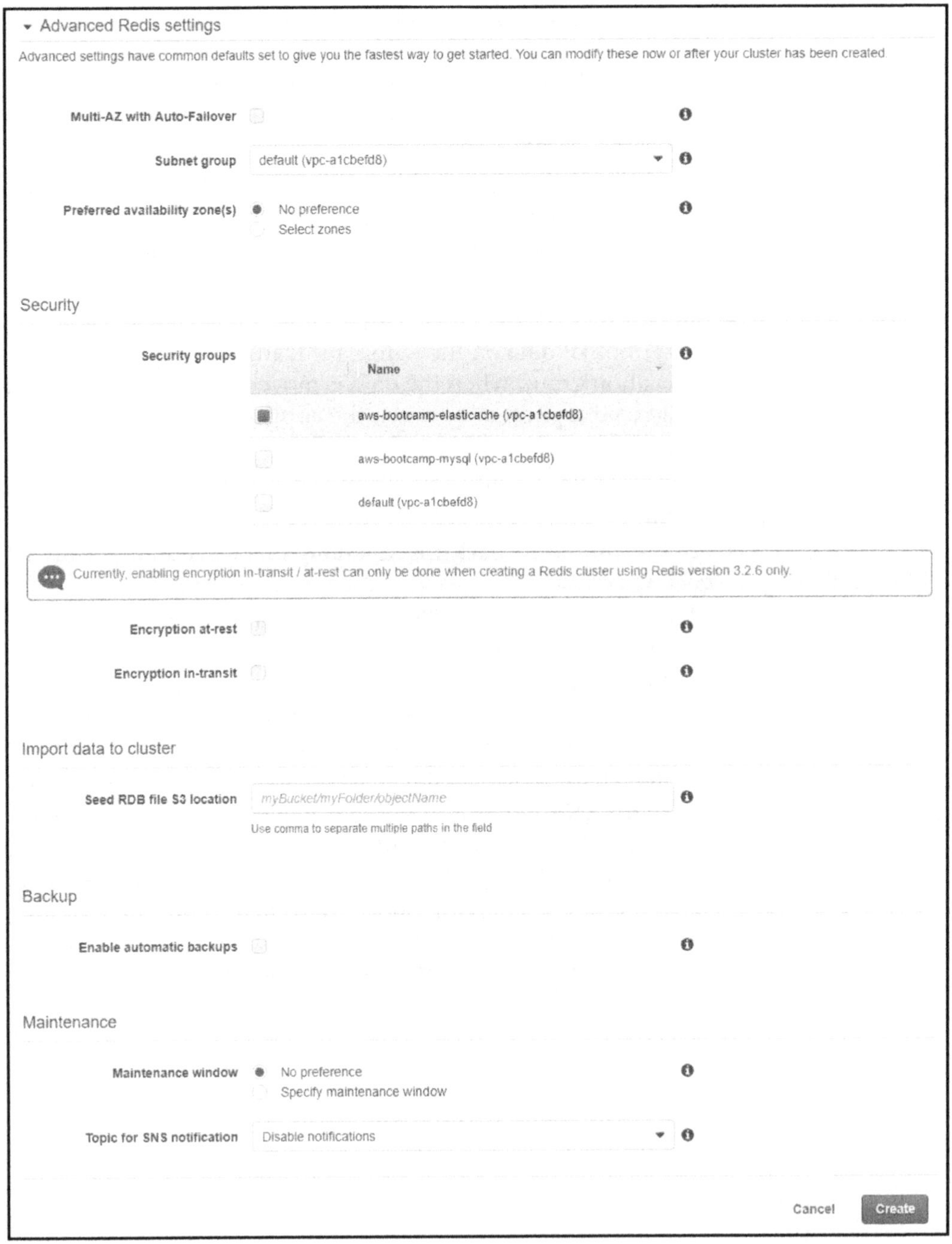

Figure 7.5: Creating Redis ElastiCache (cluster disabled) -advanced settings

For more details on ElastiCache events, refer
to https://docs.aws.amazon.com/AmazonElastiCache/latest/UserGuide
/ElastiCacheSNS.html.

Once the details have been provided, click **Create**. This will create the Redis ElastiCache.
The creation process may take some time, so initially the status will be **creating**. We need to
wait until the status is **available**:

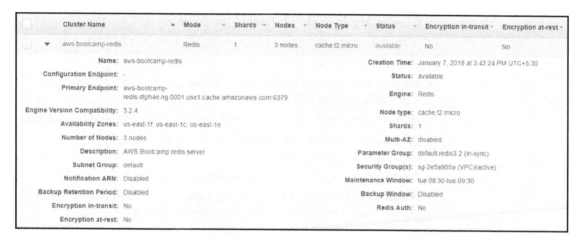

Figure 7.6: Redis cluster listing

The **Primary Endpoint** can be used in clients to connect to this Redis ElastiCache.

Creating the Redis (cluster mode enabled) ElastiCache

Let's create the Redis ElastiCache server with the cluster mode enabled:

1. Click **Redis** on the left navigation menu.
2. Click the **Create** button.
3. Provide the Redis ElastiCache details as follows:

   - **Cluster engine**: Select the **Redis** option.
   - **Cluster Mode enabled**: Enable the property.
   - **Name**: Type in `aws-bootcamp-redis`.
   - **Description**: Type in `AWS Bootcamp redis cluster`.
   - **Engine version compatibility**: Choose the default version only. Currently the default version is **3.2.10**.
   - **Port**: Type in port `6379`, on which the Redis server will be running.
   - **Parameter group**: Choose the default parameter group, **default.redis3.2.cluster.on**.
   - **Node type**: Select the **cache.t2.micro** node type.
   - **Number of Shards**: Select **2** as the number of shards. It distributes your data to store data on this number of shards.
   - **Replicas per Shard**: Select **2,** which means two replicas will be created under each shard.
   - **Subnet group**: Choose an existing subnet group or create a new one. This helps to restrict access from outside VPC:

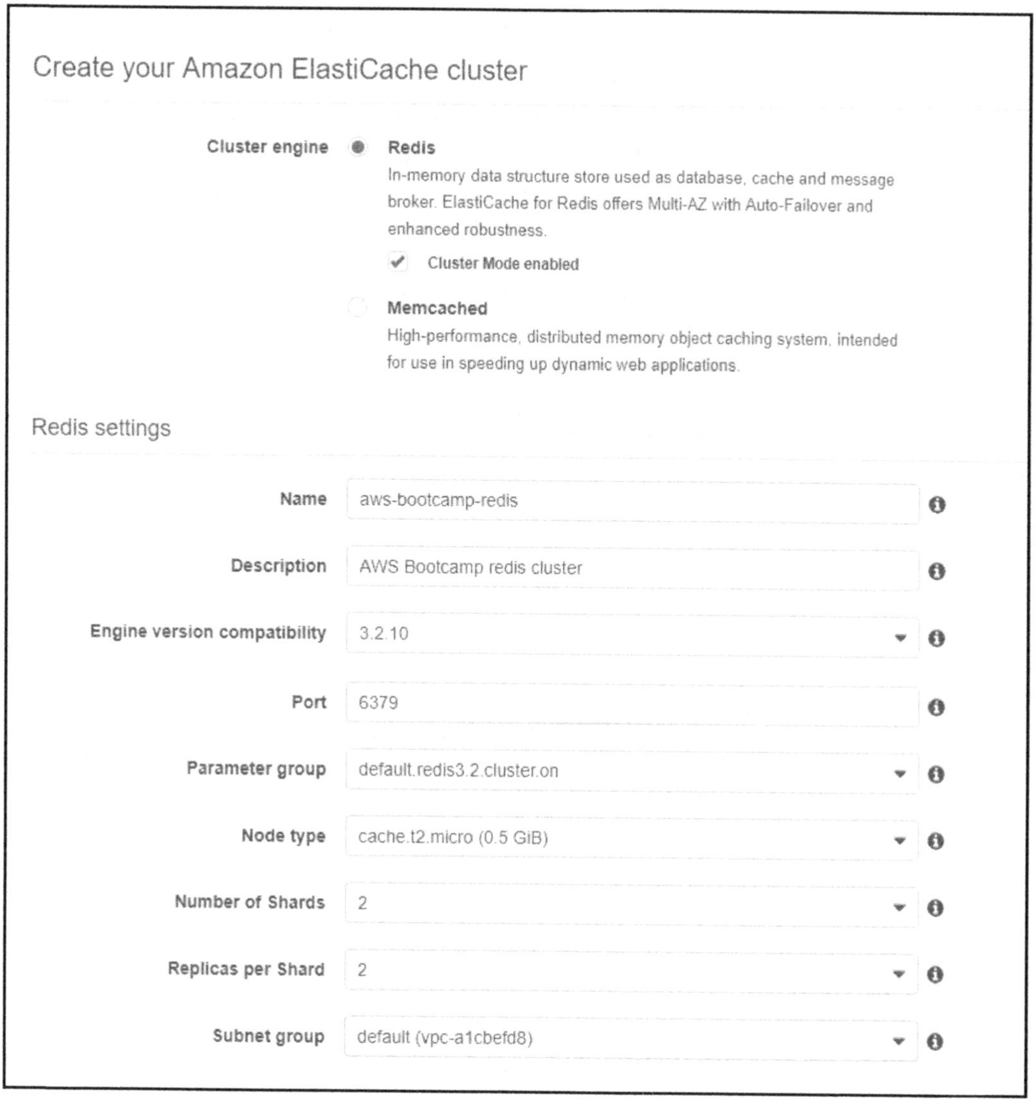

Create your Amazon ElastiCache cluster

Cluster engine   ●   **Redis**

In-memory data structure store used as database, cache and message broker. ElastiCache for Redis offers Multi-AZ with Auto-Failover and enhanced robustness.

  ✔   Cluster Mode enabled

  ○   **Memcached**

High-performance, distributed memory object caching system, intended for use in speeding up dynamic web applications.

Redis settings

Name	aws-bootcamp-redis	❶
Description	AWS Bootcamp redis cluster	❶
Engine version compatibility	3.2.10 ▼	❶
Port	6379	❶
Parameter group	default.redis3.2.cluster.on ▼	❶
Node type	cache.t2.micro (0.5 GiB) ▼	❶
Number of Shards	2 ▼	❶
Replicas per Shard	2 ▼	❶
Subnet group	default (vpc-a1cbefd8) ▼	❶

Figure 7.7: Creating Redis ElastiCache (cluster enabled)

We can also configure the following **Advanced Redis settings**:

- **Multi-AZ with Auto-Failover**: Enabling **Multi-AZ with Auto-Failover** will provide high availability in the event of primary node failures and a request will be served by the read replica.
- **Slots and keyspaces**: This defines how the distribution of slots will be carried out. By default, ElastiCache distributes 16,384 slots equally between the numbers of shards created. We can also distribute the slots as per our preference by selecting **Custom distribution**.
- **Availability zone(s)**: Although it is not mandatory to provide preferred **Availability zone(s),** it is important for managing failover if one availability zone goes down:

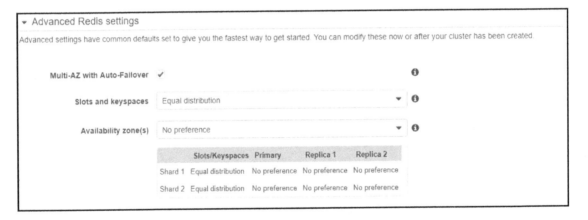

Figure 7.8: Creating Redis ElastiCache (cluster enabled) - advanced settings

- **Security groups**: Choose the security group that exposes the cluster ports for specific IP ranges. This will control access to the cluster.
- **Encryption at-rest**: Selecting this option will enable the encryption of data on the disk.
- **Encryption in-transit**: Selecting this option will enable the encryption of data on the wire. This feature is only allowed on the replication group, so that when data is moved from the primary server to the read replica, or between the application and the replication group, the data will be encrypted during the transit phase:

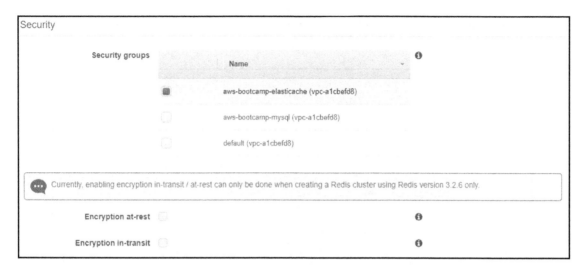

Figure 7.9: Creating Redis ElastiCache (cluster enabled) - security

- **Seed RDB file S3 location**: Provide the RDB S3 location which contains the backup file to be restored on new servers:

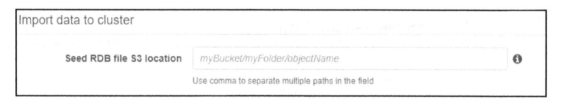

Figure 7.10: Creating Redis ElastiCache cluster enabled - import snapshot

- **Enable automatic backups**: Enabling this will automatically take backups daily.
- **Backup retention period**: If we enabled automatic backups, we need to provide the backup retention period, which means it will retain the backup for a specified number of days.

- **Backup window**: Select the backup window during which the backup will be taken:

Figure 7.11: Creating Redis ElastiCache (cluster enabled) - backup

- **Maintenance window**: Choose a maintenance window where maintenance activities, such as software patching or any cluster modification, can take place. If we don't provide a maintenance window, Amazon by default selects a particular time for this. The window should be selected at a time when your application does not have high traffic, so that your application has minimal effect.
- **Topic for SNS notification**: Select a SNS notification ARN to publish different cluster events. Cluster events can be configured so that clients that use these clusters can dynamically take actions, such as adding/removing nodes from client connections, scaling, snapshots, restoration completes or fails, and so on. For our example, we will select **Disable notifications**:

Figure 7.12: Creating Redis ElastiCache cluster enabled - maintenance

For more details on ElastiCache events, refer to
`https://docs.aws.amazon.com/AmazonElastiCache/latest/UserGuide/E`
`lastiCacheSNS.html`.

Once the details have been provided, click **Create**. This will create the Redis ElastiCache.
The creation process may take some time, so initially the status will be **creating**. We need to
wait until the status is **available**:

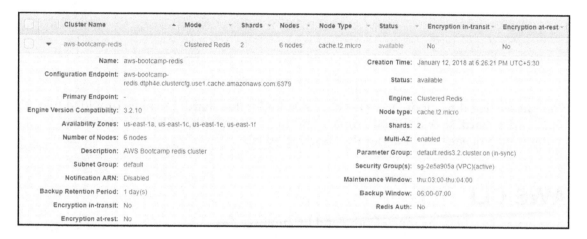

Figure 7.13: Redis cluster listing

To get details of the shards, click on the **aws-bootcamp-redis** cluster name:

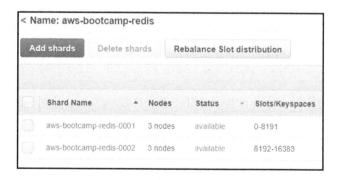

Figure 7.14: Redis cluster shard listing

While creating the Redis cluster, we have selected the **Slot/Keyspaces** as **Equal
distribution**, so you can see that **Slots/Keyspaces** are equally divided into two shards. This
helps to distribute the data between the two shards.

To view the nodes under each shard, click on **aws-bootcamp-redis-001**:

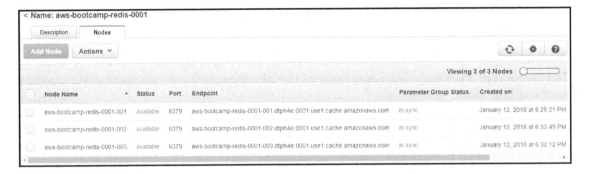

Figure 7.15: Redis cluster node listing

You can see that three nodes have been created under this shard. We have provided two replicas per shard, so one will be primary and two will be replicas. We can view the configuration of each shard under the **Description** tab.

AWS CLI

To execute the CLI script, open Command Prompt.

Creating Redis ElastiCache node

We will be using the same `create-cache-cluster` that we used in Memcached to create the cluster. The following command will create Redis with the primary node only:

```
    aws elasticache create-cache-cluster ^
--cache-cluster-id "aws-bootcamp-redis" ^
--port "6379" ^
--engine "redis" ^
--engine-version "3.2.10" ^
--cache-node-type "cache.t2.micro" ^
--num-cache-nodes 1 ^
--az-mode "single-az" ^
--security-group-ids "sg-2e5a905a"
```

Here, the `--num-cache-nodes` value has to be exactly 1, as this `create-cache-cluster` doesn't support Redis cluster creation.

Creating Redis (cluster mode disabled) ElastiCache

The following command will create Redis with the cluster mode disabled:

```
aws elasticache create-replication-group ^
--replication-group-id "aws-bootcamp-redis" ^
--replication-group-description "AWS Bootcamp redis cluster disabled" ^
--num-cache-clusters 3 ^
--engine "redis" ^
--engine-version "3.2.10" ^
--port 6379 ^
--cache-parameter-group-name "default.redis3.2" ^
--cache-node-type "cache.t2.micro" ^
--cache-subnet-group-name "default" ^
--security-group-ids "sg-2e5a905a"
```

The following are the options that can be used with `create-replication-group`:

Parameters	Optional	Descriptions
`--replication-group-id`	False	Identifier for your replication group.
`--replication-group-description`	False	Description for the replication group.
`--primary-cluster-id`	True	Defines the primary cluster identifier if already created. If the `--num-cache-clusters`, `--num-node-groups`, or `--replicas-per-node-group` options are provided, then the `--primary-cluster-id` option is not required.
`--automatic-failover-enabled` or `--no-automatic-failover-enabled`	True	If the primary fails, any of the read replicas can automatically become primary.
`--num-cache-clusters`	True	Defines the number of clusters it will have. We can provide a number of cache cluster values between 1 to 6, which includes one primary and five replicas. If we need automatic failover enabled, we need to set the value greater than or equal to 2 and if automatic failover is disabled, we can ignore this option or set the value to 1.
`--preferred-cache-cluster-a-zs`	True	Defines in which availability zone your cluster will be created. The first preferred availability zone will be used for the primary and in the same order, clusters will be created in the availability zone. Also, if we are creating the cluster under Amazon VPC, only those availability zones should be provided that are part of the **Subnet group**. When we create more than one node group this option can't be used; instead we can use `--node-group-configuration`. The format for providing values is:us-east-1a, us-east-1b,us-west-2.
`--num-node-groups`	True	Defines the number of node groups (shards). This option is useful when we want to create a cluster mode enabled Redis. We can also use this option with the cluster mode disabled but the value should be 1.

`--replicas-per-node-group`	True	Defines the number of replicas to be created per node group (shard). The value can be between 0 and 5.

`--node-group-configuration`	True	Defines the node group (shard) configuration which includes slots, primary availability zone, replica availability zones, and replica count.
		The format for providing values is as follows:
		`Slots=0-8999,PrimaryAvailabilityZone='us-east-1a',ReplicaAvailabilityZones='us-east-1b','us-east-1c',ReplicaCount=2"`
		`"Slots=9000-16383,PrimaryAvailabilityZone='us-east-1a',ReplicaAvailabilityZones='us-east-1a','us-east-1b','us-east-1c',ReplicaCount=3`
		We can also provide values in JSON format as:
		`[`
		`    {`
		`    "Slots": "0-8999",`
		`    "ReplicaCount": 2,`
		`    "PrimaryAvailabilityZone": "us-east-1a",`
		`    "ReplicaAvailabilityZones": ["us-east-1b", "us-east-1c"]`
		`    },`
		`    {`
		`    "Slots": "9000-16383",`
		`    "ReplicaCount": 3,`
		`    "PrimaryAvailabilityZone": "us-east-1a",`
		`    "ReplicaAvailabilityZones": ["us-east-1a","us-east-1b","us-east-1c"]`
		`    }`
		`]`
		The slots value has to be a key space and we need to the split key space between multiple node groups (shards).
		Key spaces can be split into 16,384 slots.

`--cache-node-type`	True	Defines the compute and memory capacity of the nodes.
`--engine`	True	Defines the name of the cache engine.
`--engine-version`	True	Defines the cache engine version.
`--cache-parameter-group-name`	True	Defines the parameter group name which defines configurations (or properties) of the cache.
`--cache-subnet-group-name`	True	Defines the subnet group name in which replication group will be created.
`--cache-security-group-names`	True	Defines the security group name that will be associated with replication group.
`--security-group-ids`	True	Defines the VPC security group IDs that will be associated with the replication group.
`--tags`	True	Defines the cost allocation tags to be attached to the replication group.
`--snapshot-arns`	True	Defines the list of Redis RDB files S3 ARNs, using which the replication group will be populated.
`--snapshot-name`	True	Defines the snapshot name which will be used to restore data to a new replication group.

`--preferred-maintenance-window`	True	Defines the weekly maintenance time window in which cluster maintenance activity is performed. The format for specifying the maintenance window is:ddd:hh24:mi-ddd:hh24:mi. Valid values for ddd are: • sun • mon • tue • wed • thu • fri • sat Also hh24 defines hours from 24 hours UTC and mi defines minutes. The minimum maintenance window should be 60 minutes.
`--port`	True	The port number on which the Memcached server will be running.
`--notification-topic-arn`	True	Defines SNS ARN on which notifications will be sent for cluster events.
`--auto-minor-version-upgrade` or `--no-auto-minor-version-upgrade`	True	This option is currently disabled.
`--snapshot-retention-limit`	true	Defines the number of days automatic snapshots need to be retained. This option is only valid for the Redis engine.
`--snapshot-window`	True	Defines the daily time range for taking the cluster snapshot. This option is only valid for Redis engine. The format for specifying the snapshot window is:hh24:mi-hh24:mi, where hh24 defines hours from 24 hours UTC and mi defines minutes.
`--auth-token`	True	The password used while connecting to the Redis cache server when the TransitEncryptionEnabled property is set to true and the database configuration file has a requirepass line.
`--transit-encryption-enabled` or `--no-transit-encryption-enabled`	True	Defines whether encryption needs to be done when data is in-transit.
`--at-rest-encryption-enabled` or `--no-at-rest-encryption-enabled`	True	Defines whether encryption needs to be done when data is at rest.

Create Redis (cluster mode enabled) ElastiCache

The following command will create Redis with the cluster mode enabled:

```
aws elasticache create-replication-group ^
--replication-group-id "aws-bootcamp-redis" ^
--replication-group-description "AWS Bootcamp redis cluster enabled" ^
--engine "redis" ^
--engine-version "3.2.10" ^
--port 6379 ^
--cache-parameter-group-name "default.redis3.2.cluster.on" ^
--cache-node-type "cache.t2.micro" ^
--num-node-groups 2 ^
--replicas-per-node-group 2 ^
```

```
--cache-subnet-group-name "default" ^
--security-group-ids "sg-2e5a905a"
```

Here `--num-node-groups` will create two shards and under each shard `--replicas-per-node-group` will create two replicas along with the primary node.

AWS SDK – Java

The AWS SDK allows us to create Redis ElastiCache with different options, such as creating a single node, a cluster disabled Redis ElastiCache, or a cluster enabled Redis ElastiCache. The cluster mode enabled and disabled settings can be created using the replication group, which we will see in a later section.

Create Redis ElastiCache node

The following code snippet will create the Redis ElastiCache node:

```
String redisCacheClusterId = "aws-bootcamp-redis";

 String redisEngine = "redis";

 String redisVersion = "3.2.10";

 int redisPort = 6379;

 String redisCacheNodeType = "cache.t2.micro";

 Integer redisNumCacheNodes = 1;

 AZMode redisAZMode = AZMode.SingleAz;

 String groupId = "sg-2e5a905a";

createCacheCluster(
    redisCacheClusterId,
    redisEngine,
    redisVersion,
    redisPort,
    redisCacheNodeType,
    redisNumCacheNodes,
    redisAZMode,
    groupId);
```

Create Redis (cluster mode disabled) ElastiCache

The following code snippet will create the Redis ElastiCache with the cluster mode disabled:

```
String replicationGroupId = "aws-bootcamp-redis";

 String replicationGroupDescription = "AWS Bootcamp redis cluster
disabled";

 int numCacheClusters = 3;

 String engine = "redis";

 String engineVersion = "3.2.10";

 int redisPort = 6379;

 String cacheParameterGroupName = "default.redis3.2";

 String cacheNodeType = "cache.t2.micro";

 String subnetGroupName = "default";

 String securityGroupId = "sg-2e5a905a";

createRedisCacheWithClusterDisabled(
     replicationGroupId,
     replicationGroupDescription,
     numCacheClusters,
     engine,
     engineVersion,
     redisPort,
     cacheParameterGroupName,
     cacheNodeType,
     subnetGroupName,
     securityGroupId);

........

private void createRedisCacheWithClusterDisabled(
        String replicationGroupId,
        String replicationGroupDescription,
        Integer numCacheClusters,
        String engine,
        String engineVersion,
        Integer port,
```

```
        String cacheParameterGroupName,
        String cacheNodeType,
        String subnetGroupName,
        String securityGroupId) {

    CreateReplicationGroupRequest request =
            new CreateReplicationGroupRequest()
                .withReplicationGroupId(replicationGroupId)
                .withReplicationGroupDescription(
                   replicationGroupDescription)
                .withNumCacheClusters(numCacheClusters)
                .withEngine(engine)
                .withEngineVersion(engineVersion)
                .withPort(port)
                .withCacheParameterGroupName(cacheParameterGroupName)
                .withCacheNodeType(cacheNodeType)
                .withCacheSubnetGroupName(subnetGroupName)
                .withSecurityGroupIds(securityGroupId);

    ReplicationGroup replicationGroup =
            amazonElastiCache.createReplicationGroup(request);
}
```

Create Redis (cluster mode enabled) ElastiCache

The following code snippet will create the Redis ElastiCache with the cluster mode enabled:

```
String replicationGroupId = "aws-bootcamp-redis";

String replicationGroupDescription = "AWS Bootcamp redis cluster enabled";

String engine = "redis";

String engineVersion = "3.2.10";

int redisPort = 6379;

String cacheParameterGroupName = "default.redis3.2.cluster.on";

String cacheNodeType = "cache.t2.micro";

String subnetGroupName = "default";

String securityGroupId = "sg-2e5a905a";

int numNodeGroups = 2;
```

```
    int replicasPerNodeGroup = 2;

createRedisCacheWithClusterEnabled(
        replicationGroupId,
        replicationGroupDescription,
        engine,
        engineVersion,
        redisPort,
        cacheParameterGroupName,
        cacheNodeType,
        numNodeGroups,
        replicasPerNodeGroup,
        subnetGroupName,
        securityGroupId);

........

private void createRedisCacheWithClusterEnabled(
        String replicationGroupId,
        String replicationGroupDescription,
        String engine,
        String engineVersion,
        Integer port,
        String cacheParameterGroupName,
        String cacheNodeType,
        int numNodeGroups,
        int replicasPerNodeGroup,
        String subnetGroupName,
        String securityGroupId) {

    CreateReplicationGroupRequest request =
            new CreateReplicationGroupRequest()
                .withReplicationGroupId(replicationGroupId)
                .withReplicationGroupDescription(
                    replicationGroupDescription)
                .withEngine(engine)
                .withEngineVersion(engineVersion)
                .withPort(port)
                .withCacheParameterGroupName(cacheParameterGroupName)
                .withCacheNodeType(cacheNodeType)
                .withNumNodeGroups(numNodeGroups)
                .withReplicasPerNodeGroup(replicasPerNodeGroup)
                .withCacheSubnetGroupName(subnetGroupName)
                .withSecurityGroupIds(securityGroupId);

    ReplicationGroup replicationGroup =
            amazonElastiCache.createReplicationGroup(request);
}
```

As we want to create Redis with the cluster mode enabled, we need to pass the relevant cache parameter group name: `default.redis.3.2.cluster.on`.

AWS CloudFormation

To create the Redis ElastiCache cluster, first we need to create the security group using the `AWS::EC2::SecurityGroup` type:

```
"AWSBootcampSecurityGroupForRedis": {
    "Type": "AWS::EC2::SecurityGroup",
    "Properties": {
        "GroupName": "aws-bootcamp-redis",
        "GroupDescription": "Enable access via port 6379",
        "SecurityGroupIngress": [{
            "IpProtocol": "tcp",
            "FromPort": "6379",
            "ToPort": "6379",
            "CidrIp": "0.0.0.0/0"
        }]
    }
}
```

Create Redis ElastiCache node

To create the Redis ElastiCache cluster with a single node, we need to use the `AWS::ElastiCache::CacheCluster` type:

```
"AWSBootcampRedisSingleNode": {
    "Type": "AWS::ElastiCache::CacheCluster",
    "Properties": {
        "ClusterName": "aws-bootcamp-redis",
        "Port": "6379",
        "Engine": "redis",
        "EngineVersion": "3.2.10",
        "CacheNodeType": "cache.t2.micro",
        "NumCacheNodes": "1",
        "AZMode": "single-az",
        "VpcSecurityGroupIds": [{
            "Fn::GetAtt": [
                "AWSBootcampSecurityGroupForRedis", "GroupId"
            ]
        }],
        "Tags": [{
            "Key": "name",
```

```
            "Value": "awsbootcamp-redis"
        }]
    },
    "DependsOn": [
        "AWSBootcampSecurityGroupForRedis"
    ]
}
```

Create Redis (cluster mode disabled) ElastiCache

To create the Redis ElastiCache cluster mode disabled, we need to use the
AWS::ElastiCache::ReplicationGroup type:

```
"AWSBootcampRedisClusterDisabled": {
    "Type": "AWS::ElastiCache::ReplicationGroup",
    "Properties": {
        "ReplicationGroupId": "aws-bootcamp-redis-1",
        "ReplicationGroupDescription": "AWS Bootcamp redis cluster
disabled",
        "NumCacheClusters": 3,
        "AutomaticFailoverEnabled": false,
        "Engine": "redis",
        "EngineVersion": "3.2.10",
        "Port": 6379,
        "CacheParameterGroupName": "default.redis3.2",
        "CacheNodeType": "cache.t2.micro",
        "CacheSubnetGroupName": "default",
        "SecurityGroupIds": [
            "sg-2e5a905a"
        ],
        "Tags": [{
            "Key": "name",
            "Value": "awsbootcamp-redis"
        }]
    }
}
```

As we created the Redis cluster with the T2 node type, automatic failover is not supported
when the cluster mode is disabled. By default, the AutomaticFailoverEnabled property
is true, so we need to set AutomaticFailoverEnabled to false.

Create Redis (cluster mode enabled) ElastiCache

To create the Redis ElastiCache cluster mode enabled, we need to use the
`AWS::ElastiCache::ReplicationGroup` type:

```
"AWSBootcampRedisClusterEnabled": {
    "Type": "AWS::ElastiCache::ReplicationGroup",
    "Properties": {
        "ReplicationGroupId": "aws-bootcamp-redis-2",
        "ReplicationGroupDescription": "AWS Bootcamp redis cluster
enabled",
        "Engine": "redis",
        "EngineVersion": "3.2.10",
        "Port": 6379,
        "CacheParameterGroupName": "default.redis3.2.cluster.on",
        "CacheSubnetGroupName": "default",
        "NumNodeGroups": 2,
        "ReplicasPerNodeGroup": 2,
        "AutomaticFailoverEnabled": true,
        "CacheNodeType": "cache.t2.micro",
        "SecurityGroupIds": [
            "sg-2e5a905a"
        ],
        "Tags": [{
            "Key": "name",
            "Value": "awsbootcamp-redis"
        }]
    }
}
```

Here, we set the `AutomaticFailoverEnabled` property to `true`, so that we can make use
of the failover strategy; that is, when the primary goes down, any of the replicas can become
the primary.

Summary

In this chapter, we learned how to create the Amazon ElastiCache infrastructure. We covered both caching servers supported by Amazon ElastiCache: Memcached and Redis. Both caching servers are open source and widely used. We demonstrated how we can create a caching server with a single node and a cluster of nodes. It is important to know the design of the caching infrastructure we need, so that while creating the infrastructure we can set the properties for the single node or cluster enabled caching servers. Also, it offers an automatic failover strategy on the ElastiCache cluster with multi-AZ deployment.

In the next chapter, we will learn about the **Simple Notification Service (SNS)**, which is used to create topics and publish messages to subscribers. We will discuss the different protocols supported for subscription and demonstrate an email protocol using an example.

Triggering Notifications

8

A messaging system provides an interface where one computer system can send a message and another system can process it. It helps computer systems to process messages asynchronously. Senders (who push messages on the messaging system) are not aware of receivers (who get messages from the messaging system). The messaging system follows a publisher and subscriber mechanism, where the publisher pushes a message and all subscribers are notified with that message. It's a way to coordinate different systems asynchronously with each other. The publisher and subscriber don't need to be on same platform and work independently, having their own architectures. The publisher doesn't need to know how the subscriber listens to the messaging system. Subscribers can listen on various protocols, such as email, HTTP, HTTPS, push notifications, and many more. For the messaging system application, Amazon offers pub/sub messaging and a push notification service.

In this chapter, we will cover the following topics:

- Topics
- Subscriptions
- Publishing messages

Amazon SNS is a fully managed notification service that works on a publisher and subscriber mechanism. SNS helps to send messages to subscribers that have different endpoints or clients. Here different endpoints/clients means the subscribers can be on different protocols, such as email, HTTP, HTTPS, SMS, **Simple Queue Service (SQS)**, AWS Lambda, and applications (push notifications). SNS is fast, easy to set up and operate, and reliably sends notifications to subscribers. SNS helps to eliminate the management of complex infrastructure, by just using a simple API to communicate. SNS follows the fan-out model, where it takes a message from the publisher and sends it asynchronously to the subscribers at the same time. Subscribers don't need to poll for the new messages, SNS will send it automatically. To communicate between the publisher and subscriber, we need to create a topic which acts as a medium.

The publisher and subscriber need to have access to the topic so that the publisher can send a message, the subscriber can add a subscription on the topic, and the subscription endpoints need to confirm the subscription.

Protocols

The following are the protocols SNS supports for subscription:

- **AWS Lambda function**: SNS topics allow us to add subscriptions for AWS Lambda. Any message published on SNS topic is delivered to the subscribed AWS Lambda so that it can process the message.
- **AWS SQS**: AWS SQS can be subscribed to an SNS topic. AWS SNS and SQS work in a similar pattern, with the only difference being that SNS follows a push mechanism whereas SQS follows a poll mechanism. From SNS, we can send messages to one or more SQS. There will be another application which will poll SQS to read messages from SQS and process ahead.
- **HTTP/HTTPS**: AWS SNS is able to send messages over HTTP/HTTPS using the POST method. While adding a subscription, it is mandatory that your HTTP/HTTPS endpoint is up and running, so that SNS will send the subscription confirmation URL. Using this subscription confirmation URL, we (the endpoint) confirms that SNS topic is allowed entry to push messages to this HTTP/HTTPS endpoint. An HTTP endpoint can be configured straightforwardly. But if we need to configure an HTTPS endpoint, SNS provides two ways to configure it:
  - **Server Name Indication (SNI)**
  - Basic and digest access authentication

- **Email**: AWS SNS supports email protocol to publish messages to email addresses. While subscribing to the topic, a confirmation is sent to an email address so that the user can confirm the subscription. Once subscription is confirmed, SNS will be able to deliver messages to the email address.
- **SMS**: AWS SNS provides support to send SMSes to mobile devices and smartphones. SNS also allows us to send a single SMS or multiple SMSes using an SNS topic. AWS SNS also allow us to set the SMS preferences, which include budget and managing delivery reports.

- **Application**: AWS SNS offers a push notification service to mobile devices and desktops. The following are the push notification services that can be used with SNS:

  - **Amazon Device Messaging (ADM)**
  - **Apple Push Notification Service (APNS)** for both iOS and macOS X
  - Baidu Cloud Push
  - **Google Cloud Messaging (GCM)** for Android
  - **Microsoft Push Notification Service (MPNS)** for Windows Phone
  - **Windows Push Notification Service (WNS)**

Topics

An SNS topic is a communication channel where a publisher can publish messages and a subscriber can get messages by subscribing to it. The SNS topic name should be unique to your AWS account. In a single AWS account, we can create up to 100,000 topics.

AWS Management Console

Go to the AWS SNS Management Console at `https://console.aws.amazon.com/sns/v2/home` and perform the following steps:

1. Click **Topics** in the navigation pane on the left.
2. Click **Create new topic**:

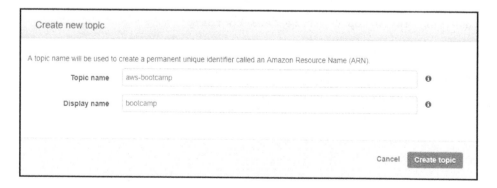

Figure 8.1: Creating a new topic

Provide details as follows:

- **Topic name**: Type in `aws-bootcamp`. We can add up to 256 alphanumeric characters, hyphens (–), and underscores (_).
- **Display name**: Type in `bootcamp`. The display name can be up to 10 characters only. The display name is used if we have an SMS subscription.

3. Once the details have been provided, click **Create topic**:

Figure 8.2: Topic listing

AWS CLI

To execute the CLI script, open Command Prompt.

The following command will create an SNS topic:

```
aws sns create-topic --name "aws-bootcamp"
```

The following are the options that can be used with `create-topic`:

Parameters	Optional	Descriptions
--name	False	Friendly name for your topic

AWS SDK – Java

To access SNS, we need to create an `AmazonSNS` object as follows:

```
AmazonSNS amazonSNS = AmazonSNSClientBuilder
        .standard()
        .withClientConfiguration(getClientConfiguration())
        .withCredentials(getCredentials())
        .withRegion(Regions.US_EAST_1)
        .build();
```

The `ClientConfiguration` and `AWSCredentialsProvider` objects are created in the same way as we mentioned in `Chapter 2`, *Configuring IAM*.

The following code snippet will create the SNS topic:

```
String topicName = "aws-bootcamp";

String topicARN = createTopic(topicName);

private String createTopic(String topicName) {
    CreateTopicRequest request =
            new CreateTopicRequest()
                    .withName(topicName);

    CreateTopicResult result =
            amazonSNS.createTopic(request);

    return result.getTopicArn();
}
```

The preceding code will create a topic with name **aws-bootcamp**. Currently, the topic doesn't have any subscribers to whom notifications can be sent. So we will see how we can subscribe to the SNS topic.

AWS CloudFormation

To create an SNS topic, we need to use the `AWS::SNS::Topic` type:

```
"AWSBootcamp": {
    "Type": "AWS::SNS::Topic",
    "Properties": {
```

```
        "TopicName": "aws-bootcamp",
        "DisplayName": "bootcamp"
    }
}
```

Subscription

Subscription to a topic will push messages to the subscriber's protocol whenever a new message is published. For subscription, we need to select the protocol and provide the endpoint of the protocol. So the endpoint-owner needs to confirm the subscription and then only SNS is able to deliver messages to the endpoint. Subscription confirmation is a URL which is received at endpoint-owner ends. This URL contains a token which will help SNS to subscribe the endpoint to a specific token and this token is valid for 3 days.

Let's see how we can subscribe to a topic using email protocol.

AWS Management Console

Go to the AWS SNS Management Console at `https://console.aws.amazon.com/sns/v2/home` and perform the following steps:

1. Click on **Topics** in the navigation pane on the left.
2. Click on **aws-bootcamp ARN**, displayed on the topic listing screen:

Figure 8.3: Topic details

3. Click **Create subscription**:

Create subscription	
Topic ARN	arn:aws:sns:us-east-1:993735536778:aws-bootcamp
Protocol	Email ▾
Endpoint	sunil.gulabani1@gmail.com
	Cancel **Create subscription**

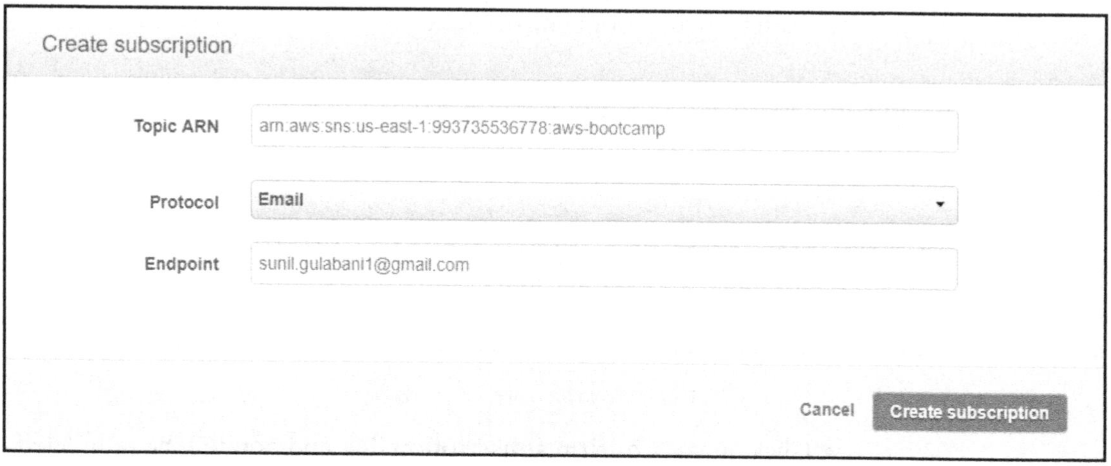

Figure 8.4: Creating a subscription

Provide details as follows:

- **Topic ARN**: By default, **Topic ARN** will be populated. Don't change the ARN name.
- **Protocol**: Select **email** protocol.
- **Endpoint**: Type in your email address `sunil.gulabani1@gmail.com`.

4. Once the details have been provided, click **Create subscription**:

	Subscription ID	Protocol	Endpoint	Subscriber
☐	PendingConfirmation	email	sunil.gulabani1@gmail.com	993735536778

Figure 8.5: Subscription listing

Here we can see that our newly created subscription is in **PendingConfirmation** state. This means that user needs to confirm the subscription using the link sent on the selected protocol. In our case, the subscription confirmation notification is sent to the email address `sunil.gulabani1@gmail.com`.

5. Confirm the subscription:

- Go to your mailbox and check you have received a mail from the Amazon SNS topic for confirmation:

Figure 8.6: Subscription mail

- Click on the **Confirm subscription** link and you will be redirected to the **Subscription confirmed!** window:

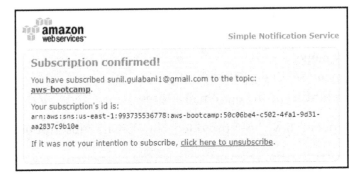

Figure 8.7: Subscription confirmed

6. Check the subscription status:

- Now the subscription has been confirmed by the user, we can see that the subscription status **PendingConfirmation** has now been replaced with the **Subscription ID** of the subscriber:

	Subscription ID	Protocol	Endpoint	Subscriber
☐	arn:aws:sns:us-east-1:993735536778:aws-bootcamp:50...	email	sunil.gulabani1@gmail.com	993735536778

Figure 8.8: Subscription listing

The SNS topic is now ready to publish messages to subscribers.

AWS CLI

To execute the CLI script, open Command Prompt.

The following command will add a subscription to an SNS topic:

```
aws sns subscribe ^
--topic-arn "arn:aws:sns:us-east-1:993735536778:awsbootcamp" ^
--protocol "email" ^
--notification-endpoint "sunil.gulabani1@gmail.com"
```

The following are the options that can be used with subscribe:

Parameters	Optional	Descriptions
--topic-arn	False	Topic ARN to which you want to create subscription.
--protocol	False	Protocol of the subscriber's endpoint. Valid values are as follows: • http • https • email • email-json • sms • sqs • application • lambda
--notification-endpoint	False	Notification endpoint with respective to protocol. Each protocol has a different format of endpoint.

The subscription endpoint has been subscribed to the topic and the mentioned endpoint needs to confirm the subscription. Please confirm the subscription by following the steps mentioned in *step 5* under *AWS Management Console*.

AWS SDK – Java

The following code snippet will add a subscription to an SNS topic:

```
String emailProtocol = "email";
String emailEndpoint = "sunil.gulabani1@gmail.com";

subscribe(topicARN, emailProtocol, emailEndpoint);
........
private void subscribe(
    String topicArn,
    String protocol,
    String endpoint) {
    SubscribeRequest request =
        new SubscribeRequest()
        .withTopicArn(topicArn)
        .withProtocol(protocol)
        .withEndpoint(endpoint);

    SubscribeResult result =
        amazonSNS.subscribe(request);
}
```

The subscription endpoint has been subscribed to the topic and the mentioned endpoint needs to confirm the subscription. Please confirm the subscription by following the steps mentioned in *step 5* under *AWS Management Console*.

AWS CloudFormation

To create a subscription on a topic, we need to use the AWS::SNS::Subscription type:

```
"EmailSubscription": {
    "Type": "AWS::SNS::Subscription",
    "Properties": {
        "Endpoint": "sunil.gulabani1@gmail.com",
        "Protocol": "email",
        "TopicArn": "arn:aws:sns:us-west-2:123456789012:aws-bootcamp"
    }
}
```

We can also add a subscription while creating the topic as follows:

```
"AWSBootcamp": {
    "Type": "AWS::SNS::Topic",
    "Properties": {
        "TopicName": "aws-bootcamp",
        "DisplayName": "bootcamp",
        "Subscription": [{
            "Endpoint": "sunil.gulabani1@gmail.com",
            "Protocol": "email"
        }]
    }
}
```

Publishing a message

Publishing a message will publish the message to a topic and then push the message to subscribers. A topic's subscribers can be on different protocols and SNS knows the format to deliver messages as per the endpoint's protocol. So from the publisher side, it will publish the data in a unified way (subject and message) which SNS understands and SNS then delivers messages as per the endpoint's format.

We can also publish messages to specific mobile devices by passing
`EndpointArn` in the `TargetArn` parameters.

AWS Management Console

Go to AWS SNS Management Console at `https://console.aws.amazon.com/sns/v2/home` and perform the following steps:

1. Click **Topics** in the navigation pane on the left.
2. Click on the **aws-bootcamp** ARN displayed on the topic listing screen:

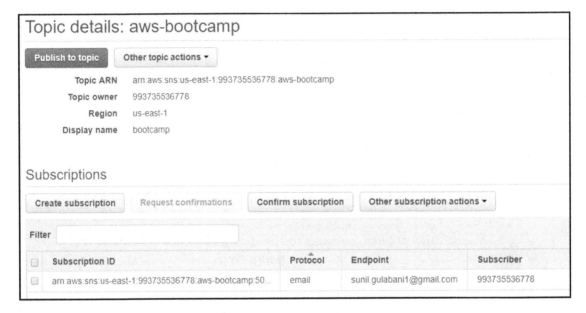

Figure 8.9: Topic details

3. Click **Publish to topic**:

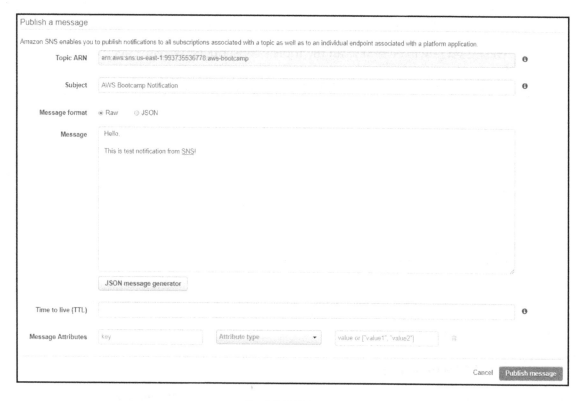

Figure 8.10: Publishing to topic

Provide details as follows:

- **Subject**: Type in `AWS Bootcamp Notification`.
- **Message format**: Choose the **Raw** option.
- **Message**: Type in the text that you want to send as the message body.
- **Time to live (TTL)**: TTL specifies the expiration time to deliver a message via push notifications to mobile devices. If the message is not delivered within the specified time, the message will be dropped and lost.
- **Message Attributes**: Provide the message attributes that will be attached to the message.

4. Once the details have been provided, click **Publish message**.

The message will be sent to all the topic's subscribers. We can check our mailbox for the message:

Figure 8.11: Notification received

AWS CLI

To execute the CLI script, open Command Prompt.

The following command will publish a message to an SNS topic and our subscriber will be able to get the message on their email address:

```
aws sns publish ^
--topic-arn "arn:aws:sns:us-east-1:993735536778:awsbootcamp" ^
--subject "AWS Bootcamp Notification" ^
--message "Hello, This is test notification from SNS!"
```

The following are the options that can be used with publish:

Parameters	Optional	Descriptions
--topic-arn	True	Topic ARN to which you want to publish message. We can either provide –phone-number or --topic-arn or --target-arn.
--subject	True	The subject will be used in email protocol while sending mail; in the case of other protocols, the subject will be included in a JSON message.
--message	False	Message body you want to send to the endpoint.

--target-arn	False	Target ARN to which notification will be sent. We can either provide -phone-number or --topic-arn or --target-arn.
--phone-number	False	Provide a phone number to which SMS needs to be sent. We can either provide -phone-number or --topic-arn or --target-arn.
--message-structure	False	Provide the message structure as JSON to send different messages to different protocols.
--message-attributes	False	Provide the message attributes that will be attached to the message.

AWS SDK – Java

The following code snippet will publish a message to an SNS topic and our subscriber will be able to get the message on their email address:

```
String subject = "AWS Bootcamp Notification";
String message = "Hello, This is test notification from SNS!";

publish(topicARN, subject, message);

........
private void publish(
    String topicARN,
    String subject,
    String message) {
    PublishRequest request =
        new PublishRequest()
        .withTopicArn(topicARN)
        .withSubject(subject)
        .withMessage(message);

    PublishResult result =
        amazonSNS.publish(request);
}
```

Summary

In this chapter, we learned the basics of SNS and its supported protocols, how to create a topics, subscribe to a topics, and publish messages to a topic using the AWS Management Console, AWS CLI, AWS SDK – Java, and AWS CloudFormation. Amazon SNS can be integrated with various AWS services, such as CloudWatch to send notifications about alarms, auto scaling groups to send notifications when any event occurs on EC2 instances, Elastic Beanstalk, and so on.

In the next chapter, we will learn about monitoring AWS resources, application performance, health checks, and more using the Amazon CloudWatch service. This is the most important part of the application because by using this service, we can ensure our application is up and running properly.

All About CloudWatch 9

Monitoring is an important aspect of the application life cycle. It involves checking application performance, health checks, resource consumption metrics, and so on. Traditionally, we need to configure external software that will monitor our application and notify the user that some problem is happening with the system; then the user can take the necessary steps to overcome the problem. Problems can be the failure of some application or hardware, high memory consumption, sudden high traffic on the applications, no traffic redirected to a distributed application, requests being processed slowly, which causes delay in response times.

Amazon CloudWatch is a smart tool to monitor AWS resources and our applications deployed on AWS. It allows us to use existing AWS resource metrics and also we can add our custom metrics, which can be used for monitoring purposes. Using the metrics, we can configure an alarm that says when a certain metric goes above or beyond the threshold limit, take certain actions, such as increasing the AWS resource capacity, adding a new EC2 instance to handle traffic, notifying a group of people that monitoring is in an alarm state so that certain actions can be taken, and so on. CloudWatch also handles monitoring in real time, which means at configured intervals, it monitors the metrics generated from AWS resources and applications and acts accordingly.

Amazon CloudWatch also provides an option to manage the logs generated from your application. We can stream the logs from AWS resources which run your applications on EC2, Lambda functions, Elastic Beanstalk, CloudTrail, Route53, RDS, and so on. We can efficiently search the logs on the AWS Management Console under CloudWatch Logs.

In CloudWatch, we can create a dashboard that can contain our custom-defined graphs and statistics or any AWS resource graphs our application uses. Dashboards help to give us insight into our application statistics using graphs and metrics.

In this chapter, we will be taking a look at the following topics:

- Metrics
- Alarms

- Events
- Logs
- Dashboard

Metrics

Metrics are a core component of CloudWatch. They are used to monitor AWS resources and our applications, and can be configured to react accordingly using CloudWatch alarms. Every AWS resource generates metrics at regular intervals, and we can also store custom metrics generated from our application. For example, our application is failing because of a database connection error and we generate metrics and store them on CloudWatch Metrics. For this database connection error metrics we created CloudWatch alarms when the number of errors crosses certain threshold, generate email notification to the group of people using SNS. So in this way we can use custom metrics as well as AWS resources metrics.

Metrics generated in a specific region can be used in that region only. We can't delete the metrics and data points. CloudWatch deletes metrics automatically after 15 months if no new data points are added under the metrics. And as data points are added under the metrics, 15-month-old data is deleted. So this helps us to view a larger picture of the application behavior.

When publishing metrics, we need to provide the following details:

- **Name**: Unique name to identify our custom metrics.
- **Namespace**: A namespace is like a category defined for a certain application. All AWS resource namespaces start with AWS/. For example, for Amazon EC2, the namespace is AWS/EC2; for Amazon RDS, the namespace is AWS/RDS.

For the namespaces of different AWS resources, please visit https://docs.aws.amazon.com/AmazonCloudWatch/latest/monitoring/aws-namespaces.html.

- **Dimensions**: Dimensions are used to uniquely identify the metrics. Dimensions can be used to filter the data. We can add up to 10 dimensions under a metric.

- **Timestamp**: A timestamp is attached to the data point being published. It is recommended to send the timestamp in UTC in `dateTime` format. We can create data points with past timestamps of up to 2 weeks and future timestamps of up to 2 hours. If we don't provide a timestamp, CloudWatch attaches a timestamp based on the request received to store the data point.

For `dateTime` format, please visit `https://www.w3.org/TR/xmlschema-2/#dateTime`.

- **Unit**: We can provide a unit of measure for each data point's value we publish. This is just to give a meaningful identity to the data. Standard units are provided, such as seconds, microseconds, milliseconds, bytes, kilobytes, counts, bits, and many more.
- **Value**: The value is the actual data point value which we need to store in CloudWatch metrics.

Let's see how we can publish custom metrics on CloudWatch using AWS SDK – Java.

Publishing metric data

To access the CloudWatch service, we need to create an `AmazonCloudWatch` object as follows:

```
AmazonCloudWatch amazonCloudWatch= AmazonCloudWatchClientBuilder
        .standard()
        .withClientConfiguration(getClientConfiguration())
        .withCredentials(getCredentials())
        .withRegion(Regions.US_EAST_1)
        .build();
```

The `ClientConfiguration` and `AWSCredentialsProvider` objects are created in the same way as we mentioned in Chapter 2, *Configuring IAM*.

The following code snippet will publish sample metrics on CloudWatch:

```
private void putMetricData(
        String namespace,
        String metricName,
        Date timestamp,
            double value,
            StandardUnit unit,
```

```
                    Dimension... dimensions) {

            MetricDatummetricDatum =
                    new MetricDatum()
                            .withMetricName(metricName)
                            .withDimensions(dimensions)
                            .withTimestamp(timestamp)
                            .withUnit(unit)
                            .withValue(value);

            PutMetricDataRequestputMetricDataRequest=
                    new PutMetricDataRequest()
                  .withMetricData(metricDatum)
                  .withNamespace(namespace);

            PutMetricDataResult putMetricDataResult =
                    cloudWatch.putMetricData(
                            putMetricDataRequest);
    }
```

Let's invoke the above code using values as:

```
String namespace = "Custom/AWSBootcampBook";
StringmetricName = "NumberOfInvocations";
Date timestamp = null;
Dimension dimension =
    createDimension("ChapterNo", "9");
Dimension dimension2 =
    createDimension(
                "ChapterName",
                "All About CloudWatch");

StandardUnit unit = StandardUnit.Count;
double minLimit = 1D;
double maxLimit = 1000D;
Random random = new Random();
double randomDataPointValue;

for(double i = 0; i <500; i++) {
  randomDataPointValue =
          minLimit + random.nextDouble()
       * (maxLimit - minLimit);

  timestamp = new Date();

  putMetricData(
        namespace,
        metricName,
```

```
                    timestamp,
                    randomDataPointValue,
                    unit,
                    dimension,
                    dimension2);
        Thread.sleep(2000);
    }
```

In this code snippet, we generated 500 random values and timestamps for publishing the data points.

To view the metrics on the AWS Management Console, go to https://console.aws.amazon.com/cloudwatch/home and perform the following steps:

1. Click Metrics in the navigation pane on the left:

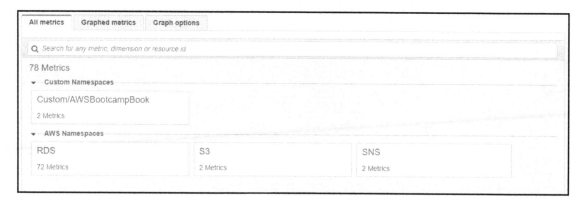

Figure 9.1: All metrics listing

Here, we can see our custom namespace is listed as **Custom/AWSBootcampBook**.

2. Click on the **Custom/AWSBootcampBook** namespace:

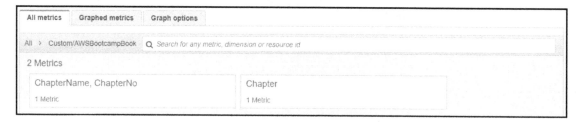

Figure 9.2: Dimensions listing

ChapterName and **ChapterNo** are two dimensions which we provided while publishing the metrics (please refer to the previous section).

3. Click the **ChapterName** and **ChapterNo** dimensions:

Figure 9.3: Metric listing

In the **Metric Name** column, we can see the metric name which we published is listed. Select the checkbox to view the graph generated by CloudWatch:

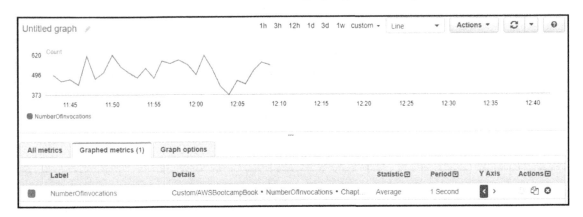

Figure 9.4: CloudWatch graph

The preceding graph shows the average number of invocations being made for 1 hour (**1h**) with a period of 1 second. To view graphs with different options, we can change them on the fly.

Alarms

CloudWatch alarms provide monitoring for our AWS resources and applications. An alarm uses a metric to monitor; if the metric's value crosses the threshold value defined for a certain period of time, an alarm action is triggered, which can be either an EC2 action, an auto scaling action, or a SNS event. CloudWatch maintains the state of change for a certain period of time. For every state of change, an alarm action can be triggered, so that we can take action properly. The following are the alarm states:

- **OK**: Metric value is within the limits of the threshold value
- **ALARM**: Metric value crosses the threshold value
- **INSUFFICIENT_DATA**: Metric value is not available or there is not enough data to identify the alarm state

IMPORTANT: We can create up to 5,000 alarms per region per AWS account.

Let's see how to create alarms using the AWS Management Console, AWS CLI, AWS SDK – Java, and CloudFormation. For our example, we will create an alarm for the RDS instance's CPU utilization. If the RDS instance's CPU utilization metric goes above 80% then an alarm should be raised and a notification should be sent to the SNS topic.

AWS Management Console

AWS Management Console allows us to create and manage the CloudWatch alarms, metrics, logs, events, and dashboard using the user interface.

Go to the CloudWatch Management Console (`https://console.aws.amazon.com/cloudwatch/home`) and then perform the following steps:

1. Click **Alarms** in the navigation pane on the left.
2. Click **Create Alarm**.

3. Select the metric for which the alarm needs to be created. Here we need to search for the metric for which we need to create an alarm. Type CPUUtilization in the search box and press *Enter*:

Figure 9.5: Selecting the metric

You can view all the AWS resources for which CPUUtilization metrics are stored in CloudWatch metrics. Select the checkbox for **DBInstanceIdentifier** of **awsbootcamp** and click **Next**.

4. Next, we need to configure the **Alarm** settings:

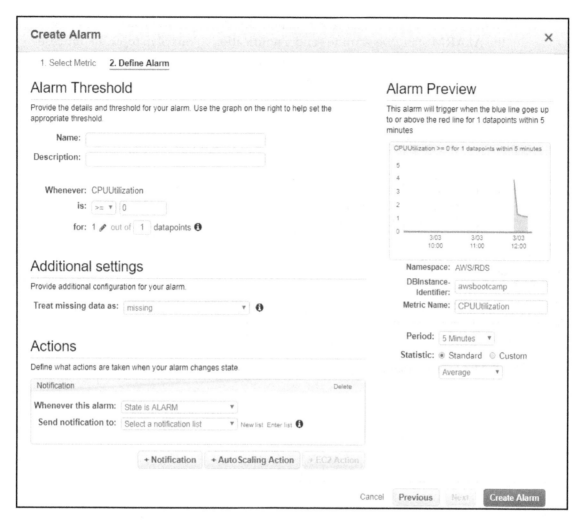

Figure 9.6: Defining the alarm

As you can see, we can provide the **Alarm** settings as shown:

- **Name**: Type in `AWS-Bootcamp-RDS-High-CPU-Utilization`
- **Description**: Type in `AWSBootcampRDS High CPUUtilization`
- **Threshold value**: Type in `80`. This means when `CPUUtilization` is `GreaterThanOrEqualTo 80`, an alarm should be raised.
- **Treat missing data as**: Select `missing`. You may select the choice which suits you best.

- **Actions**: We can provide different actions for different alarm states. For the **ALARM** state, we want to send a notification to our SNS topic. In our case, we will select the `aws-bootcamp` SNS topic.
- Keep the rest of the settings as the default ones. Once done, click **Create Alarm**:

State		Name	Threshold		Config Status	
☑ OK		AWS-Bootcamp-RDS-High-CPU-Utilization	CPUUtilization >= 80 for 1 datapoints within 5 minutes			

Figure 9.7: Alarm listing

We are done with creating the alarm, so whenever the RDS `CPUUtilization` is above 80%, an alarm action will be triggered which will send a notification to the **aws-bootcamp** SNS topic.

AWS CLI

The AWS CLI can be used to create and manage CloudWatch Alarm/Metrics/Events/Dashboard using command line scripts. All operations can be performed which are available via AWS Management Console.

To execute the CLI script, open Command Prompt. The following command will create an alarm:

```
aws cloudwatch put-metric-alarm ^
--alarm-name "AWS-Bootcamp-RDS-High-CPUUtilization" ^
--alarm-description "AWSBootcampRDS High CPU Utilization Alarm" ^
--actions-enabled ^
--dimensions Name=DBInstanceIdentifier,Value=awsbootcamp ^
--namespace "AWS/RDS" ^
--metric-name "CPUUtilization" ^
--statistic "Average" ^
--comparison-operator "GreaterThanOrEqualToThreshold" ^
--threshold 80.0 ^
--unit "Percent" ^
--evaluation-periods 2 ^
--period 300 ^
--alarm-actions "arn:aws:sns:us-east-1:123456789012:aws-bootcamp"
```

The following are the options which can be used with `put-metric-alarm`:

Parameters	Optional	Descriptions
`--alarm-name`	False	This is the name of the alarm.
`--alarm-description`	True	This is the description of the alarm.
`--actions-enabled or` `--no-actions-enabled`	True	This tells us which actions should be executed when the alarm state is changed.
`--ok-actions`	True	These are the actions that need to be executed when the alarm state is switched to OK. We need to provide Amazon Resource Names (ARNs) for the actions that need to be executed.
`--alarm-actions`	True	These are the actions that need to be executed when the alarm state is switched to ALARM. We need to provide ARNs for the actions that need to be executed.
`--insufficient-data-actions`	True	These are the actions that need to be executed when the alarm state is switched to the INSUFFICIENT_DATA state. We need to provide ARNs for the actions that need to be executed.
`--metric-name`	False	This is the metric name associated with the alarm.
`--namespace`	False	This is the namespace of the metric.
`--statistic`	True	These are the statistics for the metrics. The valid values are as follows: • `SampleCount` • `Average` • `Sum` • `Minimum` • `Maximum` For percentile statistics, we will use `--extended-statistic`.

--extended-statistic	True	We can define percentile statistics with this option. We can specify valid values between p0.0 and p100.
--dimensions	True	These are the dimensions for the metrics. These have to be in the form of a name and value pair as follows: Name= DBInstanceIdentifier, Value= awsbootcamp
--period	False	This is the time period in seconds for which statistics will be applied. The valid values are 10, 30, or multiples of 60.
--unit	True	These are the units of statistics based on the metric type.
--evaluation-periods	False	This is the evaluation period times for which statistics are compared with the threshold.
--threshold	False	This is the threshold value with which statistics are compared.
--comparison-operator	False	This is the comparison operator to compare statistics and threshold value. The valid values are as follows: • GreaterThanOrEqualToThreshold • GreaterThanThreshold • LessThanThreshold • LessThanOrEqualToThreshold
--treat-missing-data	True	This explains what action needs to be taken when missing data points are there. The valid values are as follows: • breaching • notBreaching • ignore • missing (default)

		This is effective for alarms based on percentiles. When the data points are too low to calculate statistics, we can either ignore evaluating statistics or evaluate with whatever low data points are available. The valid values are as follows: • evaluate (default) • ignore
--evaluate-low-sample-count-percentile	True	

AWS SDK – Java

The AWS SDK allows us to create and manage CloudWatch Alarm/Metrics/Events/Dashboard by programming it. All operations can be performed which are available via AWS Management Console.

The following code snippet will create an alarm:

```
public void putMetricAlarm(String alarmName,
                           String alarmActionsARN,
                           String dimensionName,
                           String dimensionValue,
                           String namespace,
                           String metricName,
                           Statistic statistic,
                           ComparisonOperator comparisonOperator,
                           Double threshold,
                           String unit,
                           Integer evaluationPeriod,
                           Integer period) {
    PutMetricAlarmRequest putMetricAlarmRequest =
            new PutMetricAlarmRequest();

    putMetricAlarmRequest.withAlarmName(alarmName);

    putMetricAlarmRequest.withActionsEnabled(true);

    putMetricAlarmRequest
        .withAlarmActions(alarmActionsARN);

    Dimension dimension =
            createDimension(dimensionName, dimensionValue);

    putMetricAlarmRequest.withDimensions(dimension);
```

```
                putMetricAlarmRequest.withNamespace(namespace);

                putMetricAlarmRequest.withMetricName(metricName);

                putMetricAlarmRequest.withStatistic(statistic);

                putMetricAlarmRequest.withComparisonOperator(comparisonOperator);

                putMetricAlarmRequest.withThreshold(threshold);

                putMetricAlarmRequest.withUnit(unit);

                putMetricAlarmRequest.withEvaluationPeriods(evaluationPeriod);

                putMetricAlarmRequest.withPeriod(period);

                PutMetricAlarmResult putMetricAlarmResult =
                        cloudWatch.putMetricAlarm(putMetricAlarmRequest);
        }
```

We also need to create `Dimension` which will be used while creating Alarm :

```
        private Dimension createDimension(
                String dimensionName,
                String dimensionValue) {
        Dimension dimension = new Dimension();

        dimension.withName(dimensionName);

        dimension.withValue(dimensionValue);

        return dimension;
    }
```

Let's invoke the preceding code using these values:

```
    String alarmName = "AWS-Bootcamp-RDS-High-CPU-Utilization";

    String alarmActionsARN = "arn:aws:sns:us-east-1:123456789012:aws-bootcamp";


    String dimensionName = "DBInstanceIdentifier";

    String dimensionValue = "awsbootcamp";

    String namespace = "AWS/RDS";

    String metricName = "CPUUtilization";
```

```
Statistic statistic = Statistic.Average;

ComparisonOperator comparisonOperator =
ComparisonOperator.GreaterThanOrEqualToThreshold;


Double threshold = 80.0;

String unit = "Percent";

Integer evaluationPeriod = 2;

Integer period = 300;

putMetricAlarm(
    alarmName,
    alarmActionsARN,
    dimensionName,
    dimensionValue,
    namespace,
    metricName,
    statistic,
    comparisonOperator,
    threshold,
    unit,
    evalutionPeriod,
    period);
```

AWS CloudFormation

AWS CloudFormation is a recommended way to create and manage the AWS infrastructure so that you have all your AWS resources at one place in form of JSON or YML template.

To create a CloudWatch alarm, we need to use the `AWS::CloudWatch::Alarm` type:

```
"AWSBootcampRDSHighCPUUtilization": {
    "Type": "AWS::CloudWatch::Alarm",
    "Properties": {
        "AlarmName": "AWS-Bootcamp-RDS-High-CPU-Utilization",
        "AlarmDescription": "AWSBootcampRDS High CPU Utilization Alarm",
        "AlarmActions": [
            "arn:aws:sns:us-east-1:123456789012:aws-bootcamp"
        ],
        "Dimensions": [{
            "Name": "DBInstanceIdentifier",
            "Value": "awsbootcamp"
```

```
        }],
    "Namespace": "AWS/RDS",
    "MetricName": "CPUUtilization",
    "Statistic": "Average",
    "ComparisonOperator": "GreaterThanOrEqualToThreshold",
    "Threshold": "80.0",
    "Unit": "Percent",
    "EvaluationPeriods": 2,
    "Period": 300
    }
    }
```

Events

CloudWatch Events can be used to track changes made to AWS resources. It may be useful for administrator to maintain a track history for the AWS resource scaling up or scaling down. Using this we can make sure that AWS resources are not being over used which may incur more charges or AWS resources scaled down which may impact application performance. So it is important to capture the CloudWatch Events and take appropriate action. We can create rules for Events, so that we can invoke the necessary actions or send notifications to concerned persons. Using CloudWatch Events, users can keep an eye on infrastructure changes so that they can compare between the old and new infrastructure and take the necessary action. This saves users time, as before we needed to write scripts which regularly checked the infrastructure, collected data, and stored it at some location. Now the entire process can be automated by defining rules and providing targets for the specific rules. The following are the main components of CloudWatch Events:

- **Rules**: Rules are used to identify the generated events and the route to appropriate targets. We can route the single event in parallel to one or more targets. Each target can then process the triggered Events and take the necessary action (if any).

- **Events**: AWS provides flexibility to generate custom events along with AWS-generated events from AWS resources. AWS resources generate events when there is a change in the state of the resource, such as a new EC2 instance being added in an auto scaling group, or an instance being started, stopped, or terminated. These types of AWS-generated events are helpful for the operational team so that they can monitor and keep track of the changes. AWS also provides the option to generate schedule events at regular intervals. For example, if an administrator need a daily report for the number of EC2 instances created/in-use by AWS Auto Scaling Group, we can create a Schedule Event and provide target as AWS Lambda Function. Lambda Function will be responsible to collect the information from Auto Scaling Group, generate report and send to Administrator.

- **Targets**: Targets are responsible for processing the event generated when a specific rule is triggered. When creating an event, we need to provide the target(s) which we need to process the event. Targets can be AWS Lambda functions, Kinesis streams, SNS topics, SQS, and many more.

Logs

CloudWatch Logs allows us to manage the logs generated from an application in a central location. This allows us to store any number of logs without storage restrictions. We can also monitor and access logs in an efficient manner using the CloudWatch Management Console. This provides an advanced search and filter capability in case we want to troubleshoot an issue. AWS resources also generate logs which can be stored in CloudWatch Logs so that we don't have distributed logs. We can define log retention days as we might not need historic logs, as per our business needs.

The CloudWatch Logs' console provides an extensive search capability where we can search logs based on filtering and patterns. It becomes easier for users to troubleshoot as log retrieval is faster based on filtering and patterns.

It also provide feature to create custom metrics based on logs. Consider a scenario where application is logging database exception like `Exception: Database connection failure`, and we want to keep a track that if such exception count is greater than 10 during 5 minutes, respective application stakeholder should be notified that something is going wrong in application.

So in this case we can create metrics based on logs and on this metrics we create CloudWatch Alarm which has validation check for count greater than 10 for 5 minutes. So if the CloudWatch Alarm state changes to ALARM it should trigger a notification to the SNS topic.

CloudWatch Logs also provides the option to stream logs in real time from Amazon EC2 or our applications. For this, we need to install the CloudWatch Logs Agent, which will be responsible for streaming logs incrementally. Apart from the CloudWatch Logs Agent, we can also use the AWS CLI, AWS SDK, or REST API to publish logs.

Publishing logs

CloudWatch Logs provides different ways to publish logs, such as the CloudWatch Logs SDK, AWS CLI, CloudWatch Logs API, or CloudWatch Logs Agent. Here we will demonstrate how to publish logs using the CloudWatch Logs SDK.

To access the CloudWatch Logs service, we need to create an AWSLogs object as follows:

```
AWSLogs awsLogs = AWSLogsClientBuilder
    .standard()
    .withClientConfiguration(getClientConfiguration())
    .withCredentials(getCredentials())
    .withRegion(Regions.US_EAST_1)
    .build();
```

The ClientConfiguration and AWSCredentialsProvider objects are created in the same way as we mentioned in Chapter 2, *Configuring IAM*.

To publish logs to CloudWatch Logs, first we need to create a log group which shares common properties such as retention of logs and permissions to access the log group:

```
String logGroupName = "aws-bootcamp";
createLogGroup(logGroupName);
........
private void createLogGroup(String logGroupName) {
    CreateLogGroupRequest createLogGroupRequest =
        new CreateLogGroupRequest()
            .withLogGroupName(logGroupName);
    CreateLogGroupResult createLogGroupResult =
        awsLogs.createLogGroup(createLogGroupRequest);
}
```

Usually a log is created once throughout the application lifecycle. So it recommended to create log group using CloudFormation script or AWS CLI.

Once we have created log group, we can create a log stream which store the sequence of events (logs) generated from applications or AWS resources:

```
String logGroupName = "aws-bootcamp";
String logStreamName = "chapter-9";
createLogStream(logGroupName, logStreamName);
........
private void createLogStream(
    String logGroupName,
    String logStreamName) {
    CreateLogStreamRequest createLogStreamRequest =
        new CreateLogStreamRequest()
            .withLogGroupName(logGroupName)
            .withLogStreamName(logStreamName);

    CreateLogStreamResult createLogStreamResult =
        awsLogs.createLogStream(createLogStreamRequest);
}
```

 Log streams can be created based on API user requests or application sessions or day-wise or hour-wise. Creating multiple log streams will help you to search logs efficiently.

Finally, we are ready to publish log events on CloudWatch Logs:

```
String logGroupName = "aws-bootcamp";
String logStreamName = "chapter-9";
InputLogEvent inputLogEvent =
    new InputLogEvent()
        .withTimestamp(Instant.now().toEpochMilli())
        .withMessage("Hello World!!!");

Thread.sleep(2000); /* This is just to demonstrate logs generated at
different timestamp */

InputLogEvent inputLogEvent2 =
    new InputLogEvent()
        .withTimestamp(Instant.now().toEpochMilli())
        .withMessage("Hello World - 2!!!");
putLogEvents(
    logGroupName,
```

```
        logStreamName,
        inputLogEvent,
        inputLogEvent2);
........
private void putLogEvents(
    String logGroupName,
    String logStreamName,
    InputLogEvent... logEvents) {
    PutLogEventsRequest putLogEventRequest =
        new PutLogEventsRequest()
            .withLogGroupName(logGroupName)
            .withLogStreamName(logStreamName)
            .withLogEvents(logEvents);
    PutLogEventsResult putLogEventsResult =
        awsLogs.putLogEvents(putLogEventRequest);
}
```

From our code snippet, we generated two log events: `Hello World!!!` and `Hello World – 2!!!`. In the next section, we will see the logs on the AWS Management Console.

Viewing logs

The AWS Management Console provides a user interface to view logs. Go to `https://console.aws.amazon.com/cloudwatch/home#logs`, where all the log groups will be listed:

	Log Groups	Expire Events After	Metric Filters	Subscriptions
○	aws-bootcamp	Never Expire	0 filters	None

Figure 9.8: Log group listing

Click the **aws-bootcamp** link to view all log streams for this log group:

	Log Streams	▽	Last Event Time
☐	chapter-9		2018-03-03 18:46 UTC+5:30

Figure 9.9: Log stream listing

Click **chapter-9** to view the logs under this log stream:

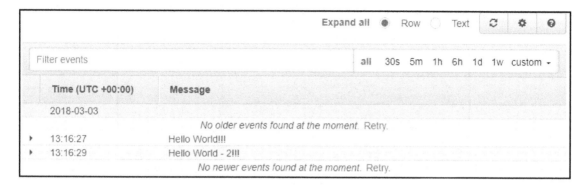

Figure 9.10: Logs listing

Here, we can see the logs that we published are being published on CloudWatch Logs. For troubleshooting, we can use this console to search and filter logs based on our criteria.

Dashboards

Amazon CloudWatch enables users to create custom dashboards which can include CloudWatch metrics or text data. We can create a dashboard which includes all the AWS resource metrics and images, which gives us an overall picture of application operations. We can monitor all the resources in one place so that we don't need to search different metric data. Dashboards allow us to show data that is available in different regions, so if your application resides in multiple AWS regions, we can get all the regions' resource data and show it in one place.

Let's build a dashboard that includes RDS `CPUUtilization` metrics.

AWS Management Console

The following are the steps to create a dashboard using the AWS Management Console:

1. Go to the Amazon CloudWatch Console and click **Dashboards** in the navigation pane on the left, or you can go directly to
   `https://console.aws.amazon.com/cloudwatch/home#dashboards`.

2. Click **Create dashboard**:

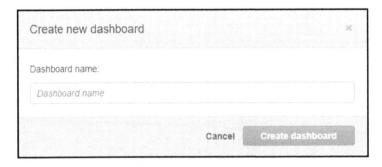

Figure 9.11: Creating a dashboard

Type in AWS-Bootcamp as the dashboard name and click **Create dashboard**:

Figure 9.12: Dashboard created

3. Add the RDS CPUUtilization widget. Click the **Add widget** button:

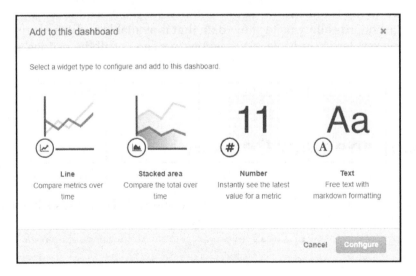

Figure 9.13: Select the widget type

4. Select the **Line** widget type and click **Configure**. The next thing to do is add a metric graph:

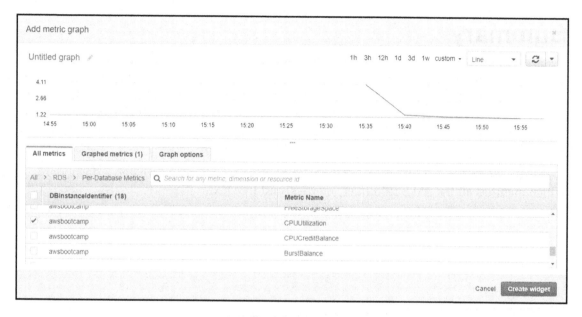

Figure 9.14: Adding a metric graph

5. Select the **awsbootcamp** RDS **CPUUtilization** metric and click **Create widget**:

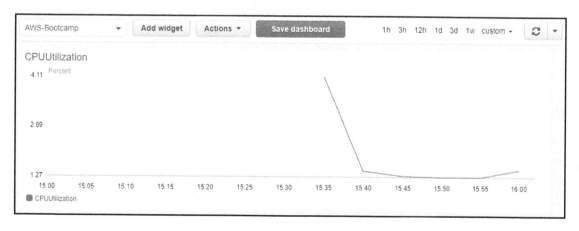

Figure 9.15: Widget added

6. Click **Save dashboard**.

This way, we can add multiple widgets and monitor all AWS resource and metric data.

Summary

Amazon CloudWatch has become a powerful tool to monitor AWS resources and custom applications. In this chapter, we have learned that we can publish custom metrics generated from our application and also create an alarm based on AWS-generated metrics or custom metrics and react accordingly. We configured events on various AWS resources and custom CloudWatch Events published and took necessary actions accordingly. We saw how to store, monitor, and access logs on Amazon CloudWatch Logs.

Lastly, to obtain the overall operational health of an application, we created a dashboard which includes all the AWS resources, metrics, and free text.

Other Books You May Enjoy

If you enjoyed this book, you may be interested in these other books by Packt:

Learning AWS - Second Edition
Aurobindo Sarkar, Amit Shah

ISBN: 978-1-78728-106-6

- Set up your AWS account and get started with the basic concepts of AWS
- Learn about AWS terminology and identity access management
- Acquaint yourself with important elements of the cloud with features such as computing, ELB, and VPC
- Back up your database and ensure high availability by having an understanding of database-related services in the AWS cloud
- Integrate AWS services with your application to meet and exceed non-functional requirements
- Create and automate infrastructure to design cost-effective, highly available applications

Mastering AWS Security
Albert Anthony

ISBN: 978-1-78829-372-3

- Learn about AWS Identity Management and Access control
- Gain knowledge to create and secure your private network in AWS
- Understand and secure your infrastructure in AWS
- Understand monitoring, logging and auditing in AWS
- Ensure Data Security in AWS
- Learn to secure your applications in AWS
- Explore AWS Security best practices

Leave a review - let other readers know what you think

Please share your thoughts on this book with others by leaving a review on the site that you bought it from. If you purchased the book from Amazon, please leave us an honest review on this book's Amazon page. This is vital so that other potential readers can see and use your unbiased opinion to make purchasing decisions, we can understand what our customers think about our products, and our authors can see your feedback on the title that they have worked with Packt to create. It will only take a few minutes of your time, but is valuable to other potential customers, our authors, and Packt. Thank you!

Index

Made in the USA
Monee, IL
27 July 2020